Around the Buoys

A Manual of Sailboat Racing Tactics and Strategies

Michael Huck, Jr.

illustrated by
Terry Greenfield

International Marine
Camden, Maine

For Michael and Logan—two able-bodied seamen.

Published by International Marine®

10 9 8 7 6

Copyright © 1994 International Marine, a
division of The McGraw-Hill Companies.

All rights reserved. The publisher takes no
responsibility for the use of any of the materials
or methods described in this book, nor for the
products thereof. The name "International
Marine" and the International Marine logo are
trademarks of The McGraw-Hill Companies.
Printed in the United States of America.

*Library of Congress Cataloging-in-
Publication Data*
   Huck, Michael.
   Around the buoys : a manual of sailboat rac-
ing tactics and strategies / Michael Huck; illus-
trated by Terry Greenfield.
       p.   cm.
   Includes index.
   ISBN 0-07-030817-9
   1. Sailboat racing. I. Title.
   GV826.5.H83   1994   93-36786
   797.1'4--dc20

Questions regarding the content of this book
should be addressed to:
   International Marine
   P.O. Box 220
   Camden, ME 04843

Questions regarding the ordering of this book
should be addressed to:
   The McGraw Hill Companies
   Customer Service Department
   P.O. Box 547; Blacklick, OH 43004
   Retail Customers: 1-800-262-4729
   Bookstores: 1-800-722-4726

Around the Buoys is printed on acid-free paper

Printed by R.R. Donnelley, Crawfordsville, IN

Design by Patrice M. Rossi

Production by Molly Mulhern

Edited by Jonathan Eaton and Christine Bartels

Contents

Acknowledgments

A lot of time has gone into collecting the knowledge in this book. I would like to thank a few of the people who have helped me along the way. Occie Gunkler's love for the sport made it possible for my early racing career to begin. Eric Hood, Peter Price, and Michael Terry provided the competition to sharpen the desire. Bob Ackerman, Bill Hubbard, and Robin Terry gave me the finest crew I've ever had at the right time, when my skills were building. Most of all, I have to thank my father, Michael Huck, Sr., who provided support and encouragement all the way through, and my mother, Durette Upton, who had the courage to let me go. All of these people are responsible for what is right in these pages. I am responsible for any errors.

Introduction

Racing around the buoys is only one of the ways people race sailboats. There are ocean, or distance, races of various types. There are match races and other specialized formats. But all the elements needed for success in any of these races are present in closed-course, around-the-buoys racing.

Racing a boat around a closed course with other boats focuses the qualities of boat handling, strategic positioning, and tactical foresight into a short, frantic, exhilarating time period. The decisions that are made have to be made right now, and the consequences of an error are immediately apparent. Equally apparent may be the chance to regain the ground lost in that error. Let me illustrate:

It was Sunday morning at Crystal Lake in Michigan. The third race of the WMYA E-scow invitational had just started, and we were over early. To make matters worse, we had fouled a boat trying to restart. We were using the percentage penalty system, in which points are deducted from your score after the race, so all was not lost, but we had a great deal of ground to make up.

The wind was blowing out of the south at about 15 m.p.h., and we knew that it was going to shift toward the west as the race progressed. We headed out to pursue the fleet.

The windward mark was set near the south shore, well away from most land effects but still under the bluffs surrounding the lake. As we proceeded up the course, we worked the right side in anticipation of a shift. We were getting some good starboard lifts as the morning air started to settle and the wind shifted toward the west. The game was to spot the puff, tack to port to close on it, tack to starboard as it hit, hike hard, and ride it until we were knocked—then repeat the process.

As we approached the shore, the gusts got more defined and hit with greater impact. The crew hung it out and had the lines for the vang, traveler, and cunningham in hand. When a puff would hit, the traveler would be eased out and the cunningham and vang pulled tighter. As the puff eased, the sails would be powered up but the crew remained out. The added depth in the sails generated enough power to balance their weight.

Other boats were coming over to us and grabbing the lifting puffs, and one tacked on our air. "We're going low," I told the crew, who responded by dropping the traveler, tightening the vang and cunningham, and sinking a little deeper in their droop hike. The other boat tried to foot with us but got hit with a puff and heeled excessively. As we squirted into clear air and entered a small header, the boat to windward fell into our backwind and tacked away. We tacked as well, and then tacked back into another lifting puff. The other boat went out to the layline and was five lengths back at the mark. We had rejoined the fleet and rounded about tenth.

The puffs were rolling down the hills and hitting the lake hard; they were spotty and clearly defined. The reach was fairly loose, and we all set spinnakers. The scows quickly jumped on plane.

There were short, sharp puffs coming through, and boats were heading high to pick them up. We grabbed one and took it low. As it petered out, we headed higher to maintain our apparent wind and managed to pick up the next shot before we dropped off plane. Boom! We were off again. Boats ahead of us were accelerating, then slowing as their puffs ran out. When we were on the leading edge of one, we went below boats; turning up, we were then able to keep going through their lees as they reaccelerated. Between puffs we went high, hiking hard when a puff hit and booming over other boats. All you could hear was "Puff above us, coming—now!," and off we'd go.

We were closing on the jibe mark and had gotten to fourth place. The lead boats were starting to jibe around the mark and were clearly having trouble carrying their chutes on the second, much tighter reaching leg. I looked to leeward and spotted the downwind mark. "Take it down at the mark," I called, and the crew went to work dropping the chute. The other boats hadn't seen the mark yet and were jibing on instinct and hope.

The first boats were blown well down the course and had to struggle to get their spinnakers down. We took off, peeling off the tops of waves and working the puffs and boat hard. We were second at the bottom mark.

The wind had shifted firmly to the southwest, and the weather leg was uneventful. We played the puffs up the west shore but were unable to catch the lead boat. The fleet was all over the lake by now, and everyone had settled into the grind-it-out rhythm of the heavy-air beat.

The lead boat rounded the weather mark, set his spinnaker, and jibed to the favored right side. But he got on the wrong side of a puff that had hit the water and spread out in a cat's-paw. The wind swung behind him and took him too far to the right before it let up and he could jibe. We jibed at the mark and caught the other side of the puff, a header that took us down the course. After it ran out we were able to continue over to the right side on a favorable angle. With clear air all the way down the course, we didn't jibe back to starboard until we had crossed in front of the other boat.

Our only task on the last windward leg was to stay between the boat behind us and the finish while protecting the right side. We were able to let the other boat off fairly easily and cover loosely. If he tacked to starboard, we could wait until the next puff came, then tack with him. If he tacked to port, we went with him immediately. By waiting for the starboard lift and tacking on it, we were able to slowly extend our lead.

Crossing the finish line, we indicated to the judges that we were acknowledging a foul. With the 20-percent penalty, we scored a sixth place even though we had won the race. Obviously, had we not won the race the score would have been worse.

How were we able to start behind everyone, sail through the fleet, and win the race? Well, first of all, it was a long race, and we had the boat tuned correctly for the conditions. We knew where we wanted to be in 15-m.p.h. air, placed the boat in that configuration, and sailed it. Second, we knew what to do as a crew. Sail controls were adjusted automatically at the proper time with no instruction, no questions, and in many cases no signal from the helm. Third, when tactical opportunities came along, we executed the tactic we wanted. In so much wind, most people weren't worried about their tactics, which made ours much more effective. We knew the course and considered the next legs before we were on them.

Sure, we got some breaks. The downwind puff that headed us and lifted the boat ahead of us was not something you could have forecast. But we made sure that when we got a break, we got all of it.

Some of the moves we made were decided before the race started, and some were made on the fly. The purpose of this book is to outline the basis for such decisions and equip you with some techniques to take advantage of whenever possible. We will go through the prerace process of assembling the information that will suggest your strategy. And we will dissect the race into segments and illustrate some of the approaches and tactics that work for each.

We start with selecting a boat because some people aren't familiar with the characteristics of the different boats on the market and don't know how to get the best boat for their purposes. Then we'll look at the sails and the various factors affecting boatspeed. You don't have to know a great deal about aerodynamics to take advantage of some of the simple sail-shaping adjustments used while racing. Those adjustments are important, though, and make the difference between a successful maneuver and one that doesn't quite cut it.

The balance of the book is a segment-by-segment look at the race. In discussing tactics and other considerations, I've attempted to bring all aspects of sailing to bear on each situation encountered. We want the correct sail trim at the correct time for the correct maneuver to get us to the correct position. The rest takes care of itself.

Sailboat racing has been a passion with me for as long as I can remember. I hope the information in this book will help you enjoy the sport as much as I do.

Chapter 1

The Boat

T he first step in a successful racing program is a close look at your equipment, and for the sailor, the basic piece of equipment is the boat. The choice of a boat is a highly personal one. Sailing is a multipurpose sport, and a boat can be used as an excursion vehicle, for entertainment, as a weekend retreat, or all of the above. If the boat is to be raced as well, two major concerns are the type of racing to be done and the makeup of the local fleets.

When you consider the racing you want to do, you need to think about who will be sailing with you, how much traveling you might want to do, and what level of competition you eventually want to reach. The answers to these questions may change as you become more involved in the sport. They will help you choose a boat from the hundreds available. You only need to visit a boat show to see that sailboats vary widely in configuration.

One year we were in Clearwater, Florida, for a Kahlua Cup race, a 120-mile overnighter that attracts a great number and variety of boats. There were seven guys aboard an Olson 30—a light, relatively quick boat that can be a real handful for its crew—and we were all there for the challenge of pushing the boat hard all night. Late in the night, while sailing upwind, we fell in beside an Irwin 65, decidedly not your typical race boat. Sitting on the rail, we could smell microwave popcorn. Obviously, the crew of the Irwin was there mainly for the adventure of being out all night, and only secondarily for the race. As a matter of fact, when I mentioned the smell of the popcorn to one of the women on board the Irwin the next morning, she said, "Oh yes, that's when we were watching movies on the VCR!" Incidentally, we both agreed it was a great race.

It makes little sense to acquire a boat that is completely unlike anything you will be sailing against. If you want to compete, you must at least be in the ballpark. A look at the fleets racing locally will show you that somewhere in your area there are people racing the kind of boat you are looking for. Even in Oklahoma sailors get together in cruising boats to race up and down the many lakes and reservoirs of the state. If cruising boats race in the middle of the prairie, you should be able to find a fleet within reach that races boats that match your desires.

One-Designs

Most people start racing in one-design classes. *One-design* simply means that all the boats are substantially the same, so the contest focuses on the skills of the crews. Modern one-designs are typically light, fast, and easy to maneuver, and they place a premium on boat handling. The winners will be the people who have spent the time in the boat to perfect their skills. The crew that can tack and jibe well, execute good starts, and make the fewest tactical errors will win. The aim of the one-design philosophy is to eliminate other variables.

There are one-designs—including most scows, the Soling, and the Star—that require a great deal of physical ability to sail competitively. On the other hand, if speed and sailing on the edge are your cup of tea, you may want to consider one of the lighter boats that hang the crew over the side on a trapeze: 505s, International 14s, and catamarans provide all the excitement anyone could desire. Other boats reward positioning and tactics more than raw boatspeed, and these boats make for great family fun as they do not require linebackers for crew. Highlanders, Flying Scots, and the Ideal 18 have been designed expressly for this. Their regattas resemble huge family reunions.

A dinghy one-design. (Photo by Carol Singer)

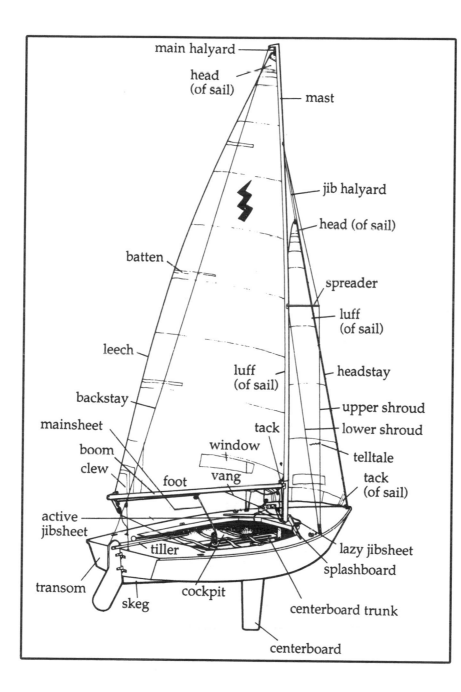

main halyard

head
(of sail)

mast

jib halyard

head (of sail)

batten

spreader

luff
(of sail)

leech

luff
(of sail)

headstay

backstay

upper shroud

lower shroud

mainsheet

tack

window

telltale

boom

vang

clew

foot

tack
(of sail)

active
jibsheet

lazy jibsheet

tiller

splashboard

transom

centerboard trunk

skeg

cockpit

centerboard

Trailering—portability—is another concern. Many new designs emphasize ease of traveling and setup. Retractable keels and deck-stepped masts make traveling with a boat a much more pleasant experience.

Most small training boats are one-designs. They are purposely made as simple as

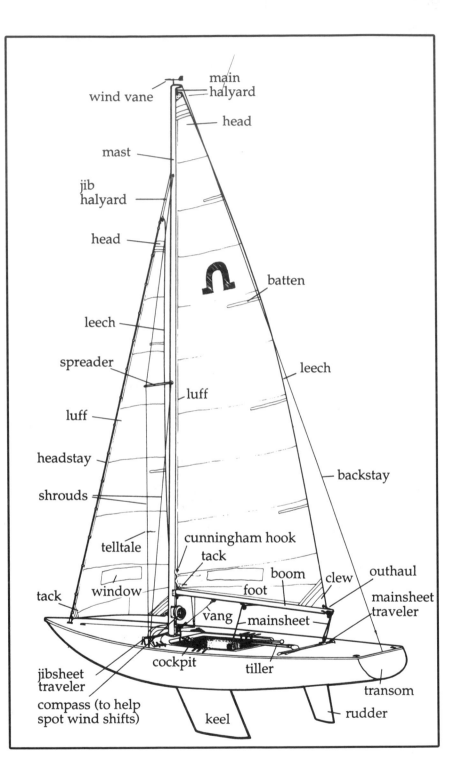

The Soling, a class of racing keelboat. (Illustration by Brad Dellenbaugh)

wind vane

main halyard

head

mast

jib halyard

head

batten

leech

spreader

luff

leech

luff

headstay

shrouds

backstay

telltale

cunningham hook

tack

boom

clew

outhaul

tack

window

foot

mainsheet traveler

vang

mainsheet

jibsheet traveler

cockpit

tiller

transom

compass (to help spot wind shifts)

keel

rudder

The International One-Design is a beautiful class of small keelboats—heavy and comfortable, slow to maneuver but with good straight-line speed in a breeze. These boats place emphasis on tactical thinking and careful sail shaping. Their big, deep cockpits make them excellent all-purpose family boats. (Photo by Story Litchfield)

A Laser on a fast run, with centerboard up. (Photo courtesy Laser International)

possible to place the emphasis on good steering and basic sail trim. Keeping the distractions to a minimum forces development of the important skills and curbs that primate's desire to fiddle with things. When your only tools are the mainsheet and tiller, you'll learn to use them well.

The simplicity of these boats can be misleading. The tighter the rules governing the boat, the more likely it is that someone has discovered the hot setup within those rules. The Sunfish is a good example of this. With its deceptively simple rig, this boat must be set up a certain way to be competitive. It is well worth your time to ask some questions and discover those few important settings early in the game. No sense reinventing the wheel.

At the other end of the spectrum, there are one-designs that require a great deal of crew input to be sailed well. They can be optimized for every nuance of wind and sea condition, and they need to be adjusted for changing tactical situations. Such boats are frequently compared with an automobile. They need to shift gears to adjust to changing conditions.

All these adjustments affect the major components of the boat's rig and are designed to present the best sail shape for the purpose at hand. Although the types of adjustments are usually specified by the rules, how they are used depends on a number of factors, which vary with boat and crew. Sail shape and crew weight are the two major variables. Flatter sails or a heavier crew will require that the boat be set up differently from one with full sails or a flyweight team.

The challenge of coming up with the right combination is one of the attractions of this kind of racing. It requires a team effort and rewards crews that work well together. Most of the sailing done in the Olympics is in boats of this type. The best example is probably the Star. Designed in the early part of this century, the Star in its modern version has a myriad of adjustments and a flexible rig; sailing it has been likened to tuning a piano upside down with your eyes shut.

In terms of complexity, many boats fall somewhere between the Star and the training dinghy. The idea is to get one that enjoys popularity in your area, and then go out and do it!

PHRF and Other Handicap Racing

The nice thing about handicap sailing is that it allows different types of boats to race against one another with some objectivity in the results. This includes boats that might also be used for a family cruise. The boats are timed around a course of known length, then a factor is applied to produce a corrected time. The way this correction factor is derived is the basis of the different rating systems, or rules.

One of the most popular and simplest to administer is the Performance Handicap Rating Formula, or PHRF, which rates boats based on their observed speed relative to each other. The handicaps are determined regionally, based on reported race results, in an effort to eliminate local bias. If one boat is determined to be 30 seconds per mile faster than another, and it crosses the line 12 minutes ahead after a 24-mile race, then the two boats are tied.

This system has its drawbacks. Because it is based on actual performance, it rates crews as well as boats. For example, a new boat, well sailed, ends up with an artificially low rating. This may be OK for that particular crew but would make it difficult for an average crew to be competitive. Also, boats may have a significant design advantage in certain conditions, but may find themselves at a disadvantage when these conditions don't exist. To alleviate such problems, ratings are reviewed periodically; as a boat gains in popularity, enough people will be sailing it to give a statistically meaningful sample.

The International Measurement System (IMS), another popular rating system, develops correction factors directly from the physical characteristics of the boat as they affect the boat's expected performance. Advances in computer software, measuring techniques, and aero- and hydrodynamics have made this possible. Most production boats have to be measured only once, and then a master certificate can be used for the entire production run.

Other systems in use include the International Offshore Rule (IOR) and the various meter boat formulas. These are rule-based systems in that the handicap is developed from a rating formula, and new boats are designed around the formula. The designer tries to fool the rating system into classifying the boat as slower than it actually is. Quasi–one-design racing is currently developing between boats that share similar ratings. This type of racing, called *level racing,* pits boats of substantially different design but essentially equal rating against each other.

Let's take another look at a handicap fleet. Theoretically Joe Turtle, aboard the *Weekend Retreat,* can race against Richard Hare's PDQuick 38 and be assured that he has just as much chance of winning as if he had been on a similar boat. What actually happens is a somewhat different story.

You see, Richard not only has a quick boat, he has assembled a crew of Romanian circus performers who have no fear, do not require any mechanical advantage in the rigging, and are led by a psychic who knows of windshifts not yet apparent to the mere mortal. Joe, on the other hand, is sailing with a client whom he wants to entertain and impress with his well-rounded personality.

This problem is solved by placing each of these sailors in a class that more accurately reflects his goals. Richard sails in the RR (rabid racer) class, while Joe sails in the Zoned MO (multiple occupancy) class. Each of them is happy, comparing his skills to those of others who share the same outlook and approach. Both are competitive, and both desire to be at the top of their respective groups; they are now able to compete on fairly level playing fields.

Catamarans and Other Multihulls

Racing multihulls is one of life's great pleasures. Some of us had to be dragged kicking and screaming into the ranks of these speed demons, but once you try it you can get hooked in a hurry. The great top-end speed of these boats and their quick acceleration put a premium on getting and maintaining boatspeed *at the appropriate times.* Speed management is the key; you literally have to know when to go fast and when to go slow. Your tactical decisions will be concerned with when to trade speed for pointing ability and vice versa. Multihulls severely penalize the sailor who places himself in disturbed air. Tacking away is costly because the parallel hulls of a catamaran do not want to turn easily. Achieving and maintaining clear air must be the first concern; getting to the correct side of the course takes a close second. Sailing cats isn't quite as radical in this respect as iceboat sailing, but since the goal of both is to tack as little as possible, it is important that you hit the correct side right off the line. The difficulty of turning a cat requires special consideration when approaching marks; you must anticipate what is going to happen in front of you.

Catamarans are sailed mainly as one-design classes. Most look simple to set up but are ultrasensitive to the tune of the rig. The boat is so light that small differences of power produced by the rig create large differences in speed. Doing your homework and asking questions will push you up the learning curve quickly. Above all, you must spend time with the boat. The differences between monohulls and catamarans really crop up when switching from one to the other, and although the same strategic principles apply, only experience will show you which tactics are appropriate for your boat at what times.

The Prindle 19 offers lively sailing. (Photo courtesy Starcraft Sailboat Products)

Sailboards

The first sailboard race I saw had an interesting start. Many people were using the maneuverability of the board to move back and forth over the line, slowly drifting toward the port end but just shooting forward a couple of yards over the line each time, then backing up. This went on until the gun sounded and they were off. It reminded me of a running race. Since then, boardsailors have adopted starting tactics much more like those of other boats. I guess the sight of someone hitting the line at speed when you are just filling your sail has an educational effect.

Sailboards and other radical sailing craft have traits that require adjustments in your tactics. The idea, as always, is to put your opponent in a position where he can only react to what is happening, but the characteristics of the boats involved determine what that position is. The rules and conditions of the race are the same for any sailing craft. For the most part, we apply the same weapons to gain an advantage and consider the same factors in planning a strategy.

If your boat moves slowly and turns quickly, you can keep your options open a little farther into a situation. If, however, you are moving fast and can only turn slowly, you must be more aware of what is happening in front of you and know how you are going to attack it.

The physics of sailing don't change from one boat to the next. You first want to decide what type of boat is going to fit the style of sailing you want to do, and then apply those physical principles to that boat. In the next chapter we will look at the forces that drive a sailboat, so that we can manipulate them to advantage in the situations one finds on the racecourse.

Questions

Q What kind of boat should I be looking for?

A As I've said, there are so many boats on the market that finding one that suits you should not be a problem. The table on page 10 illustrates some of the characteristics of popular one-designs. Chances are there's a boat being raced in your area that shares some of the characteristics of one of these. Use the table to determine the type of boat you need, then look around to see where similar boats are being sailed.

Some boats popular in your area probably aren't included in Table 1-1, but at least the list will give you some insight into the variety of boats on the market.

Table 1-2 shows some of the more popular dual-purpose racing cruisers under 30 feet long, with their PHRF ratings. It is more difficult to select a small keelboat or handicap racer than a one-design because of the larger variety available, and the

TABLE 1-1.

Popular One-Designs

Name	Sailplan	Number and weight of crew	Comments	Similar boats
Sunfish	lateen single sail	1 110–190#	good training boat with great racing	Phantom, Sailfish, Optimist
Laser	single sail	1 150#+	Olympic class, worldwide racing, responsive	Force 5, US 1, Contender
Coronado 15	sloop no spinnaker	2 trapeze 250#+	popular husband-wife boat	Sweet 16, Holder 14, Buccaneer
JY 15	sloop no spinnaker	2 250#+	no trapeze, tight one-design control	Vanguard 15, M-16, Lido 14
505	sloop spinnaker	2 trapeze 275#+	high-performance dinghy	470, M-20, Fireball
Flying Scot	sloop spinnaker	3 550#+	family oriented, large racing organization	Highlander, Catalina 22, Ideal 18
Lightning	sloop spinnaker	3 550#+	planing hull, strong class	Y-Flyer, Tempest
Scows	varies	varies	a boat for any need, 16' to 38', strong class organization	E-scows, A-scows, MC-scows
Star	sloop no spinnaker	2 375#+	complex boat, Olympic class, athletic boat	Flying Dutchman, Soling, Etchells 22
Catamarans	sloop varies	2 trapeze varies	great beach boats, good racing, hair-raising performance	Hobie Cats, Tornado, NACRA, Prindle

local fleets are likely to be a mixed bag. Since these boats are raced in handicap fleets, I suggest you look at the rating band containing most of the boats in your area and find something that fits within the band.

Boat mfg. and length	PHRF rating	Characteristics
Catalina 22	270	family cruising boat, swing keel
Santana 23	172	smaller racing boat, lightweight
Wavelength 24	163	small racing boat, fixed keel, lightweight
J-24	171	small racing boat, fixed keel, strong fleet
Hunter 25	231	family cruising boat, fixed keel
Cal 25	223	family cruising boat, fixed keel
B-25	138	racing boat, lifting keel, lightweight, recent design
Hunter 28.5	184	midsize, family cruising boat, full accommodations
Olson 30	105	narrow, light racing boat, fixed keel, strong fleet racing
Tarten 10 (32')	126	midsize racing boat, one-design racing
C & C 38	128	full-size offshore cruiser, full accommodations

TABLE 1-2.

Some Popular PHRF Boats and Their Ratings

Chapter 2

Moving the Boat

Most people understand the basic forces that move a sailboat. Buddy Melges—Olympic gold medalist, world champion in several classes, and the patron saint of scow sailors—always used to open his talks with a discussion of lift and airplane wings. He never focused on the pure physics of lift, instead moving quickly to the more practically important subject of how pilots change their wing shapes for various purposes, and how racing sailors should emulate them. The racing sailor has got to understand the lessons of induced drag and lift.

For the sailor, lift translates into pointing ability, and drag means that the pointing ability will come at the expense of straight-line speed. This is the important point to understand. A shape that creates a lot of lift generates a correspondingly high amount of drag. At times either side of this trade-off will become more desirable. You've got to realize how you need to set up the boat to maximize certain characteristics in tactical situations. For example, if someone tacks right over you and he is not quite on your air, how do you set up to drive out from underneath him? How do you then start up to squeeze him, feed him bad air, and force him to tack? Depending on the situation, the sails can be adjusted to trade off lift (pointing ability) or speed (footing ability).

We'll look at these factors briefly here and illustrate how they fit into the general picture once we are on the racecourse. There is plenty of literature available that describes how sails are made and the principles behind their operation. Here, we need only know what we can do to our sails to increase the range and effectiveness of our racing tactics.

Sails and Sail Controls

The sail comes off the floor of the sailmaker's loft with a lot of its shape built in. Sailmakers assume a great deal when they lay out a sail. They plan for a certain

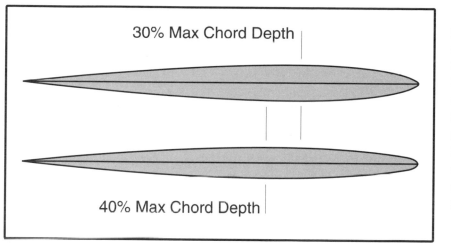

30% Max Chord Depth

40% Max Chord Depth

The airplane wing above produces high lift. (With a sail, high lift translates into pointing ability.) This ability comes at the expense of a lower top speed, but this shape will provide good acceleration. The bottom foil will move at a high speed without creating much drag, but will falter at slow speeds.

amount of mast bend, both fore and aft and sideways, and they take into account the average wind speed, sea conditions, and other external factors affecting the desired

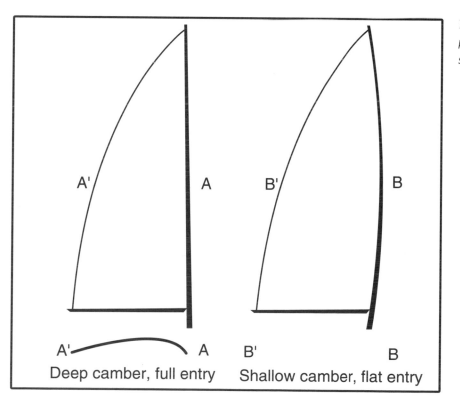

A'

A

B'

B

A'

A

B'

B

Deep camber, full entry

Shallow camber, flat entry

The rig can be adjusted to produce many different shapes from the same sail.

shape of the sail. They then design the sail to optimally fit this set of conditions, but to be adjustable to other conditions. You can alter the shape of your sails by changing the rig. This process of adjustment is called *tuning the rig*. It allows you to adapt a sail designed for a wide range of conditions to the conditions prevailing on the day of the race.

Sailmakers will have a good idea what the adjustments should be for a given set of conditions, and their advice will give you the general parameters. Following the instructions that come with the sails will save you from redoing someone else's work.

Once the rig is set up, the sail controls change the look of the sail to match slight variations in conditions and our own changing requirements as tactical situations evolve.

The boat moves through a balance of forces. In any given condition, for any given crew and sail combination, there is an optimum balance to be attained. As we sail, we are constantly adjusting the elements within our control to balance the forces outside our control. When a puff hits, we hike to balance the increased force of the wind. If the wind is strong enough, we adjust the sails to bleed off excess power and maintain that elusive balance. When the wind backs off, we readjust the sails to increase their power output. We are thus constantly dancing around the balance point, which itself changes with the wind.

Proper mainsheet tension is the single most important factor in sail trim and the most obvious sail control. Too little tension on the mainsheet, and much of the airflow across the sail simply spills off the leech; too much tension and the battens poke up to weather, restricting the air and causing it to pile up in the sail. The sail works best when as much air as possible flows across it while remaining smoothly attached to the sail. In other words, the wind has got to follow the curve of the sail—rather than detaching itself in confused, turbulent, power-robbing eddies—while moving as fast as possible.

The rule of thumb for mainsheet tension is to align the top batten of the sail with the boom. Telltales on the leech of the sail help indicate proper trim. If they are flowing straight aft, the airflow is attached on both sides of the sail. If they curl over, the air on the leeward side of the sail cannot follow the curve of the sail, and the sheet should be eased. Telltales placed at intervals down the leech will indicate the effects of twist on the sail.

Besides the mainsheet, we have a number of other tools to achieve balance. By tugging and pulling on the fabric of the sail, we can work on its shape and adapt it to the changing wind. The four most common adjustments are the outhaul, cunningham, boom vang, and traveler.

The cunningham, and for that matter the outhaul, acts by pulling along one axis and drawing material from the other axis. As the cunningham pulls down on the luff, cloth from the center of the sail is pulled toward the mast. This decreases the cloth available for the middle of the sail, flattening it. As the cloth moves forward, it brings the point of greatest draft, or the deepest part of the sail, with it. You don't have to

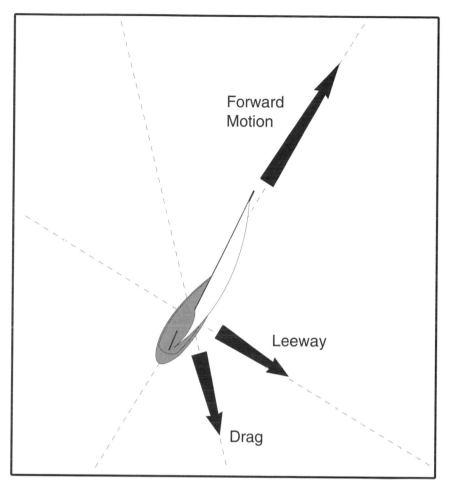

Forward
Motion

Leeway

Drag

All movement of a sailboat is the result of the balance of the forces shown.

be an aerospace engineer to appreciate that this reconfiguration of the foil will have an impact on the forces created by the sail. The sail is going to generate less power and less drag, and the angles of the resultant forces will change.

Why less power, you may ask. Remember that in a puff the input to the sail increases, and the sail produces more power overall. The heeling moment of the boat has to be controlled to keep the underwater drag on the hull from building up, and if shifting crew weight outboard is insufficient to accomplish this, the power output of the sails will have to be decreased. Tightening the cunningham to flatten the sail will do this, and also reduce the drag generated by the sail. This will allow the boat to use more efficiently the power it does develop. It also allows you to sail lower than you might ordinarily without creating excessive heel, a useful effect when driving out from underneath a boat to windward.

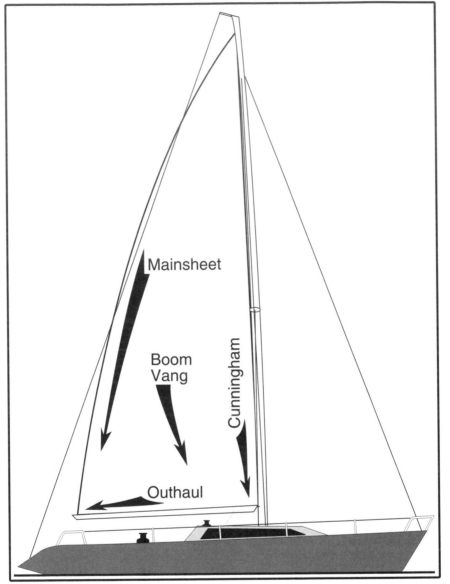

The outhaul acts in much the same way along the foot of the sail. Most modern mainsails are constructed with additional material along the foot that folds against the boom when the outhaul is tight. This fold, or *shelf*, opens up when the outhaul is eased to provide more exposed area off the wind. Pulling the outhaul out to the band on the boom should shut this fold and begin to pull on the cloth in the lower part of the sail. Pull farther, and you affect not just the fold but the sail as a whole. The outhaul will actually open the top of the sail when it is tensioned properly.

Most people understand the advantage of using these tools to flatten the sail in heavy air. However, they also work well in light air. Because the sail works by having air pass over it, reducing the curve, or flattening the sail, will allow the wind to make the passage more easily and produce some lift. Some is always better than none.

The vang acts in several ways. In some designs, it acts to induce greater mast bend. This has an effect similar to the cunningham. The bend in the mast reduces the draft in the sail, giving us a flatter sail.

On some boats the vang may not be strong enough to bend the mast. In these cases, the vang will only keep the leech tight and regulate the degree of twist in the sail. If the lower leech is trimmed more closely to the boat's centerline than the upper leech, the sail has twist; some twist can be desirable, but it must be regulated. Furthermore, when a sail is vanged, it can be more closely controlled by the mainsheet. As the sheet is eased, the boom travels out in a horizontal direction, adjusting the angle of attack of the entire sail. If there is no vang, or insufficient tension on the vang, the boom will rise as the sheet is eased. This will make the sail fuller and increase its power—doing exactly the opposite of what you intend when easing the sheet.

The traveler also can be used to alter the angle of the sail plan to the wind. For example, you might move the mainsheet lead to leeward on the traveler, thereby moving the main boom outboard without adjusting the mainsheet. The sail now makes a smaller angle to the apparent wind, so that the wind experiences a smaller change in direction when it reaches the sail and therefore fails to build up a great deal of force in any particular direction. By decreasing the angle of attack, you have decreased the amount of lift produced by the sail. Again, this is most useful in depowering a sail. You want as much power as you can use, but no more. Otherwise the boat will heel excessively and spill air anyway, creating a lot of drag both from the sails and from the hull passing through the water while heeled. In light air, the traveler can be moved to windward to maintain the angle of attack with a lighter mainsheet tension.

Not all boats have all of these controls, but sailors have used their ingenuity to devise substitutes as needed. A strong vang and an active mainsheet can function like a traveler, and halyard tension can substitute for the cunningham. The rules governing the class you are sailing dictate which controls can be used. When a control is allowed, you should make full use of it. When it is not, you should determine what the control does and try to substitute for it within the rules.

This applies also to sail-shaping controls we haven't mentioned yet, such as headsail barber haulers, jib cunninghams, topping lifts, etc. All such controls allow for more precise and effective use of the sails. The barber hauler merely allows the lead of the jib to be placed more outboard for reaching. Jib cunninghams perform the same function for the headsail as a cunningham does for the main. A topping lift can support the boom to take its weight off the sail.

Understanding the use of sail controls in tactical situations is as important as understanding how they affect your straight-line speed. In any given situation, you may want to force your way into an advantageous position. You may want to give up a little speed to get higher relative to another boat; or you might need to sacrifice some pointing ability to speed away from someone. The informed use of controls will allow you to extend your ability to place your boat where you want it.

We are not going to talk about finding the best settings for your boat. We are concerned here with using controls to further a tactical plan, and the adjustments we discuss will be relative. The important idea is to be able to make adjustments right when they are needed. This means that the controls must be led within easy reach of the crew in their sailing positions. Furthermore, they must have sufficient mechanical advantage to be adjusted without a lot of grunting and shifting weight. Pulling someone off the rail or in from hiking to depower the sail defeats the purpose of the adjustment.

Imagine yourself coming off the starting line. Someone has started above you with a little room and is slightly faster. You also have some room to leeward, but you are overpowered. Having the right setup means you can apply a little more cunningham, a tighter vang, and slightly ease the traveler, all without taking weight off the rail and causing the boat to heel further. You crack off a degree or two to accelerate, then readjust the controls to the pointing mode and squeeze the life out of the boat above. You simply can't do this if your boat heels and slows down during the adjustment.

Questions

Q How can I tell when my boat is set up properly?

A That depends on what is meant by "properly." Different boats require and allow various ways of adjusting their rigs for maximum performance. Before the race, setting up generally consists of mast and shroud tuning. In general, all boats will benefit from a mast that is straight athwartships (from side to side). This is a good starting point. The fore-and-aft angle, or *rake,* depends on factors that vary a great deal.

Shifting the center of force in the sail plan by angling the mast is an option in some one-designs. A slight degree of weather helm is desirable, and mast rake can contribute to it. In general, sail plans are more efficient when the leech of the main is more vertical; raking the mast aft helps. If the rake is so extreme that the main can't be trimmed without the boom hitting the deck or the mainsheet going block to block, you've gone too far. On PHRF boats, which are usually masthead-rigged, the forestay and jib luff determine the degree of rake. The base of the mast can be moved to allow more rake, but its range of movement is limited.

Rig tension will be regulated by the amount of prebend specified by the sailmakers. Most boats have the shroud chainplates aft of the mast, and in the absence of any other loads, increasing the tension on the shrouds will force the mast to bend. It will also tension the headstay without your having to apply backstay tension. Bending the mast like this has the effect of flattening the sails. Overtensioning the rig will result in sluggish acceleration and mediocre light-air performance; undertensioning will hurt boatspeed, make it difficult to keep the boat in the groove, and cause overpowering.

Most boats require that the adjustments discussed here be made on shore before the race. Some boats will allow you to change, say, rake on the water, so you can experiment right up until race time. The only sure way to know if your boat is set up correctly is to sail against another boat in a practice situation and play around with all controls available.

Q How can I sail through gusts better?

A Gusts are localized wind increases. You can use your sail controls to adjust for these changes in wind speed. If you need to depower for a gust, you should execute the following sequence: As the gust approaches, tighten the cunningham to flatten the sail, drop the traveler to reduce the angle of attack, and haul on the vang to keep the boom level if the mainsheet has to be eased. As the puff hits, ease the mainsheet slightly to spill the first impact, then resheet to help the boat accelerate.

If the puff is not overpowering, you might not use the sail controls, but you would still want to give a slight ease of the mainsheet. This allows the sail to become fuller and more powerful momentarily so that it can accelerate the mass of the boat. As the boat reaches speed, you retrim to reduce drag and achieve a higher top-end speed.

Q How can I accelerate out of tacks better?

A This is an important skill, as we'll discuss later. The thing to remember is that tacks will slow the boat; in order to accelerate again, you need to apply more power. This means that you've got to come out of the tack with the sails eased slightly. As the boat starts to regain speed, gradually trimming the sails will reduce drag and further increase acceleration. The quicker the boat reaches top speed, the faster the trim can be. For heavy boats this process can take a few seconds; for light one-designs it may just be a quick seven inches out and in—zoom!

Q How can I point higher? And how can I foot better?

A From a sail control point of view, these questions are just opposite sides of the same coin. The solution is likely to lie in the rig tune, particularly as it affects headstay sag. Start monkeying around with the boat in a systematic manner and see what develops. Go first to someone who doesn't have these problems and ask him or her what he or she is doing. That will at least give you a direction to pursue.

Beyond solving basic tuning problems, you must use the controls available to you when trying to point higher or foot faster than you would if there were no other boat close by. Pointing requires more lift, and the sails should be made fuller to provide the extra lift you need. This can be done through a combination of sheet easing and slacking the sail controls. The traveler can be pulled up farther to increase the angle of attack of the sails.

Footing more than usual requires the opposite response. The sails need to be flatter and the angle of attack may need to be decreased. Keep the traveler down, the sail controls tightened, and the mainsheet played to reduce heeling. Keeping the boat on its feet is important, as the object of footing is to develop higher speed, and heeling increases the underwater drag.

Chapter 3

Elements of the Race

Once the boat and crew are ready to go, it is time to start considering the particulars of the race to be sailed. I have always been blessed—or cursed, depending on your viewpoint—with a nature that demands that I wake very early on race days. Rather than tinkering around the house, I go to the water. I spend some time getting a feel for the current weather conditions so I will be able to monitor their changes as the morning goes on. This in turn will allow me to make some predictions about the weather pattern for the rest of the day, predictions that provide the basis of my strategy for the race.

Strategy is defined as the larger plan for the race. It takes into account, for example, the expected weather, the size of the fleet, and one's current standing in the race series. Strategy will dictate the type of start to use, the side of the course to favor, and the cues to look for on the racecourse.

A successful strategy depends on a number of elements that sometimes can't be strictly defined. Consider some of the variables relating to the expected weather and the location of the course. Can you expect a steady wind throughout the race, or is it likely to swing as the afternoon progresses? Are there currents to be dealt with? Are they going to change with the tide, and how will that mesh with the expected windshifts? Can you accept a slightly adverse current to gain from an expected windshift?

On the east coast of Florida, these considerations are pretty straightforward. The wind shifts clockwise as the day moves on, and there is a small tidal current that becomes a factor only when calling the laylines. Consequently, the correct strategy is to sail on the east side of the course early in the upwind leg and late in the downwind leg. This in turn determines where to start and how to finish the race. As long as you are on the correct side of the course, protecting the expected shift, you can't be too far off.

It is rarely this simple. For instance, no one can time the wind exactly. It may shift all at once, or it may oscillate back and forth. An unexpected weather system may overcome an expected shift altogether. Also, the simple strategy laid out above

21

As the sun heats the land and the rising air begins to draw more air in from the sea, the surface wind direction along the east coast of Florida will shift toward the east and begin to build.

ignores any action on the part of your competition. During a race, you must be able to adjust at any moment to accommodate previously unconsidered or discounted factors.

Your job in formulating a strategy is to account for all possibilities and work them into your plan. In doing so, you should concentrate on the implications of the most predictable factors and pay less attention to relatively uncertain aspects. You can

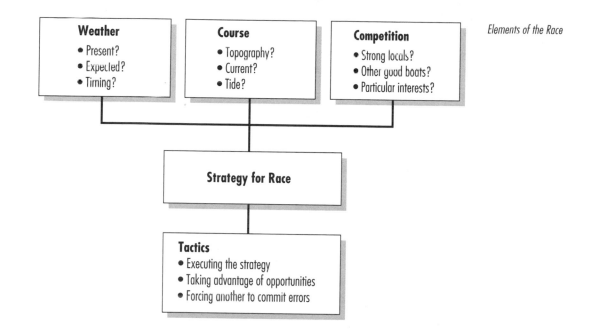

see this principle at work in most professional sports. Contrast college football to the pro game. The pros formulate a more conservative game plan and stick with it longer. They know that when the chips are down, playing to their strengths will pay off. Their game plan, or strategy, focuses on those things they know will happen, discounting the things they hope will happen.

The accompanying flow chart lists the elements that go into the strategic plan for a race. The order of the elements may shift, but they all must be included for the plan to be complete. We will now discuss the various elements in more detail.

Weather: The First Element of Strategy

It is essential that you know what conditions to expect during the course of the race. As weather systems sweep across the country, they cause the wind to behave in certain predictable ways. For example, the counterclockwise flow around a low pressure cell will dictate conditions up and down the frontal path. If you have a sense of the relative strength of the front and the speed at which it is approaching, you can infer roughly how and when it will affect the local environment.

If you are sailing in familiar waters, you can probably make a fair prediction just by walking outside and looking at the sky, then feeling the wind strength. Comparing what you see with previous days will probably give you an indication of how close a front might be and how soon it is likely to arrive. If you are sailing in a new place,

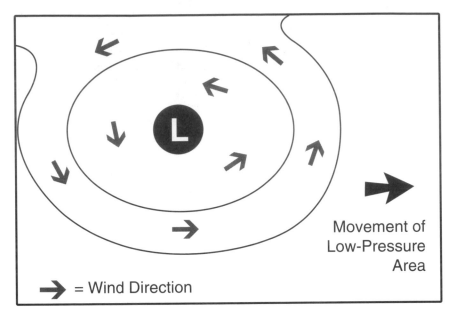

Movement of
Low-Pressure
Area

= Wind Direction

you will have to pay closer attention to the forecasters, because you need their input to develop a feel for how fast conditions are changing. But even though 24-hour forecasts by themselves will help, several days of observation of your own will enhance your ability to interpret what they are telling you and relate it to what you see during the race.

Rarely do the weather changes associated with a system reveal more than tendencies—a broad picture. To use the football analogy again, tendencies represent the opposing team's likelihood to do certain things. Coaches develop defenses around these tendencies, but the players still have to react to what actually occurs on the field. Similarly, knowing that the wind is likely to *back,* or shift, counterclockwise as the front approaches, you should work the left side of the course as the race progresses; but your assessment shouldn't lead you to blast over to the left corner at the earliest opportunity and then bewail the fact that the shift wasn't there yet. You don't want to be the one who stands at the end of the dock throughout the postrace party waiting for that shift so he can run in when it finally comes and say, "I knew it would fill in from the left!" The people around the bar just don't care.

It is important to formulate some expectations for the wind, then try to confirm them shortly before the race. Getting out to the course before the start and sailing while reading the compass is the best way of doing this. Watching the upwind headings change out on the course gives you some solid data to use in creating a strategy for that first leg. Despite the value of such estimates, however, I would never want to make a blanket statement about future weather conditions. I know I have to retain enough flexibility to adjust to actual conditions during the race.

The Playing Field: The Second Element of Strategy

Common Courses

Always know the course. The course most often used for important races with good race support is the Olympic Triangle. This race starts at the downwind mark, proceeds around the triangle, then has a windward-leeward component, and finally

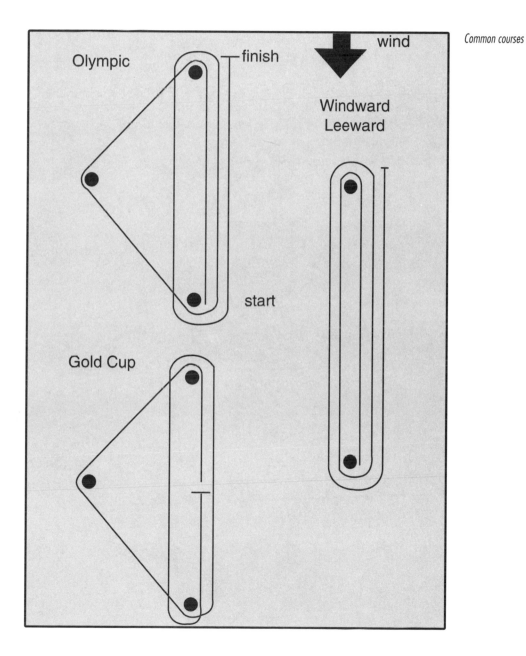

Common courses

finishes back at the weather mark. Because the starting line and finish line are different, the Olympic Triangle requires a mobile committee and creates difficulties in multiclass regattas.

Increasingly common now is the Gold Cup–type course. This is the same as the Olympic course except that the start/finish line is located midway between the downwind and windward marks. The first and last windward legs are abbreviated, but the race starts and ends in the same place so that multiple races can be run quickly.

We are also seeing now a number of windward-leeward courses that completely eliminate the reaching legs of the triangle. Such courses place a premium on staying in phase with the windshifts.

As sailboat racing grows in popularity, a number of other new courses are being tried and judged on their appeal for participants and observers. The course for the 1992 America's Cup races (windward, leeward, windward, reach, reach, reach, windward, leeward), regardless of what its drawbacks may have been, was an example of this kind of experiment.

For instructional purposes, I've organized this book to follow the legs as they are sailed on the Olympic course. A change in the order of the legs will not affect the basic considerations discussed here.

Windshifts Caused by the Land

Just as important as weather-associated shifts are those caused by topographical features. Wind bends as it is deflected over and around points and bluffs. In some instances it will even reverse its direction. The lakes of the Midwest are prime laboratories for this type of effect. There was a steep bluff where I learned to sail, about 300 feet high. The wind would leave the water to rise over the bluff long before it reached the shoreline. The mark was set fairly close to shore, and sailing into it was like entering another planet. It didn't matter how hard it might be blowing in the middle of the lake; if the wind was straight into the bluff, there was no wind around that mark.

The topography of the shoreline has a strong and predictable effect on wind direction.

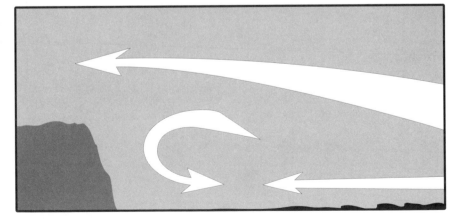

Rarely are topographical effects so dramatic. But changes in wind direction of 20 degrees or so as the wind blows across points or the mouths of small bays are fairly common, and they can have considerable impact on a race. The marks are generally close to these features, and as you approach them you will have to take account of the change in wind direction. Thus you might plan to play the shifts up the middle of the course until the last quarter of the leg, then get on the side benefited by the expected shift and take that layline into the mark. If the expected shift hasn't taken effect yet, plan to tack short of the apparent layline to leave room for it later. With shifts of this magnitude, short-tacking the last 100 yards or so can produce dramatic results. For reaching legs, the plan may be to go low initially to avoid a wind shadow from a bluff and obtain steadier air farther out in the lake.

It's difficult to predict such topographical effects, because they will vary with wind strength and with even slight differences in wind direction. On Spring Lake in Grand Haven, Michigan, the yacht club is on a point that narrows the lake to about 250 yards across. This makes for exciting race watching because the whole fleet has to fit through this bottleneck. Standard practice is to sail right into the docks at the club, tack, and take the lift out beyond the point into the wider part of the lake. The problem is that if you are one or two boatlengths short of the point, you may have to sail straight back out into the lake on a big header and try the whole sequence again. Even worse is the possibility that a big puff may lift right over the point and over you, to the benefit of your rivals. If this happens, muttering about fate won't do the trick. All you can do is hope that the next capricious breeze finds you instead of them.

The only way to handle such adverse situations is to maintain a conservative plan and not get rattled. If you've played the percentages correctly, you will eventually experience your moment of reward. It may not come until the next race, but it will come. The worst thing you can do is to start going from corner to corner chasing the last leg's miracle shift. You can't ignore what happens out on the water, but you need to consider any new factor in relation to decisions you've already made. Does it change the picture? Is it a persistent condition or just a temporary anomaly? The new element should really be significant, like an indication that a front has arrived or the early onset of a sea breeze, if it is going to make you modify your basic plan.

Current and Tide

Somewhat more predictable than the wind are the effects of current and tides. Accounting for current can be extremely disorienting, because it may not give you many visual cues. I remember going like a banshee through the waters of the Mississippi once while looking over at the same tree for what seemed like hours. On a larger body of water, I might never have known what was happening until the boats that had avoided the strong current had crossed in front of me.

So the key to making current your ally is knowledge of its relative strength. You want to be where the current is strong when it is going in the direction you want to

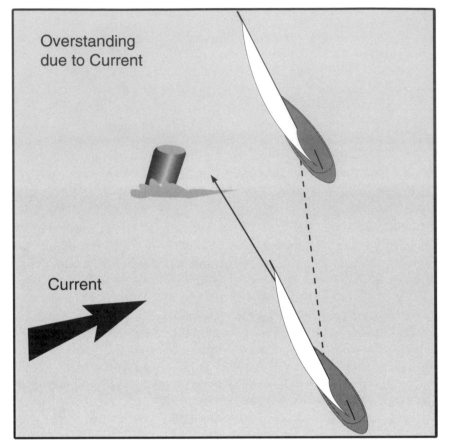

Overstanding due to Current

Current

go, and where it is weak when you have to work against it. If it is sweeping across the course, build the drift into your calculations of the laylines. Simple, right?

Tidal flow will change over time. It may either augment or work against the prevailing current. Frequently, the tide will move across the current produced by a river emptying into a bay. This will create all sorts of interesting phenomena. Look at the tide as the oscillating shift of the current world; at least the moon is more regular than a frontal system. You should be well informed about changes and anticipate their effects.

Finally, the topography of the bottom affects currents much as surface landforms influence the wind. The current will be stronger in deeper water and on the outsides of curves. My suggestion: If there is going to be significant current, get to the site early, sail around a lot, and tie the crustiest-looking local to your boat for advice while you do it. This will at least give you some hands-on information to integrate into the overall plan. The worst thing you can do with the current is ignore it. Who knows, you may be the first one to slip an anchor over the side while trying to go downwind against an unfavorable current in light air. This will give you an instant advantage over those with positive waterspeeds but negative groundspeeds. It's better than an oversize chute.

The Competition: The Third Element of Strategy

You will rarely enter a race completely ignorant of the competition. It may be the first race of the series and you have an idea who might be fast, or it may be late in an important championship and there's a boat right there that you've got to beat. Obviously, you are going to approach these situations in different ways.

In the first instance, you will go with your own assessment of the fastest way to get around the course. You will do so by staying in touch with the rest of the fleet but cheating toward what you've decided is the favored side of the course. You have to maintain the ability to execute your strategy: you have to be headed toward the side you want to go, you have to be in clear air, and you want to be able to hedge your bets. If you think you have uncovered some mystery that has eluded the rest of the fleet, who are over on the opposite side, you may need to reevaluate. Stay on your favored side, but play it closer to the rest of the fleet. If you are correct, you'll still gain some advantage, but you will avoid disaster if you are mistaken.

In the second case, you'll have to consider where your rival is whenever you make a move. In fact, your strategy may be reduced to simply sitting on the boats closest to you and letting the rest go where they may. Let your knowledge of the conditions tell you the best side to cover from; protect the advantaged side, and don't let yourself be drawn off to the point where someone else can emerge from the pack. If you are forty-second and your rival is forty-third, chances are that the first-place finisher will gain substantial ground on both of you, throw-out and all.

In general, the better you are doing in a series, the more conservative your strategy should be until it is time to go for broke. Remember that at a high level of play, more games are lost than won. You need to concentrate on not making mistakes. Let your competition make the fatal error. Your job is to capitalize on it, but you have to be in the ballpark to do so.

Having said that, there are moments when you need to roll the dice and go for it. Second is pretty nice, but winning requires a bold move from time to time. If you have sailed consistently well, you may not ever need to shoot a corner, but if you do, shoot it on purpose and take the verdict with good humor.

Tactics: The Final Element of Strategy

Just as the race can be a step in a series, tactics are the steps we take to execute a given strategy. We use tactics when we deal directly with other boats and the unique situations presented at each point in a race. It is possible to have the best strategy in the world and not be able to carry it out because of weak tactics. On the other hand, good tactics can sometimes be successful without a strategic overlay. Simply pass boats at every opportunity and you're bound to be close to the top by the end. (One could argue, of course, that this fits with the general strategy of starting first and increasing your lead!)

Tactics are either offensive or defensive, and are classed according to where in the race they are used. For example, there are tactics designed to get a good start and there are tactics to pass a boat on a free leg of the course. The chapters that follow will outline these tactics, among others. The prerequisite to using them effectively is a tactical frame of mind.

The tactical mind always looks ahead: it analyzes situations and projects them into the future to identify opportunities and vulnerabilities. This is the mindset used by great chess players; learning to adopt it is one of the big challenges of sailing. Recognizing a tactical opportunity early allows you to place yourself in an advantageous position. You might even determine the outcome of a situation by placing

The Racing Rules

The rules governing the sport of sailboat racing come in a book of 158 pages. The very idea of so many rules can be a little intimidating, but it needn't be. The portion of the book concerned with tactics and the conduct of competitors consists of just 3 pages of definitions and 16 pages of rules. The rest of the book covers administrative concerns and contains appendices for particular types of races. You need to refer to these additional regulations if you are about to plan a race, adjudicate a dispute, or participate in one of the specialized races covered, but complete understanding of the entire book is not a prerequisite for successful racing. Unfortunately, many people merely glance at the book and then decide they'd rather wing it.

We will look at the rules, including those governing the rights and obligations of yachts when they meet, as they bear on the topic under discussion. As we look at a particular part of the race, the appropriate rules will be mentioned by number and briefly summarized in a sidebar. Note that these summaries are only commentary, not a substitute for the rules themselves. You will find that once the appropriate section of the rule book is identified, reading the rule is not so daunting a task.

The rules define the nature of the tactics we have available to us. The two greatest tactical opportunities, the start and the mark roundings, are governed by a series of rules, an understanding of which is critical in turning these tactical situations to our advantage.

yourself in a position so superior that your opponent will concede rather than try to defend, which allows both of you to move along to the next episode with a minimum of fuss. This is your chance to practice what Sun Tze calls the essence of generalship: to win your battles by not having to fight them. Miss the opportunity and you may still be able to execute the maneuver, but it will cost you more in terms of time lost to the rest of the fleet.

Of course, successful use of the tactical mind presupposes a thorough acquaintance with your boat and the range of tactical options available to you. The only way to achieve this is through practice and plenty of time on the water. You may practice with other boats or by yourself, going through the adjustments necessary to shift gears as you might when defending or attacking another boat. The key is to be able to make these moves almost intuitively, with little premeditation. You must have the full range of tactical options immediately accessible to you, and move to the correct option without being distracted from monitoring the overall situation. I know that I am spinning my wheels when I am racking my mind for an answer to a problem on the racecourse. The solution must suggest itself.

We have to find out what works before we can make it work for us. The sections that follow will provide the basic knowledge; your job is to make it part of your tactical mind.

Questions

Q   How can I anticipate conditions for a course that hasn't been set yet?

A   No matter what type of course will be used, the influences of local terrain can be anticipated, and you need to understand the probable effect of the current and anticipated weather changes on the sailing area; you can then predict the effect on the specific legs as they become known. For instance, you may have planned to beat against a tidal flow, only to find that the course is going to take you across it. You know that the flow will set you toward the east, so you can adjust your perspective. You may have determined where the current would have been weakest in order to sail against it; now use this knowledge to decide if you can carry a spinnaker on that leg. Having a firm idea of the elements of strategy will help you in any situation.

Q   What if two elements indicate opposite actions?

A   This is more common than not. We once started a Mug race, a race from Palatka to Jacksonville, Florida, on the St. Johns River, expecting the wind to come in from the east and on the favored end of the starting line. The current was running along with us and was stronger on the west side, toward the middle of the river and away from the favored end. In this case, the current was the dominant factor. The boats in the middle got the constant push, while the wind filled in and faded out.

The solution to such problems is to get out early and make the call. Had we had more time to evaluate the current, we might have had better results. As it was, we went with what we could see and ignored the current. Wrongo!

Q What is the purpose of figuring out a strong strategy when the conditions on the racecourse may not be the same throughout?

A Your strategy gives you the framework you need to evaluate the choices you have on the course. Any decision is better if you have a baseline to judge it against. As we will discuss later, there will be moments when one element of your strategy will outweigh the others, and there will be times when either side of a decision offers advantages. Your strategy will tip the scales in favor of one course of action, making the decision more timely. You will act purposefully instead of sticking around to see what happens.

Q How can I develop a strategy to deal with puffy, shifty conditions that have no rhyme or reason?

A The short answer is that your strategy will consist of taking advantage of opportunities as they present themselves. At least you have realized that there is no consistency in the conditions and that you will have to be flexible. This will place you in a much better frame of mind if your competition gets a favorable shift, because you'll know that you could get the next one. You'll also know you have to be looking far ahead to spot emerging opportunities. It's no coincidence that even in the hairiest crapshoot, the good sailors always seem to end up on top.

Chapter 4

Before the Race

E ach race you sail can be part of a larger plan. Even weeknight beer-can races have a role in preparing you for an important series or testing some new technique. This means it is always worthwhile to get to the racecourse early. Besides, it is tough enough to get a crew together for the race itself, let alone for practice on nonrace days. The time before a race is an ideal practice opportunity.

There is much to be done in the time immediately before the race. After the boat has been thoroughly checked out to eliminate the possibility of mechanical breakdowns, and everything you will need on the water has been placed aboard, you should focus on the surrounding conditions.

On the Water

This is the time to take a close look at the sailing area. Time spent on the course before the race will pay off in the accuracy of the assumptions you make as you formulate your strategy. I once sailed a catamaran regatta off the beach south of Cape Canaveral, Florida. The cape extends about four miles into the Atlantic, but was well north of the racecourse. Even so, as the sea breeze went over the cape it shifted from the east toward the north. This shift favored the left side of the course, overriding the expected shift to the right caused by the buildup of the sea breeze. Everybody figured this out after the first leg, but everybody also reached the first mark behind the guys who had figured it out before the race.

When you get into the boat, it is time to test your strategic assumptions. Compare actual conditions with what you expected. If there are differences, can you explain them? Sail both sides of the course to get a feel for any advantage of one over the other. Sometimes there may be more air on the side you thought might not be favored. The puffs may be coming in from one direction, and you will want to use this information in planning your upwind leg. Discuss the options with your crew.

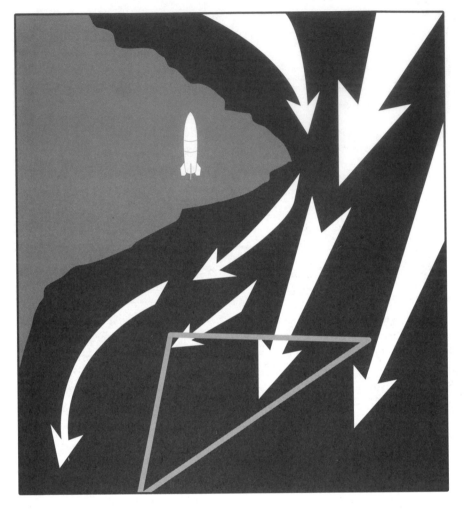

Cape Canaveral is fairly far from the racing area, but it has a significant effect on the wind. The shift toward the left would be unexpected if we were merely considering the sea breeze.

If there is consensus on the race strategy, everyone will expend that much more effort to make it work. Just sailing hard for a while will settle the boat and put you in a competitive frame of mind.

While you're at it, you may want to run through a few drills to sharpen the crew. A couple of spinnaker sets and a few quick tacks will loosen things up. If there is some confusion in the crew about tasks and roles, now is the time to get it straightened out. Every sport has its warm-up routine, and sailing should be no exception. The more extreme the conditions, the better everyone will feel if you've done all the maneuvers you can expect before the race.

Now is also a time to locate the competition and try to find out what they have in mind. Most people telegraph their intentions. One fellow I know simply runs through the line at the committee boat time after time. He probably still wonders why he can never get there at the start.

On the other hand, try to hide your own intentions. A little deception never hurts. If conditions are stable enough that you can make your choice of starting position early, stay away from it for a while. Not only does this keep your intentions masked, it also gives you a read on conditions elsewhere in the starting area. This widened awareness will come in handy if conditions suddenly change.

Planning the Start and the Early Part of the First Leg

The requirements for a good start are fairly straightforward. All you have to do is execute the start that will get you to the first mark first. That is not always the start that finds you at the windward end of the line, nor is it even necessarily the start that gives you the favored end of the line.

The most important aspect of the start is where it places you after you've traveled 100 yards from the line. Can you tack? Are you headed toward the favored side of the course? Will the first shift put you on top of the fleet, or will you be buried by the boats who may have given a little bit at the gun but were free to tack on the first puff?

When you are out sailing around before the race, you have to sample the wind. It will have its own feel. The wind can be rhythmic in its cycles of direction, or it can be sporadic, shifting quickly and without much warning. You can pick up on this

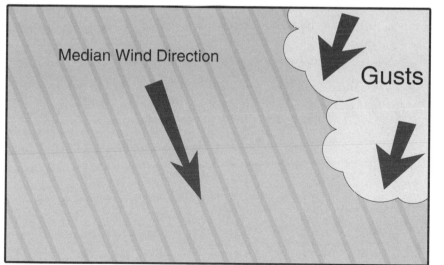

In this instance, the gusts are all shifted to the right, indicating the direction of the new incoming wind. This unstable condition can persist for some time and can be sailed as oscillating shifts.

by carefully monitoring the impact of the puffs. Sometimes the major shifts announce themselves with a burst of wind. If the shifts are sporadic, they will most likely come in hard.

Now you have to relate those shifts to where you are in the starting sequence. By this I simply mean that you establish what phase the wind is going to be in as the starting gun goes off. We need to be able to secure the most advantage from what the wind will do right after the start. Getting this first jump, having the freedom to tack, and being the first one into the shift will determine as much as anything the success of the first leg, and perhaps the race.

Now is the time to integrate what you have seen on the water with the weather data you've acquired on shore. Use the forecast only as a framework to analyze what is taking place on the water. You have to play the cards you are dealt. It is much more important to be right at the time of the start than later, when the forecasted wind finally emerges. You have to plan the start and first leg based on your own hard data.

Gathering these data is your first task. As you are sailing around working the bugs out of your crew, start timing any oscillations you can detect. This may not always be easy. The heading of the boat may move for various reasons, from wind velocity increases to momentary calms in the wave pattern. The way to get an accurate idea of the timing of the oscillations is to take compass headings at regular intervals for at least 40 minutes. You need to take enough readings to obtain a reasonably complete sample. If the oscillations are longer than 10 or 15 minutes, they won't be much of a factor on the leg itself, but they will tell you which way the wind will be going at your start.

A rough estimate of how long each phase lasts can be an enormous advantage if you can relate the timing to your starting sequence. The message here is that it is easy to know what to do with a shift; what is difficult is to know when to do it. Immediately after the start, when the boats are close together, that first shift can put you over a lot of boats very quickly.

A good way of determining the favored side of the course is to pair up with another boat and sail the course on opposite sides. This will give you a sense of what side of the course is advantaged. It may not be the one indicated at the starting line. If this is the case, you have to plan your start to allow you to get over to the good side as soon as possible, before the other boats.

Wind direction often oscillates with wind velocity. The harder puffs or the stronger wind will come in from a somewhat different direction; as the wind backs off, it will swing back to its original direction. These shifts can be subtle, and their effects are sometimes mistaken for the impact of wind velocity on the apparent wind. We can confirm that there are actual shifts by trying the puffs on both tacks. The velocity effect should be the same; that is, a velocity lift affects both tacks more or less equally. If the puffs are shifting, how are you going to use that to your advantage?

Puzzling out the conditions can be frustrating, and you are seldom going to get an unmistakable read on the situation. That's the way things should be, though; if

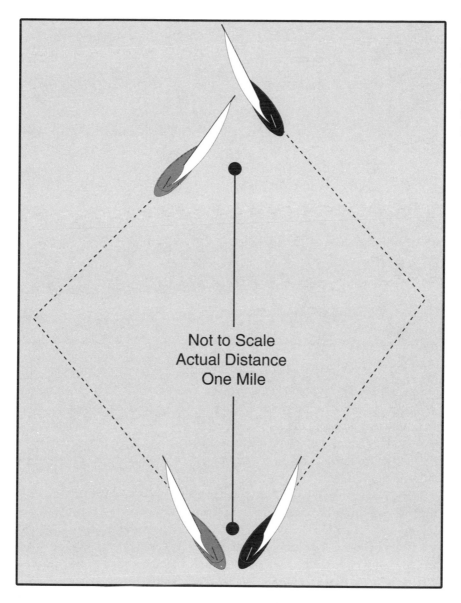

Not to Scale
Actual Distance
One Mile

developing a winning strategy were easy, everybody would do it. We are aiming for the unique insight, or the special timing, that elevates us above the competition. Most people can find their way down to the favored end of the line, but they often get trapped in the stacks of boats who have the same idea. What we need to do is to work backward from the first shift to the start and see how we can avoid a similar fate.

Let's begin by assuming that we have a relatively square line and a square first leg.

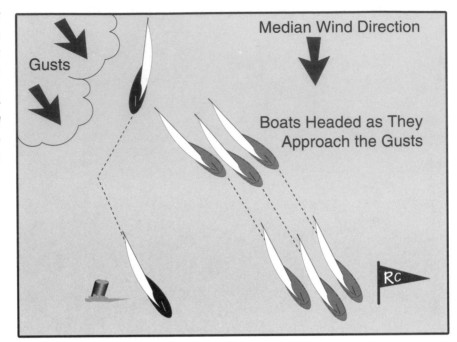

A typical fleet start would have a gaggle of boats trying to hit the line on starboard tack at or near the committee boat. Having concluded our observations, we realize that the wind increases and shifts to the left, then dies off and swings to the right. We want to be the first boat entering a backing, or counterclockwise, phase, and with about two minutes to go, we see some air coming onto the course—the backing shift moving across.

Now, rather than carving out a hole for ourselves in the crowd, we may want to allow ourselves to be squeezed out in front early, so that we can sail down the line and engineer a start farther down toward the new wind. If there isn't enough room to sail down the line in front of the fleet, we can try to duck out of line and head low for a hole farther down. Even better, if we were anticipating this possibility, we may have been approaching the port end of the line on port tack, and are now able to swing into the hole farthest down the line as our expectations are confirmed.

In the opposite case, with the first shift coming in from the right, one of our goals is to maintain the ability to flop over to port tack immediately after the start. This means that we have to be near the committee boat or have a wide enough gap between us and the boats to windward so that we can tack quickly, take a transom or two, and emerge into clear air heading for the shift. Techniques to get us to these spots will be discussed in the next chapter. Right now, we are concerned with what we have to know to decide where we want to be at the start.

Seeing opportunities and getting your boat to where you can take advantage of

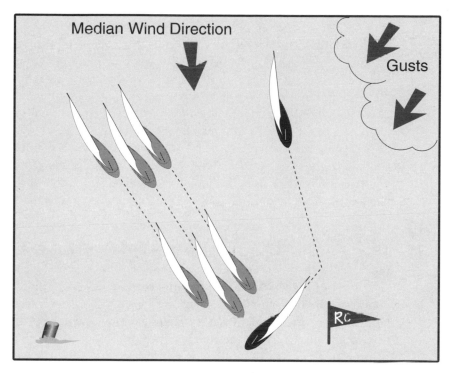

Median Wind Direction

Gusts

When the wind goes right, we may have to duck a few boats to get to it.

them are two very different things. Generally, the smaller the fleet, the more time you have to make your move. There will be gaps where you need them, and you can easily move from behind other boats into the front row. In larger fleets, it takes longer to establish your spot. Once you are there, you can't suddenly bolt and expect to get another spot where you see an even greater advantage. Once you are locked in, you have to postpone any strategic move until after the start.

What your start should do for you is get you on the side you've decided is correct without your having to swim upstream. Planning alone won't execute your start, of course, but it may make things easier for you by placing you in a relatively unpopulated position.

Questions

Q How can I tell a real oscillation from ephemeral shifts?

A The quick answer is that you can't. A single puff is just that, a localized area of increased wind that may have a different direction from the median wind. You need a series of readings that show a consistent bias toward one side or the other to define an oscillation. This is why it is so important to get out early, especially in unfamiliar territory.

If oscillations are present, your compass readings will show wind movement toward one side, then they will start to recede, pass the median, and increase to the other side. Remember that when you start your readings, you may be on one side already; you won't know your median yet. For example, you may start looking at the compass during the extreme right-hand phase and find that it continually moves left. By the time the wind reverses and starts to move right, you may be in the starting sequence. You'll have to pick a median value, then keep your eyes open. When you see readings similar to when you were first watching the compass, even after the start, you'll know you are at the beginning of another oscillation. If this sounds like a lot to keep in your mind, have someone else keep track of it.

Q What is the most important element in prestart planning?

A There are several elements of planning and preparation that are crucial. In the previous chapter we discussed the importance of strategy, including consideration of the wind, the current, and the competition. Another important area is boat preparation and rig tune. These tasks can be accomplished before leaving the harbor. Even if a significant amount of adjusting can be done while on the water, the rough settings should have been determined beforehand.

But your primary task before the start is to observe the extent and timing of the windshifts and use these observations to select a location on the starting line. After that, you are free to concentrate on what you need to do to get there. If the situation cannot be pinned down in the early going, at least you know what the variables are, and as time winds down to the start, you can continue to watch the critical factors and perhaps will still have time to adjust.

Q What if the area I want to get to for the start is crowded with boats?

A You might have to respond to this situation by avoiding that area. If things are so skewed that the entire fleet is likely to end up in one spot, you need to adjust to take account of the crowd—clear air is a valid reason for starting away from an advantaged location. We will discuss specific techniques for dealing with other boats in the next chapter.

Q What if the situation is so fluid that I can't tell where to start?

A That uncertainty itself can be the basis for a plan. If conditions are changing rapidly, you have to make sure you are not pinned in place and will be free to tack or continue as the situation demands. You may want to announce to your crew that things are going to be interesting. They should keep their eyes peeled and alert you to any changes. Flexibility in this case is not an indication of indecision; it is a strategy itself.

Chapter 5

Starts

I'd always had trouble with starts until Harry Melges III (the son of Buddy Melges), president of Melges/Sobstad Sails and winner of multiple E-scow national championships, explained his technique to me: "I pick my spot, and start from there." Aha—how much simpler that is than contemplating all sorts of strange rituals and complicated decision trees!

To gain anything from this insight, however, we have to probe a little deeper. How do you find the right spot, and once you've found it, how do you start, juggling all the requirements of clear air, boatspeed, and room to maneuver?

Finding the Line

The first step to a good start is to determine the exact location of the starting line. If race committees could draw a stationary chalk line on the water, it would make things a lot easier. As it is, the only way to locate the line is to define it in relation to easily seen landmarks on shore. Sail down the line with one end directly over your bow and the other directly over your stern, then extend the line beyond each end to some landmark. This is called *establishing a range*. The idea is that when either end of the line is lined up with the landmark beyond it, you are on the line.

After establishing the range, you can tell where you are in relation to the line anytime two of the marks are visible. Then use the extension to give you a reference as you sail up to the line.

If the line is offshore or there are no landmarks to use for a range, the process becomes much more difficult. There is no substitute for a foredeck crewmember with good eyesight, because this person may be able to establish an effective range with items on the committee boat itself. Once the starting flag has been identified, other masts or flags can be used to determine where the line is. If you are starting at the leeward end and can't see the committee boat, your proximity to the leeward end

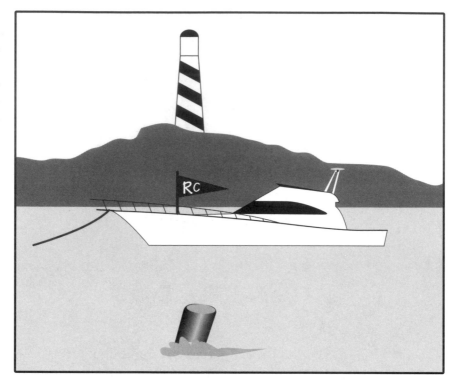

should be gauge enough. If you are starting in the middle and can't see either end, you had better get going, because you are too far back.

If you are sailing dinghies and no one can be sent to the bow for a look, remember to keep your bow just a couple of feet ahead of your windward competitor's. Put the time you've spent practicing to work, and beat him off the line with quicker acceleration and a greater knowledge of your boat's capabilities.

Determining the Favored End

Choosing where on the line to start involves several variables. The first is the spatial relationship of the line to the first mark and the wind direction. Starting lines are supposed to be set up nearly perpendicular to the first leg. In practice, most lines are set up slightly angled to favor the port end. If they were perfectly square, the result would be a large number of boats trying to start right at the starboard end. The jockeying for position would result in a high number of general recalls as boats are pushed over the line from behind. The race committees of the world try to give us some incentive for starting down the line by placing the port end closer to the mark.

The easiest way to spot which end is favored is simply to point your boat head-to-

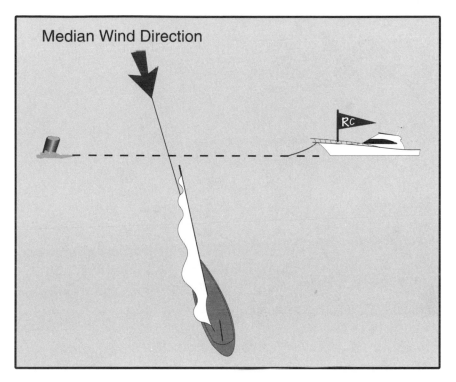

Median Wind Direction

RC

Once the boat is head-to-wind, the end of the starting line that the bow is pointing toward is the favored end.

wind while on the line. The end of the line your bow points toward becomes the favored end. Whether or not the windward mark is straight upwind, starting at the favored end of the line will put you closer to it. Even though you probably will not sail straight out to the layline and tack, the advantage you gain will carry through the leg. If the wind oscillates and starts to favor the other side, you can carry your initial advantage across the course and gain even more by tacking on the new shift.

What might be a nearly even line when the sequence begins may be favored at one end by the time the starting signal is given. As we discussed in the last chapter, you have to keep an eye on this and check the line frequently to get a feel for the wind's oscillations.

If one side of the course is favored by topographical shifts or current, the favored end of the line will be the end that allows you to take advantage of those shifts first. In other words, if the port end is favored at the moment but you expect a shift to come in that will favor the right side of the course, you'll want to start where you will be free to move right. That may mean trailing the pack of boats trying for a pin-end start. Indeed, you might even want to start at the starboard end. Tacking to port sends you out to the right side of the course, and you will be first in line for the expected shift. Remember, you want to be on top at the windward mark, not necessarily at the start.

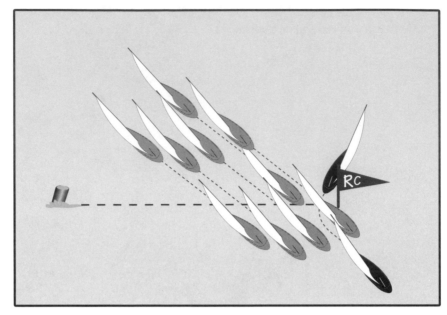

A quick tack is
sometimes necessary
to salvage a poor start.

Setting Up the Start

After you have determined where you want to start and what you want to do immediately after the start, how can you secure the desired position at the line and maintain your ability to sail where you want from there?

In a small fleet, it is easy to open up a gap or move into an already existing one. In the period prior to the five-minute gun, study the actions of your competitors; most boats are likely to line up for the start fairly early. See which ones seem to be paying attention to the area you've picked for yourself. If there aren't too many, you can approach the line from the left on port tack, tack underneath them a little later in the sequence, and hold them in place until you are ready to go. The delay in acceleration you've caused them will allow you to start with a good lee-bow position. This will force them to tack earlier than they may have wanted.

Getting them to tack does one of two things. If you want to continue on starboard tack because you anticipate the left side being favored, it forces them to the wrong side of the course. If you want to go right, then they will clear the way for you to tack and act as blockers through the fleet. A parade of port tackers crossing from the left has an interesting effect on approaching starboard tackers. They wonder why everyone is going right, start to look over there, and either slow down or tack early to maintain their position on the right side of the fleet. Either way, your chances of crossing the fleet are enhanced.

You can execute the same start in a larger fleet, but it becomes more difficult to punch through on port tack and tack into a position in the front row. You've got to

The first two rules cover most situations when yachts meet. Rule 36 is the fundamental opposite-tack rule—when two boats on opposite tacks meet, the starboard tack boat always has right of way. Rule 37 is the fundamental rule for boats on the same tack; it states that when boats are overlapped, the leeward boat has right of way, and if they are not overlapped, the boat clear ahead has right of way. The third, Rule 38, puts limits on the rights of the leeward yacht to luff or sail above a close-hauled course before clearing the starting line (after the start, Rule 39 applies instead). Rule 38 states that the leeward yacht shall not sail above close-hauled when the windward yacht is mast-abeam (see below) if doing so forces the windward yacht to alter course, and further, the leeward yacht or a yacht clear ahead must luff *slowly* if another yacht will have to alter course to keep clear. This rule recognizes that although boats are moving at slow speed before the start, the transition from privileged to burdened yacht can take place quite suddenly. Any move to take advantage of a newly acquired privileged status must allow the burdened boat ample room and opportunity to keep clear. The intent is to prevent another boat from slipping up underneath you and executing a quick luff with the sole objective of creating a foul.

The common tactic of a leeward boat holding a windward boat head to wind before the start must cease immediately when the gun sounds. Thereafter, the rules restrict the leeward boat from luffing above his proper course. Specifically, Rule 39 states that a leeward boat must sail his proper course after clearing the starting line if at any time during the currently established overlap the helmsman of the windward boat has been mast-abeam of the leeward boat—that is, directly abeam of the other boat's mast. Since most leeward overlaps that exist at the start have been initiated by the leeward boat's coming up from behind the windward yacht, this is commonly the case.

Rule 42 governs all obstructions and marks, but 42(a) defines the special role of the starting mark as an obstruction and gate, and specifically how the starting signal changes the relationship between the leeward and the windward yacht at that mark. This is the well-known "antibarging rule," which exempts a leeward yacht from having to give room to a windward yacht at a starting mark. After the starting signal, however, the leeward boat may not sail above close-hauled or above the compass course to the next mark to deprive the windward boat of room at the mark.

Together, these rules work to make the process of creating a hole at the line a slow and deliberate one.

get into position on starboard tack earlier and be more aggressive in carving out your spot. Ideally, you want a gap of at least a couple of boatlengths below you to allow for acceleration, while your bow is a couple of feet in front of the boat to windward to allow for clear air. Maneuvering at low speed is critical to the success of this strategy: you've got to be able to turn your boat without having it move too far in any direction.

Effective maneuvering at low speed is the hallmark of a good starting helmsman. It takes close coordination with the sail trimmers to turn the boat without either killing its speed entirely or suddenly filling the sails and taking off. As the boat sits luffing on the line, slightly trimming the headsail will turn it off the wind. As soon as the rotation is underway, the sail has to go back out and be continually eased as the boat turns farther off the wind. This allows you to rotate at a snail's pace, without picking up speed down or toward the line. A turn in the opposite direction, back toward the wind, is initiated by handling the mainsail in the same way. Using the rudder here would brake the boat; then sails would have to be trimmed to reestablish forward movement, and the boat would move farther faster than you might have intended. Try steering with the sails—you'll like it.

A word to the boat above you to watch your transom when you turn down will keep him from getting as close as he may want. Since he is trying to build his own acceleration ramp, he will be more than willing to maintain some distance to weather. The real problem will be the boats coming up from behind who will want to fill the gap between you and the boat to leeward. This will ruin your ability to build boatspeed as you make your run at the line.

Dealing with this threat means accepting some trade-offs. As boats are coming up and threatening to establish an overlap, you can turn down the line, thus occupying a large part of the gap. The other boat may then aim farther below you so

Turning your boat while holding position will preserve the gap beneath you. You are vulnerable here, but you can simply sheet in and go if pressed. It is unlikely that anyone will be coming up too hard early in the sequence.

that when you turn back up, the gap reappears. Again, the trick is to do this without picking up speed. If the other boat persists, you can quickly build some speed, cross his bow, and then lose the speed by taking a hard turn back toward the wind. This is the trade-off: you've maintained control of the area directly to leeward, but you've lost some distance down the line. Consequently, you ought to set up in a place that will put you where you want to start after having repeated the maneuver a couple of times.

Closer to the start, it may not be possible to execute this maneuver at all due to the large number of boats trying to push up to the line. But if the fleet has been a little leery of pushing the line, there should be plenty of room in front of the other boats.

You must resist being pushed toward the line at any cost. The boats coming from astern are going to start shouting for their rights as leeward boats long before they've established an overlap. Ignore them. The rules don't provide for people *attempting* to establish an overlap. They do require, however, that a boat, having established an overlap, gives the windward boat ample room and opportunity to respond. Take it. Also, remember that the leeward boat cannot luff beyond a close-hauled course until he has established an overlap beyond the mast-abeam position, even before the start. You may have to prepare a quick rules brief as the stampede starts up, but the time you gain by holding your position is going to translate into distance you can use to accelerate.

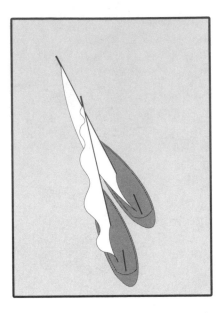

A leeward boat cannot luff past close-hauled until he passes mast-abeam.

Time to Go

There has been a spate of basketball analogies in sailing lately, and I'm going to use another one here. What you need to do in the final seconds before the start is like a baseline dribble to the basket. After the first step, the player leans on his defender to force him off balance and get him to move away from the basket. Once he succeeds, the player then shifts direction for an unimpeded two steps to the hoop. Your timing must be the same. You lean on the guy to weather to open up your ramp to the line, then break and go for it. No matter who has stacked up underneath you, unless they are close enough to lean on you, you will get some room to accelerate. Meanwhile, the boat above you can only wait and follow you down, but he is already that fatal half-step behind.

After you have reached your best speed, it is a simple matter to squeeze the windward boat until he disappears. If you want to tack to port, it is a good idea to start squeezing up early and hard. This may entice your competitor to do the same to boats above him or to tack and clear a lane for you. If you want to continue out to the left side of the course, concentrate on accelerating away from the other boat while gassing him with your backwind. Knowing where the line is and how long it will take you to get up to speed is imperative if this maneuver is to be successful.

The simple port tack approach can also be used for starting in larger fleets. As described earlier, this tactic consists of approaching the line from the pin end on port tack and sailing until you reach the spot you want or until you see a gap that can comfortably accommodate your boat. The larger the fleet, the earlier you will have

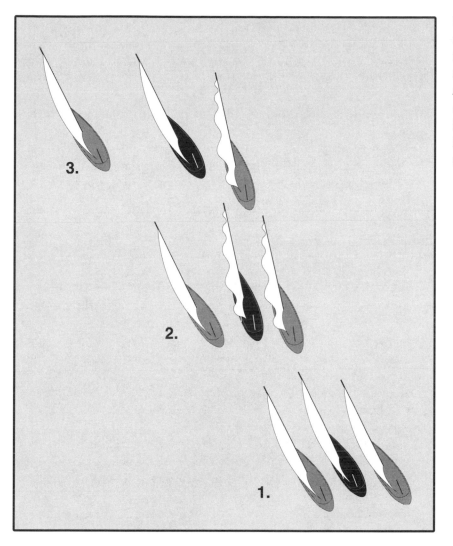

to tack over to starboard. I find this works best when I am dealing with a port-favored line and I want to sail beyond the cluster of boats crowding the pin, or when the line is square but has a great many boats stacking up at the starboard end. The gaps are going to form where the crowd thins out. Sailing on port tack gives you a better idea of where they are.

You need to approach the line nearly close-hauled. This will reduce the size of the turn you have to make when you tack over to starboard and allow you to preserve some speed for maneuvering. A complete 180-degree turn would cause your boat to stop, and you'd have to expend some of the gap just accelerating to regain steerage. Besides, coming up from an angle makes the gaps more visible. Point your bow directly at the boat to windward of the gap you are heading for. When he tries to close it by accelerating, tack into it before he can pick up too much speed. If he gets going too quickly for you, force him to pass, and tack into the gap that opens to windward of him.

A word of warning: If you use this technique in a very large fleet, tack over early. Don't continue down the line looking for the next good gap. Even if there is one, the air behind an intervening cluster of boats may be so disturbed that you can't get to it. The fleet is also going to develop rows as boats fill in behind the ones who are already set up. Get in there early, and once you get there, start building your ramp.

One time I was starting a race at the MC-scow national regatta on Lake Geneva, Wisconsin. I had decided I wanted to head left until the first header and then take a long port tack to or near the starboard layline. Sailing left first would take me to the western point defining a large bay perpendicular to the nominal wind direction. Experience had shown me that there would be a large shift there. The fleet was sizable, and I wanted to be sure I could get off the line cleanly, so I elected to start about two-thirds down the line. I sailed on port past the clump of boats lining up for a shot at the pin end, found a nice wide hole, and tacked. I still had nearly one and a half minutes before the start. Immediately someone who was reaching down the line was all over me. I luffed him once and realized that this guy was going to really tie me up. I allowed him to sail over me and encouraged him to accelerate so that he would end up well down the line. As he sailed by, I moved toward him once more; he put on speed and pulled way low after he cleared me. This got him going pretty fast and sent him on his way. Boom! I had clear air and, with the midline sag, plenty of room to accelerate as well.

A good start comes down to control. Are you controlling the boats around you or are you being forced to respond to what they are doing? Having control implies that you know where you are going. In the example above, my competitor was trying to control what I did, even though I had all the rights granted by the rules. Had he stayed close above me, my start would have been controlled by his position relative to mine. If he had gone early, I would have had to go with him to preserve my clear air.

Starting at the pin end is particularly interesting. Anyone coming up on port tack will find room to tack underneath the crowd. As the crowd drifts down the line, the last person in will be forced to tack too close to the pin and be early for the start. If you find yourself in that position, recognize that you have to halt your drift toward the mark first. A low-speed luff will stop the pack from coming down. If the entire mass of boats is early, there will probably be a recall, and when you're pinned down this may suit your purposes fine. Assuming there is no danger of a black flag (which disqualifies everyone who is over the line before the gun), consider blasting out early. Even if there is no general recall, you should at least get the three or four closest boats to go with you. Then you will be on the inside of the wheel when you spin around the mark to restart. If there is any kind of breeze, you should

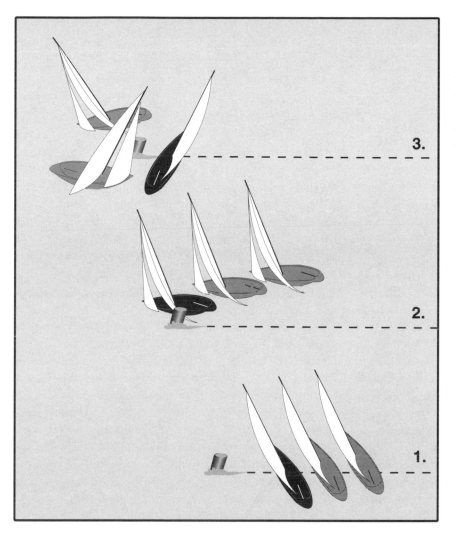

When you have to go over early, take someone with you. They might leave a hole for you to shoot through on port. Time this so that you will still make it back to the line nearly on time.

also have built enough speed to shoot through a gap in the line of starboard tackers. They will all be pinching and moving fairly slowly as they try to raise themselves out of the pack. You will end up above them in what should be pretty clear air, able to tack back onto starboard or continue on port, depending on your assessment of the next shift.

This maneuver actually works best when the port end isn't so favored that everyone immediately tacks over to port. The key to your success is to penetrate the line of starboard tackers without having one tack right on your air or use you as a blocker. Incidentally, you may find the comments of the boats you take over the line extremely entertaining.

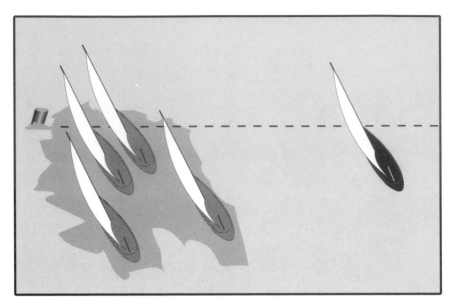

If the pin is crowded, only the boat farthest to leeward will get away cleanly. Starting slightly above the pack allows us to sail our best speed in clear air while the rest of the fleet is pinching in slop.

A safer tactic to use when the pin end is favored is to start just to weather of the pile-up that will form at the leeward end. There should be a good area in which to build speed between the guys at the buoy and the people who are going to try to start near the committee boat no matter what. If the wind is continuing to shift toward the left, there is a good chance that everyone at the pin will sail all the way out to the lay-line. Being closer to the center of the course gives you the ability to tack over at will, in clear air. Of course, if the wind swings right, you are on the inside of the shift and will gain accordingly. But you planned it that way, didn't you?

There are several other starting techniques, including dip starts and timed runs. Modern race administration has more or less eliminated dip starts by applying the one-minute or around-the-ends rule, which requires that any boat over the line within one minute of the start must round one end of the line to start properly. Timed runs break down in all but the smallest fleets. I believe the key to a good start is to keep it simple. I also believe the primary cause of a bad start is indecision. If you wait until things sort themselves out, you'll end up being bounced around. It doesn't take many boats to cut the air so badly that you can't get to where you want to go. Some people don't like the pressure of getting in early enough and then standing their ground. Well, the only alternative is to stay away from the crowd. It is better to be slightly out of position with clear air than to be waiting for the dust to clear at the favored end while letting boats from either side slide up and over you.

What if you do become trapped in the second or third row? If you have some time left, it may still be possible for you to work your way up to the line. Think of yourself as a crowbar levering boats apart to give you space.

Establish an overlap to leeward, then slowly luff the windward boat. When he

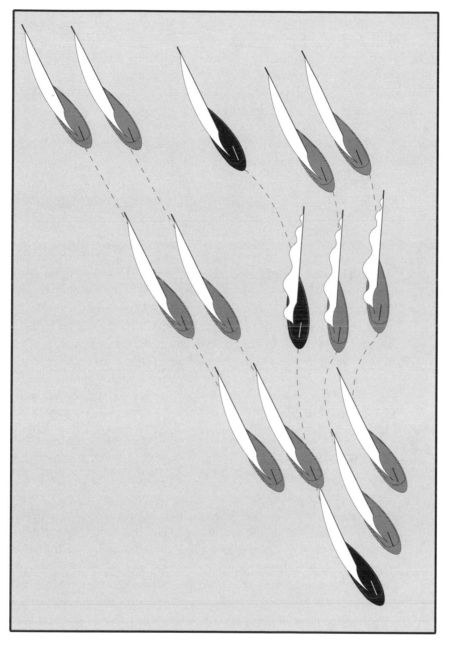

By luffing the boats to windward you can create a gap in which to accelerate toward the line.

starts to respond, pull off a bit and gain some speed. This will move you up in line. Repeat the luff and pull off again. If you can do this smoothly, you can continue to work up against the windward boat until you are at least bow-to-bow. Remember he will want to avoid being pushed toward the line and may let you in next to him. This same technique will allow you to open up some space to leeward and, if you are aware of the line, beat him to the punch when it is time to go.

If this doesn't get you into the first row, you'll need to bite the bullet and tack out of there as soon as possible after the start. Sailing in dirty air while the leaders pull away is a losing proposition. While you are continually bounced around in your search for clear air, they will be free to tack at will, hit the shifts, and disappear. This is another reason why starting where they ain't sometimes works out to be best. If you aren't first across, you can end up paying a big penalty for the privilege of crossing the line at the favored point.

Questions

Q What if I can't determine which end is favored?

A Well, if there is no obvious favored end, you have the entire line to work with. Think about what you learned when you were sailing around before the start, and make a decision about the side of the course you want to be on after the start. Then execute a start that will get you there. Also, make sure the weather mark isn't over on one side of the course. If the line is not square, start closer to the favored end. If the leg is square, start looking for your competition and try to get an advantage over them right away. In the absence of a clear bias in the line, just go over your prerace strategy to identify some relevant factor and use it to select a starting spot. But *do* pick a spot, if only to give you a framework for your prestart maneuvering.

Q When I get ready for the start, everything seems to go well until the last minute, but then the fleet streams in around me and I'm stuck with bad air and nowhere to go. How can I prevent this?

A It sounds as if you are at least picking the right spot. You have to either get there later in the sequence or take a more aggressive stand in protecting your air. If the fleet streams in around you, you are probably not on the line. As they come up, work on the boat to weather and stay with him. If you are not comfortable with his approach to the line, try to slow him down. If boats are coming up from below you, make sure you respond to them when you need to and not before. Use the speed you have to scallop your way to the line. Taking digs to windward will open up some space below you. Finally, practice accelerating your boat so that you aren't left on the line when everyone starts to move.

Q I always get into trouble by being early at the line. How can I regulate my speed without losing steerage?

A I like to do S-turns if I need to slow down because it keeps water moving over the foils. Being early is a relative problem. If you are already in your spot, someone would have to force you to move. This has its advantages. Discourage boats coming in from below you by turning your boat down the line when they look as though they are coming toward you. Keep your sails out and your centerboard up (if you have one). As the boats coming up hail to initiate a luff, remember that you have room and opportunity to respond. Turn your boat up using main trim if you have little forward speed; use your rudder if you have too much forward speed. Avoid turning up so far that you go into irons or can't get down.

Q I always seem to be late for the start. How can I improve my timing?

A Being late at the start is usually a matter of not knowing where to start and not being able to get one's boat up to speed quickly. Force yourself to decide on a location and stick with your choice. Right or wrong, you need a target to move effectively. Accelerating is an acquired skill. Practice some standing starts when you are sailing around before the start, or make it the focus of a practice session. And if you are afraid of being over the line early—well, the last I heard they weren't executing people for being over the line. An occasional restart might be no worse than consistently starting in the second or third row.

Q What is barging?

A *Barging* is an attempt to force your way in from a windward approach at the starboard end of the starting line. The boats already there have rights as leeward boats. A barging boat will try to wedge himself between those boats and the mark or committee boat. If he is hailed and luffed before he overlaps the committee boat, he can be forced to go to the windward side. Once he overlaps with the committee boat, he cannot be forced to hit it. Barging is a constant temptation, because as boats cluster at the starboard end they tend to move down the line. This opens a hole for boats entering late, and you can enter this hole without barging if other boats would have to luff beyond head-to-wind to stop you. A good tactic making use of this hole is to come into the line slightly low with good speed and, when you reach the back of the pack that is there, shoot head-to-wind right at the mark or committee boat. Make the turn gradually so that any boat above you has room to respond, and make sure you have enough way on to get you to the mark. Timing is everything here, because you have to surge up into the gap, then turn off and reaccelerate. In big fleets, there will probably be too much traffic for this approach to work, but if the crowd forms early enough, they have to drift down the line or go over it.

Chapter 6

Sailing the First Leg

OK, we're off the line in good shape. We've sorted out the boats around us, and we have room to tack or to continue without anyone trying to squeeze us. The couple of boats who got away underneath us are safely tucked in, and they either have to duck us or keep going. Now what? Let's say we notice a large number of boats aiming for the other side of the course and we are slowly being headed. What does this mean? What should we do next?

The first important consideration is to keep the boat moving fast. All the practice and equipment, the measuring and tweaking will not help if you start swiveling your head while pinching the boat. You should have the early part of the first leg planned before the start; once you are underway, you need to focus on the plan's execution. The boats are still close together at this point, which gives you a chance to consolidate a good position or recover from a less than stellar start. You can accomplish this by concentrating on boatspeed as you execute your plan.

Boatspeed Development

The mechanics of sailing upwind are fairly simple. Trim in the sails, and steer the boat to maintain attached airflow across the sails and to keep the underwater foils working. But there are many subtleties involved in maximizing your speed in the process.

Tuning a boat for upwind speed requires an individual touch, since the adjustments needed vary with crew weight, sail shape, mast stiffness, etc. We all operate in the same physical environment, but the constraints it imposes are different for each boat and crew. Certain helmsmen sail their boats consistently high and require a setup that allows them to do this. Others foot more and optimize their rig accordingly. These preferences also need to be reflected in the final tune of the boat. For starters, use the ballpark estimates provided by the sailmakers or consult others familiar with a particular boat.

The way to achieve superior speed is very simple—too simple for many people. It means going out and experimenting with your sail controls, sailing by yourself if necessary but ideally together with another boat. After you have established a baseline, start changing rig tension, changing sails, or using one particular control to extremes. Do all of these things, but do them systematically, one at a time. After a particular control has been sufficiently explored and adjusted to its most advantageous setting, move on to the next.

Even in this day of sophisticated computer programs, the staff of Melges/Sobstad Sails will be out on Lake Geneva testing sails boat-on-boat, because that is the only way of confirming the merits of a new sail design. They can see a difference on the water very quickly. Sailmakers know whether they are headed in the right direction with a particular change by making it and trying it. It's also a hell of a way to get out of the office, but hey, somebody's got to do it.

Some ground rules have to be in place to make the best use of the time you spend improving your speed. Try to suppress the impulse to exploit an advantage while you are in the process of systematically testing adjustment combinations. Of course, after a piece of equipment or a tuning technique has been evaluated, the boat-on-boat fun can start, for this too should be practiced.

Two boats working together can develop all the skills needed for successful fleet racing. Drills to accomplish this include timed tacking and pure straight-line drag racing. The drills start with both boats even and continue until one gains the advantage. Then positions are switched, and the drill is repeated.

These drills and practice sessions seem like work, but the truth is that spending time in the boat thoroughly honing your skills is the one sure way to improve performance. The purpose of the intensive drills is to shorten the time you need to attain a given skill level. You don't have the luxury of unlimited time when you are preparing for a particular race, but there is certainly no limit to the level to which you can develop your skills in the long run.

Having said that, let us consider the impact of boatspeed on tactical situations. Sailing is a game of inches. I don't mean the margin at the finish line but the difference between a neutral and an advantaged position. To get to the controlling position you must be able to do the most with what you've got. If a puff comes by, use it to accelerate the boat to its full potential; if you need to tack in front of another boat, go in and come out of the tack with maximum boatspeed. The less time spent regaining full speed, the more time to exploit the lee-bow position.

Most of the tactical maneuvers on an upwind leg are either initiated or ended with a tack. You've got to tack to cross boats as you consolidate a good start, and you have to tack right on someone to force him over to the disadvantaged side or to control him while approaching a mark. It is a skill that requires practice.

A good tack usually has some rolling elements in it. The turn is started by allowing the boat to heel. The shape of the hull then moves the bow to weather without your having to turn the rudder. As the bow approaches the eye of the wind, the

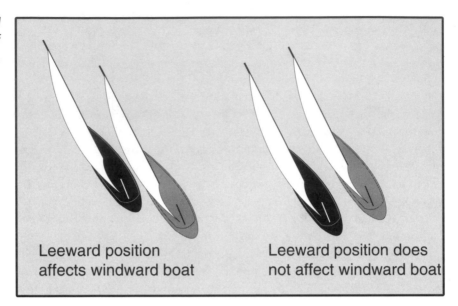

Attaining the safe leeward position is a matter of inches.

Leeward position
affects windward boat

Leeward position does
not affect windward boat

Starting a roll tack properly allows the shape of the boat and the center of effort of the sails to steer the boat around, rather than the rudder.

rudder can be used to encourage rather than initiate the turn. The crew use their weight to accelerate, or emphasize, the roll toward the new leeward side as the sails lose the air. Then they flatten the boat on the new tack, with the roll back to windward forcing air through the sails and accelerating the boat on the new tack.

Pretty simple, isn't it? Now try it after your tactician has called for a tack across the bow of a boat that almost certainly has you pinned. If you want to succeed, it has to be the same smooth, clean tack.

The importance of good tacking is illustrated by a certain tradition at the E-Scow Blue Chip regatta. The Blue Chip regatta is an all-star event open to scow sailors who have qualified by placing at one of the regional or national regattas earlier in the season. The organizers always invite a well-known sailor from outside the class, give him a first-class boat and crew, and let him have a go at it.

The first thing the invited guest does is sail the boat around and tack, tack, tack. He then sets the chute and jibes, jibes, jibes. In lake sailing, the ability to execute clean tacks time after time is the key to sailing the shifty breezes. The seasoned mystery guest appreciates that, and spends his short practice time trying to get his tacks up to speed.

The Blue Chip races themselves give good tacking practice. All 25 or so boats have gotten to the party by proving their boatspeed. They tend to arrive at the first mark all at once. Trying to get into line from port tack at these races makes you a believer in good tacks.

Another component of overall boatspeed is the ability to react promptly to changing conditions, such as an increase or decrease in wind or an alteration in the wave pattern. A quick change in the boat might also be necessary if you set your sights on a new goal, for example, getting into a certain position relative to another boat.

A wind gust gives you an opportunity for gain. It will swing the apparent wind aft for a bit and accelerate the boat forward. Handling the puff well can give you that extra foot or two you need. In the last few feet of the gust's approach, ease the sails slightly. This gives them a fuller shape—that is, more power that you can use to move the boat. Remember, the wind has to accelerate the mass of the boat; more power in the rig allows this to happen quicker. Then, as the boat is about to reach a steady speed, trim the sails back in. This flattens them, reducing the drag they produce and allowing the boat to achieve a higher top end. So you can reach a greater top speed faster with this "ease-and-squeeze" technique. It doesn't take a large ease to give you results. Using this initial surge of power to head closer to the wind allows you to levitate to windward if that is where you need to go.

If the gust is so hard that it will require the crew to hike, or hike harder, get them out there before the force is felt. The extra righting moment will work to squirt the boat forward rather than heeling it. But no matter how hard it is blowing, your crew should preserve the ability to throw a bit more weight out. You must adjust the rig by using the controls available to you, so the boat can be sailed on its lines in the median wind and the crew can give you the extra oomph when you need it.

Easing slightly into the puff presents a more powerful shape to the wind, making it easier for the boat to accelerate. Once the speed is up, trimming flattens the sails, reduces drag, and allows a greater top speed.

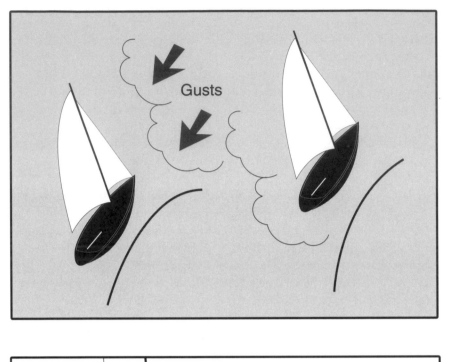

Get the crew hiked out before the puff hits. The added righting moment will translate into greater speed.

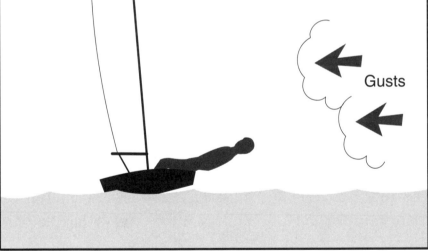

Most boats are somewhat overpowered; the impact of a sudden gust may heel them quickly. This is something you must prevent. Depowering when necessary keeps the boat moving forward instead of sideways. Once the underwater foils stall from heeling, it will take some time for them to reestablish a smooth flow and regain lift.

Depowering a typical boat may involve tightening the cunningham, dropping the main traveler, adding more tension to the vang, or applying more backstay. It may in fact require all of these adjustments. Once again, this depends on the boat you are sailing, your style of sailing upwind, and the availability of the appropriate controls. Your practice sailing should reveal the combination that works best for you.

Practice should also give you the ability to make these adjustments without looking at the sails. There are many things going on while you are sailing upwind, and you have to be aware of all of them. You cannot afford to get distracted. When you look into the boat, you lose touch with the situation around you for the time your head is down and the time it takes to reorient yourself as you look up again. Learn to recognize the effects of what you are doing by the change in the feel of the boat. Yes, practice will allow you to do this.

Confident in our speed, we can look at the racecourse now and make sure we are headed quickly in the right direction.

Getting in Phase

Our study of the wind before the start gave us some idea of the pattern and magnitude of the shifts we can expect. A look at the morning weather map has alerted us to the possibility of any dramatic weather-related shifts, and we've examined the sky to get early indications of a weather change, if any. A prerace sail up the course has given us a feel for how topography might affect the direction of the wind. Now, after the start, the question is, are we using all this information correctly?

If the wind is oscillating, are we on the advantaged tack? If we are, is this advantage waning or will it persist? The quick rule of thumb is to sail toward an expected shift. By moving toward the shift, you maximize its benefits. If you expect the wind to move left, sail to the left and tack when the wind goes over. That is referred to as being *in phase* with the windshifts.

To be in phase from the beginning, try to monitor the wind direction in the final minutes before the start. This is easier if there are other starts before yours. Get a good look up the course to see what kind of wind is coming down it. Some oscillations announce themselves with a puff; you can spot these and adjust your start to take advantage of them. Head for the shift off the line, and swing over to the other tack when you get to it. If you keep this up for the entire leg, you should be in pretty good shape at the weather mark.

The danger we face after the start is that we are going left, for example, when the wind is about to shift to the right. Then, as we recognize the advantage over to the right, we might head over in that direction just as the wind is preparing to swing back. This is referred to as being *out of phase* and will cause some gray hairs. After all, you've got to tack sometime, and there is an urge to get over to the side that looks good in hope that it will remain that way.

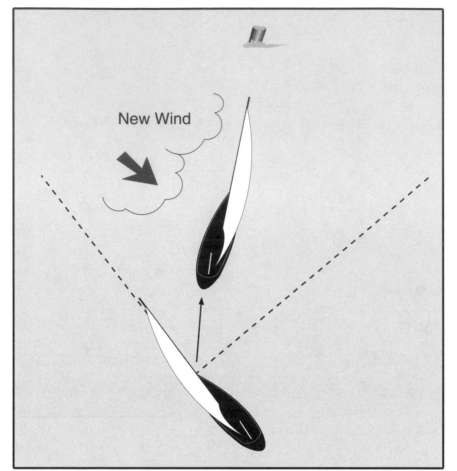

New Wind

The problem is that when you concede and head over to the other side—in this case to the right—you do two things: you give up the boats over on the right by crossing behind them as you meet near the middle of the course, and you give up the potential advantage you have when the wind swings back to the left. In the context of the entire race, however—even an entire series—it might not be so bad to reestablish contact with the fleet. You can limit and perhaps partially recoup your loss by being careful as you converge with the fleet.

If you are likely to experience a couple of oscillations before you reach the weather mark, you have no choice but to get back on the correct side of the shifts. You can gain back some of the distance lost by coming toward the middle and then working back to the left prior to the shift. The key is not to let the boats going across from the right get on your left. Work in the left center, and then lead the fleet back to the left side. This will get you to the next shift first and allow you to use that lever-

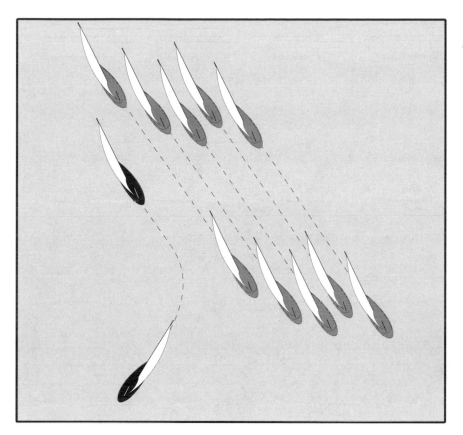

When you are out of phase, come back to the fleet and tack underneath them onto the favored tack.

age to close the gap between you and the boats who hit the first shift correctly.

The advantage gained by being in phase with the shifting wind clearly outweighs every other factor in racing success; it almost seems pointless to discuss anything else. Getting in phase if you are not must override every other consideration. Bad air, other boats, waves, and other hazards will have to be dealt with after you regain the proper relationship with the wind direction.

Boat-on-Boat Upwind

Tactics on the first leg of the race should focus on positioning. Early in the leg, your first priority must be to position yourself in clear air, then get in phase with the wind. Much depends on the start you've had. If you are in clear air, you need to move to keep it. If you are heading in the right direction, you'll want to keep going; but recognize the need for a tack at some point and start looking for your lane.

If things have gone well at the start, there are a couple of points to keep in mind.

RULES 36, 37, 39, 41, 43

Complementing rules 36 and 37—the basic rule governing boats on opposite tacks and the same-tack rule giving the leeward boat rights (see Chapter 5)—the rules governing sailing to weather discuss tacking and jibing. The important point rules 39, 41, and 43 have in common is that it is illegal to tack too close to another yacht. If you tack so close to another yacht that he has to take action to avoid hitting you before you have completed your tack—that is, before you have fallen down to your proper course on the new tack—then you have tacked too close. If you are able to complete your tack, then the oncoming boat is overtaking and must keep clear. This becomes relevant in crossing situations and also at the mark.

Rule 43 specifies the procedure for requesting and granting room to pass obstructions. The significant point is that while the yacht wanting to pass must properly request room, the other yacht is obligated to honor the request. If he feels the request has been made incorrectly, he must take recourse to protesting the yacht that made the request.

Also important are the restrictions placed on the leeward yacht by Rule 39. This rule applies particularly to the period right after the start, but it has clear tactical implications beyond. The rule restricts the attempt of a leeward yacht to force a windward yacht to tack by luffing him. If the leeward yacht luffs above his proper course, he must continue the luff and tack *without* interfering with the windward yacht. Note that a leeward boat in a safe leeward position will have a proper course higher than a nearby windward boat, due to the effect of the leeward boat's backwind on the windward boat. The windward boat will not be able to point as high as the leeward boat and will have to slow or tack.

Most of the other boats on the course will not be able to realize their full speed right off the line. They will be sailing in chopped-up water and chopped-up air. Boats also will be squeezed together, and they will be sailing higher than normal in an attempt to build some separation between themselves and others.

This will make them appear to be pointing quite well, but in reality they will be developing more leeway than normal and their path may well be below the course they would sail in the absence of other boats. If you can resist the urge to point up with them, the extra speed you attain will counteract the leeway. You can pull away and have them slide into your wake. If anything, you should start by footing slightly to build boatspeed. This is why the boat on the pin end often gets away cleanly.

Every boat has a best speed to windward. Your job off the line is to place your-

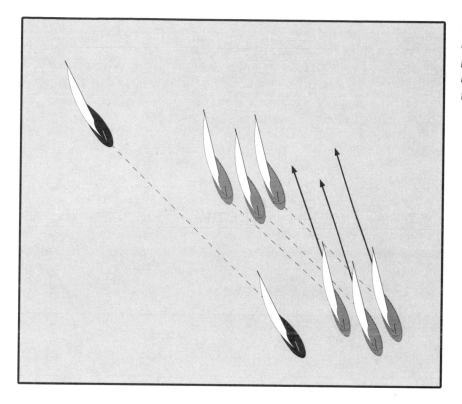

Coming off the start, the boats that can sail without pinching are going to put lengths on those that are tangled in traffic.

self where you can develop this speed without interference. If you are sailing your best speed and those around you aren't sailing theirs, you will either beat them to the mark or beat them under the handicapping system. Of course, other boats will also be trying to achieve their best speed and to prevent you from reaching yours.

Obviously, if there is a boat to leeward clearing his throat, you have to sail high to stay clear. Remember that the surface of the water is probably lumpier than usual near the start, and fuller sails and careful steering can minimize the input of the waves and give you the power you need to grind over the other boat. More powerful sails enable you to steer higher with more power in a situation like this. If the leeward boat is slower through the waves, you can drive over him. He will quickly fall to a mast-abeam position, and you can resume a normal course. He'll probably want to tack about then anyway.

Setting up for lumpy conditions right at the start can also be an advantage. The crews in catamarans often move slightly aft in lumpy seas. If the waves in the starting area are large enough—maybe from spectators or other fleets waiting for their turn—moving aft to lift the bows slightly might give a catamaran those inches that are needed.

If the boat to leeward persists in squeezing up, or if he is a little ahead, tacking away may be the only option you have. If his bow is out in front of yours, you won't be able to grind over him. As the two of you slow, the rest of the fleet will be sailing away down the course. Neither one of you will profit from a sustained battle at this point in the race. Unless it is late in the series and the leeward boat is trying deliberately to drive you back in the fleet, he will probably knock it off once he has established a safe leeward position.

Clearing Tacks

Right after the start the fleet is as close together as it will ever be. We can benefit from this fact if we find it necessary to clear our air with a short tack. Remember that the majority of boats will be bunched near the favored end of the line. This mass of boats will create a large area of disturbed air. A short tack to a position over the fleet,

Getting into clear air is worth taking a few transoms, and even going the wrong way for a moment. This is also a consideration at the windward mark when the fleet closes up again.

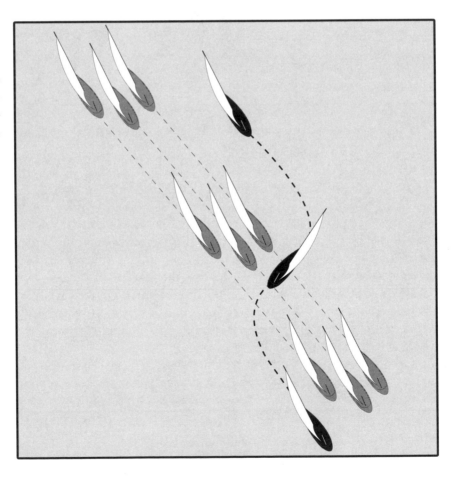

even if it is temporarily out of phase, can pay off. This will work best when the fleet is likely to stay on starboard tack for some time after the gun. Sailing in clear air above the other boats is worth taking a few sterns. While the other boats are sailing higher or lower than they might want, you'll have the ability to sail fast.

The sooner you can make this call the better. If a lane opens up, take it quickly, but with the knowledge that you will be going back at the first opportunity. After all, if you are going in the wrong direction when you tack to clear your air, you want to get back in phase as quickly as possible after you have accomplished your purpose.

A variation of the clearing tack can also be used if you've come out ahead on start. Consolidating your lead when you are able to cross the other boats puts you in control. If the wind is fairly steady and there is no compelling reason to be the boat farthest left, a tack across the fleet restores your options. Working back to the middle of the course allows you to take advantage of any shift that develops. It also places you between the mark and the rest of the fleet. Whatever happens, they will still have to come back to you.

The timing depends on the wind. If you get the first whiff of a knock, take the hitch. As you start to cross boats, check the persistence of the wind you tacked on. If it fades, you'll want to get back over to starboard tack to sink deeper into the shift and protect the left side of the course. If the shift continues and builds, you can take it back to the middle of the course.

Reading the Wind and Water

Spotting the wind on the water is something every racing sailor must do to enjoy consistent success. You need to be aware of three properties of the wind: its velocity, direction, and duration.

Velocity concerns us because we have to make adjustments to keep our boat moving at its greatest efficiency. The boat will need to be accelerated, the crew will want to hike harder, and we will want to be ready to depower if the incoming wind is too much. Velocity also gives us an indication of a change in direction.

It is easy to see a puff moving across the water. The area of disturbed, dark water travels right down the course. If you are sailing upwind, the puffs tend to come from two directions: they either arrive head-on or they come in from the weather side. If you can see the area of dark water moving *across* your course, it will be a lift. If it approaches head-on and just gets bigger, it is undoubtedly a header and you may want to consider tacking.

The duration of the puffs is important as well. A small, isolated puff in light air may just be a harbinger of the main event. Beware of such sucker puffs, which come and go, drawing you away from the body of the shift. The sea breeze shift is a good example. It announces itself with a number of small puffs that may die out quickly, before the real breeze comes in as a long-lived block of air. All oscillating shifts

If the puff just gets larger, it is a header. If you can see it moving across your bow, it is likely to be a lift.

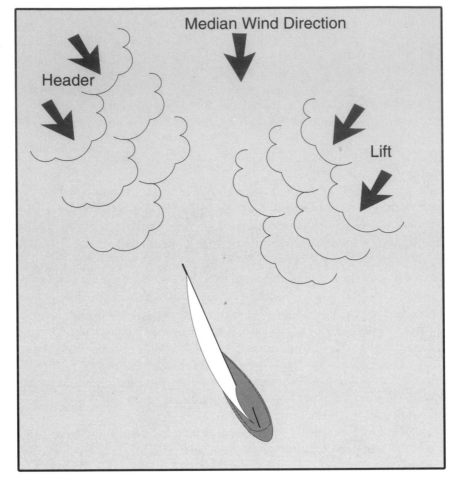

Median Wind Direction

Header

Lift

have to be judged on duration. You want to tack over on a shift that is going to last at least long enough to justify the loss of speed incurred during the tack.

As you start thinking about tacking to port, you have to pick your spot with all three of these aspects in mind. You want to go back toward the middle riding a lift, but you need to be sure that the shift will stick around long enough to get you where you want to go. Similarly, you don't want to give up a great deal of velocity if you can avoid it. If the wind looks stronger and more sustained a few hundred yards ahead, it makes sense to get deeper into the shift before tacking. Remember, that shift is approaching at its own speed plus your speed toward it. It doesn't take long to move into a more consistent area of wind.

After you have decided that this is indeed the time to get back to the middle, the only factor that might delay you would be a boat that has just passed; tacking too soon might place you directly in his backwind. Even then, he had better be right there to delay your tack. Any boat coming in from the left side will be riding the lift, and will probably cross in front of you if you continue. Tacking before the other boat crosses does two things for you: it gets you on the lifted tack, and it puts you that much closer to the next shift favoring starboard. This assumes that the wind is oscillating back and forth, not shifting permanently in one direction. Our earlier study of the weather should have tipped us off on this possibility.

Crossing Boats on the Weather Leg

After the first third of the leg, the fleet has sorted itself out a bit. There are lanes of clear air, and boats on either side of the course are starting to consider heading back to the middle, if they aren't doing so already. Your crew has warned you of several crossing situations coming up.

Your next move at this point depends on a number of factors besides the tack you happen to be on. Evaluate your position relative to the course and the wind. Do you want to continue on your tack, or are you thinking about getting over to the other tack anyway? Are you heading toward a big wind or current advantage, or are things fairly neutral and you just want to maintain your clear air?

The fundamental rule governing crossing boats is simple: the boat on starboard tack has the right of way. He is free to proceed on his course, while boats crossing on port are forced either to go around him or to tack over onto starboard. Let's put ourselves in his position and consider a number of possible scenarios.

We will look at the best case first. We are sailing on starboard with a lift. Some boats are attempting to cross close by on port tack. We want to continue on starboard until the wind starts to back, which we think will occur sometime later in the leg. The boats on port can either continue or tack underneath us.

The last thing we want is for one of these boats to attempt to cross in front of us, decide he can't make it, and camp on our lee bow. If one of them seems about to do this, it is easiest to just wave him by. You can also start footing a little more to increase the likelihood of his continuing on. If he decides to tack anyway, resume your normal course as he starts his tack. You will have put a nice distance between the two of you, and you can sail on without having to suffer in his bad air. The extra boatspeed you picked up while footing may allow you to drive over him and place him in your disturbed air.

Any boat that looks as if it is going to pull off and pass behind you should be encouraged to do so. This means that you should alert him to your presence fairly early. If he recently tacked over to port, he is likely to continue on that tack for a while. In that case, he is heading in the wrong direction and has in effect conceded your position. On the other hand, if he tacked in the early part of the shift, you still gain by crossing him, driving deeper into the shift, and getting on the inside.

Dealing with boats on starboard crossing us while we are on port tack requires somewhat different tactics. We have to give way in any close situation, but ducking a starboard tacker can initiate a whole series of bad crossings. If we duck just a single boat, the encounter may be without consequence, but if there are a number of boats following him and we have to duck them all, we've just given away a great deal of our hard-earned windward position.

As always, the first decision we have to make is whether to continue on port or to tack and head back to the left. If we elect to tack, we want to have clear air or force the starboard tack boat back in the other direction. Our choices are to tack early and well clear of the other boat, or to close with him and tack onto his lee bow. The risks are, respectively, that he will be on the inside of us, with any favorable shift extending his lead, or that he will drive over us and we will fail to establish a safe leeward.

Here in the first leg, the decisive factor should be where we are on the course. If we are already on the left side and we want to work back into the middle, we should continue right. If we are close to crossing him, we can ask whether he wants us to cross or tack. Because he will not want a boat on his bow, he may wave us across. If he doesn't, we can plant a tack right on him, preparing to tack back to port after he does. But if we want to pass behind him, we should slow down early rather than being forced into a major last-second course change in order to duck him. By slowing down and keeping our course changes to a minimum, we preserve distance to windward and maintain greater control over our boat and the situation. If our opponent attempts to cross and then tack on us, our acceleration should break us through his bad air and may give us the safe leeward position. If he crosses easily and tacks on us, he was too far away and we shouldn't have worried about him.

On this first leg, we want to be able to take what we consider the best course upwind. We do not want to get involved with other boats unless we can engage them on extremely favorable terms. So we won't worry about tacking right on anyone's air or trying any really aggressive tactic until later in the race.

Leverage

When you are able to tack to port before other boats can cross, you put a very powerful force to work for you. I'm talking about the concept of *leverage* on the upwind leg. Simply stated, leverage is the advantage you gain by reaching a favorable shift earlier, and sailing in it longer, than your opponent. It operates by placing you on the inside of the shift relative to the competition.

Leverage requires some lateral separation between the two boats involved—that is to say, separation in the direction perpendicular to the *rhumb line*, in this case the straight line between the start and the windward mark. If you pass close behind a boat on starboard tack who continues, then tacks over to port on your hip, you can use leverage to close the gap or even pass him. Shift your boat into a high-speed mode, and try to increase that horizontal separation. As you enter the next shift, you can tack back to starboard and sail a converging course as the other boat sails on toward the shift. When it reaches him and he tacks over, you have now placed yourself on the inside of the wheel. As the shift continues, your position gets better and better. To prevent your competitor from doing the same as the wind swings back, trade some of your inside advantage for boatspeed and work to decrease the separation between the boats. As you are lifted on the inside, make sure that your boat is sailing at its maximum speed, and resist the temptation to stuff the boat as far into the lift as possible. Your opponent will be trying to close up, and will likely squander his chance for leverage on the way back. Ideally, when the wind does shift back, you'll be able to place him in your backwind as you tack over. If you haven't quite gotten there yet, remember the cardinal rule: *Stay in phase!*

Persistent Shifts

In the middle of the leg, the strategy outlined above works well if the wind is shifting back and forth fairly regularly. A permanent shift will give the leg a significantly favored side, however. If you are facing this kind of one-way street, how can you improve on your position coming out of the start?

Let's say that we have been thorough in our prerace activities, and we know that the left side is the ticket. We get off the line and start the drag race out to the corner. There are two favorable positions. The first is to be the farthest out to the left, gaining the most advantage and tacking on the layline to the mark. The second, which has the greater chance of success going for it, is to be the first boat to tack coming out of the corner, short of the layline. This position provides us with clear air for the long port tack and lets us take advantage of any shifts that occur along the way. Even a persistent shift has oscillations within it. By tacking early, we largely avoid getting stuck on the layline, and we can use any significant headers to consolidate our position relative to the boats that headed out farther.

To pull this off, we need a clear lane to tack—a goal we should have been working toward right from the start. This means we need to squeeze any boats that might be overlapped close by to windward and try to get them to take a clearing tack early. Otherwise, even though they may be falling back due to our bad air, they can hang on and keep us pinned until they tack, which will probably be about the time when we wanted to go.

Sailing this first weather leg really comes down to two simple rules—stay in phase, and get and keep clear air. It can be a chance to build on a good start or recover from a bad one. The decisions you make early in the leg will set the tone for the rest of the race.

Remember, at this point we aren't focusing on any other boats in particular. We want to place ourselves in an advantaged position relative to the fleet, where the air is free and unobstructed, and we want to maintain that position. When we encounter other boats, we need to be careful. We can't spend much time battling with them, because the fleet is so packed that we risk giving a lot of boats the opportunity to pass us while we deal with just one. We need to induce our competitors to tack away from our air or to pass on, leaving us unmolested.

If we got off to a good start and picked the correct side, we should be approaching the windward mark at or near the top of the fleet. Conversely, if we were buried at the line, or we misread the wind coming up the leg, our comeback can start with a smart approach to the weather mark. The fleet has to come together again to round this mark, and it will be possible to pass a number of boats all at once. In the next chapter, we will consider how we can get a leg up coming into this mark.

Questions

Q I've started on the favored left side of the starting line but want to get to the right side of the course quickly. How shall I proceed?

A Well, if you need to go right immediately, you have to ask yourself, how favored was the left side of the line? You need to plan to be either on or at least headed toward the favored side as soon after the start as you can manage. If you have time to reach the right side, set your boat up to point as high as possible and squeeze the boat above you; if you can force him to tack, he will become a blocker across the course. If there isn't a boat above you, you should tack over and be prepared to take a couple of sterns. Then, if it looks as if someone may want to tack on you, try to confuse him so that he tacks too early or too late to affect your air. If you are coming from the left on a nice left shift, most of the other boats will catch it below you and tack before they reach you. You will be fairly safe in tacking onto port riding a solid lift.

Q Suppose I am working back to the middle and notice that the boats coming in from the other side are working a big lift. How do I know whether I should continue on to get above them, or tack short of them and move back outside with them?

A If the wind has been oscillating and these other boats are in phase, tack short if you expect another oscillation. Sail until you get the shift, then tack and take the lift. You will be farther outside and ready to jump on the reverse phase of the oscillation. If this is a completely new wind, however, and the layline to the weather mark is not a factor yet, cross behind them and get on the inside of the shift. Then if the wind continues to shift around, you will be on the inside of the persistent shift and in the favored position.

In the first case, you were caught out of phase and are seeking to get back in; in the second, you are dealing with a persistent shift, such as the sea breeze arriving, and have to sail toward it to take advantage of it.

Q When is a good time to consolidate and tack across the fleet?

A The best time to consolidate is when you have been hit with a significant header. If you are to leeward and ahead of the other boats, you will encounter this new air first. Tacking to take advantage of it will give you the heading you need to cross the other boats. You need to make sure you are truly in the shift before you tack, especially if it comes right off the line. If the knock comes immediately, wait until it passes to the boats above you. When they start to tack away, or fall down toward your course, take a tack across them. In light air you have to watch out for the sucker puff that just gives you a hint of what's in store. If you act prematurely on the hint, you'll be stuck until the real thing comes along.

Q Every time a puff hits me, the boat just heels and seems stuck in the water— there is no real acceleration. How can I change this?

A For one thing, it sounds as if you are not reacting until the puff hits you. Poor acceleration can be a result of many things, from rig tune to sail shape. Even if all your equipment is in apple-pie order, poor technique will ruin your speed. A puff is a sudden increase in power, just as if you had stomped on the gas in your car. Your car accelerates, but to accelerate quickly it first drops into a lower gear. You can create the same effect with your sails. When the puff hits, drop them into a lower gear, for example by easing the mainsheet slightly. The wind power can then accelerate the boat. Do not pull on the sail controls—cunningham, boom vang, etc.—until the boat is responding to the stronger wind. This technique, which I referred to as the "ease and squeeze" earlier in this chapter, works coming out of tacks, when being hit by puffs, or any time the boat needs to be accelerated quickly.

Chapter 7

Rounding the Windward Mark

We've been working up the left middle of the course. After tacking with the first few shifts, we've recovered from a second-row start; we now find ourselves back in the upper third of the fleet. The windward mark has come into view, and two more tacks should get us there. Ahead of us, boats coming in from the deep left side are heading for the starboard tack layline, where they'll meet the boats coming back from the right.

The fleet, which has been all over the course on the way upwind, converges now, creating a wall of disturbed air. The boats that were on the layline first can only watch as new arrivals slide up and tack underneath them. As these boats start pinching up to "gas" those above them, the boats above pinch up in an effort to maintain clear air, and the whole train starts to grind a little more slowly.

There are both hazard and opportunity aplenty at the weather mark. The hazard is that we get caught in the mass of boats moving up the layline, our position locked, in which case we can only hope there won't be a lift that lets in all the boats that have tacked short underneath us. The opportunity lies in being one of those boats. But what if we *are* one of those boats and the lift doesn't materialize? Well, that's another hazard.

Finding the Laylines

The *layline* is the imaginary line representing the fastest course around a mark on a single tack. It is not stationary, however; rather, it changes position depending on the wind. A windshift may move the layline to weather or to leeward of your course—but either way your preliminary calculations are gone with the wind. If you try to tack on the layline while still far from the mark, chances are excellent that the layline will shift away from you at least once.

In the case of the windward mark, there are two laylines—one for each tack.

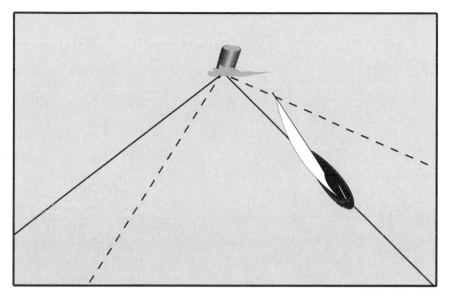

Let's assume for the moment that we're approaching the windward mark on the port tack layline. Our optimum course is close-hauled: pointing as high as possible with no loss of speed. That's what sailing a windward leg is all about. But a lift will move our optimum course above the mark, and a knock will place it below the mark. In either case we are no longer on the layline but either beyond it or short of it. We'll explore the consequences in a moment.

There are numerous advantages to approaching the mark on starboard. Most courses leave the mark to port, so rounding the mark is simply a process of bearing away and moving down the reach. You have the right of way over boats trying to come in on port tack, so you can sail to the mark without worrying about having to avoid your competition (although some people will be quite insistent about trying to get in line, and a quick luff may be necessary to avoid a late tacker trying to force his way in). Your crew also has time to prepare to raise the spinnaker or put the boat in reaching trim for a quick getaway at the mark.

The port tack layline also has advantages. It attracts a much smaller crowd, which means you can move faster and maintain clear air longer as you sail into the mark. Your added speed may enable you to take some time finding a gap through the starboard tack boats, or to tack into line late, and still come out better than you might have if you'd been locked into the starboard tack parade. And after the first leg the fleet spreads out, leaving plenty of room to tack around the mark if the port tack approach is favored.

Neither layline is a place you want to be too early, because then your options are severely limited. Once you are on the layline, three things can happen to you, two of them bad. As mentioned, the laylines move as the wind shifts. A lift will cause you

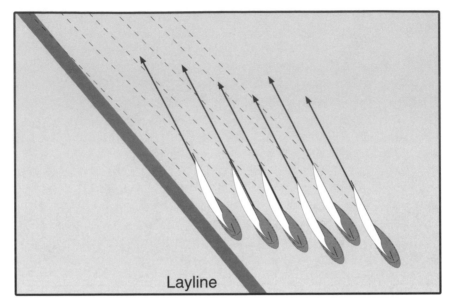

Layline

to overstand, sailing farther than you need to, whereas a header will leave you short of the mark with little room to maneuver. In other words, you can only reach off in the case of a lift, and you are too close to the layline to tack over to the advantaged side in the case of a knock. The third possibility is that the wind stays the same, which will merely preserve the status quo.

In contrast, tacking to take advantage of a shift while other boats are held on the layline can instantly move you around a clump of boats. These boats would have been on your nose otherwise, fouling the air and presenting an impassable obstacle between you and the mark.

Sometimes the layline provides an irresistible temptation. But consider the following scenario: You've played one side of the course and find yourself only five or six boatlengths inside the layline, heading toward it. You continue, then tack over with the mark in your sights. You start to drive for it, but another boat comes up and tacks in front of you. No problem, you say, and squeeze a little higher to gain clear air. Now another boat fills in the gap between you and the first; so you start to pinch a little more. Then another boat fills an opening in front of them, and they all start to head up. Pretty soon the whole line is moving slowly and starting to slip sideways. It could become a struggle for you just to make the mark now. Boats that have waited to move to the layline are sailing beyond you, then tacking and pinning you, leaving no room for you to tack.

After this nightmare has happened once, you will err toward overstanding, and now everyone will tack underneath you and proceed merrily around the mark. So resist the temptation to sail out to the layline. The farther you are from the mark, the

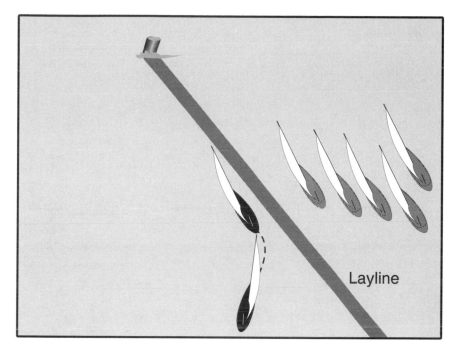

As the pack heads higher, a boat underneath can tack and be lifted right to the mark.

Layline

more difficult it will be to hit it correctly. If you have practiced tacking, the prospect of a quick sequence of tacks to gain some advantage at the mark should not be discouraging.

If you are short of the layline but close to the mark, there is the danger of other boats first crossing you, then tacking on your wind. You can avoid this by pinching slightly as they cross. This will lead them to go farther than necessary to interfere with your wind. When you come back down to your proper course, you will be ahead of their wind shadow and find that you have clear air.

If there have been regular oscillations in the wind direction, use the last shift favoring port tack to move over to the starboard layline. Ideally you should wait to tack onto starboard until the wind starts to veer, tacking below the crowd then and using the lift to make the mark. This maneuver will succeed more often than not and rewards the patient skipper who enters the line late.

Approaching the mark from the port tack layline is an interesting experience, but not a real problem if you are in the lead. You still may want to spend a short period on starboard tack to build speed for the reach, but a quick tack at the mark followed by a slightly higher course leaving the mark should get you to speed anyway.

If you are not in or near the lead, the port tack layline can be real trouble. You have to find a gap in the line of boats approaching on starboard tack, but if you start reaching down the line, these boats will be coming at an angle close on the bow,

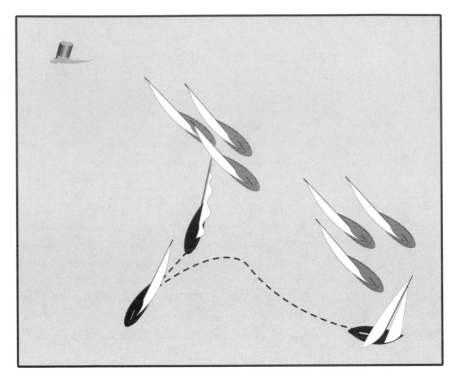

Look for a gap when approaching on port tack. If necessary, slow down to preserve your angle. Tack short, or shoot through if you can't tack into the hole.

and gaps will be extremely hard to spot. Also, you would have to make a sharp turn into any gap you see, and that would slow you considerably. To avoid these problems, you need to start footing early so you can work down the line without substantial course alterations. You want the starboard tack boats to be crossing at nearly 90 degrees; that way you can pick out the gaps more easily. If no gap is immediately apparent, slow down by easing your sails rather than turning away. This keeps the boats crossing at nearly right angles, and your tack onto starboard can be made more quickly, through a smaller angle. You may have to wait for the gap you want. Remember that the greater the stack of boats coming in on starboard tack, the more likely it is that the tail end of the line has overstood the mark significantly. Even in disturbed air, you may be able to tack underneath the line and still make the mark.

Once you have identified a promising space, there are two options. You can tack below the approaching boat, or you can continue through the gap and tack late, overstanding the mark slightly. The first option works well when there isn't a large gaggle of boats trying to round in front of you. You can afford to stay low awhile, build some speed, and give the boat above you a sharp luff to get around the mark.

If you go beyond the line, you can get set up in the passing lane for the reach, build a lot of speed, and be in a position to blanket the boats immediately ahead on the early part of the reach. This really works well if there is a knot of boats going around at once. Bunched boats tend to move relatively slowly because they are concentrating on each other rather than on their trim. The crews are often busy preparing to hoist the lightsails, and they are relatively helpless.

Your team should come into a mark ready to put pressure on the other boats and make the most of the situation. As I've said, you can pass a lot of boats in a short time at the mark, but this presumes skilled, well-rehearsed boat handling by your crew. It's worth the effort, though: coming into the mark with the confidence that you can put the boat where it needs to be and won't have to wait for the rest of the crew to catch up is a gratifying experience.

Getting into Line

So now we have sailed two-thirds of the first weather leg, and let's say we find ourselves in the top quarter of the fleet. We are not in a position to be content: if the leaders round the mark alone, they will pull away during the reach and be difficult to catch. We need to get into that first bunch. Approaching the mark, we want to use leverage in our favor, and prevent others from using it against us. If the wind is shifty, we want to jump on each little one of its variations. This will allow us to cut the corners on those who are slower to tack or who may be held in place by other boats. We may have to duck some boats to tack as aggressively as we want, but we can use each duck as an opportunity to build speed and then trade that speed for more separation.

Ideally, we should be in phase with the wind and out of phase with the other boats. If the mark is close to shore, this is easy to accomplish. As the wind hits the water, it bounces or spreads out in cat's-paws. A cat's-paw puff allows boats on opposite tacks to be lifted by the same wind; you must try to be on the side of the puff that will take you more directly to the mark. This can be done by keeping the body of the puff to windward, thus placing yourself on that important outside edge, as well as on the correct tack. If the puff seems to be filling the area immediately ahead of you, you may need to get ready to tack. In really puffy conditions, you can play hopscotch right up to the mark.

As traffic builds near the mark, it becomes less likely that you will be able to take advantage of each and every puff. You may have to take a header, either because of other boats or because you've worked too far over to one side and need to get back to the middle of the course.

Make the most of this adversity. Too many people start to lose their mind in such circumstances. Remember, this is only the first mark. If the wind direction is changing frequently, relief is probably in the next gust. Get in position to benefit from it, and make the most of your boatspeed. Tack when you can, and always take the opportunity to dig in toward the middle. Getting back to the middle gives you the ability to take advantage of the next shift.

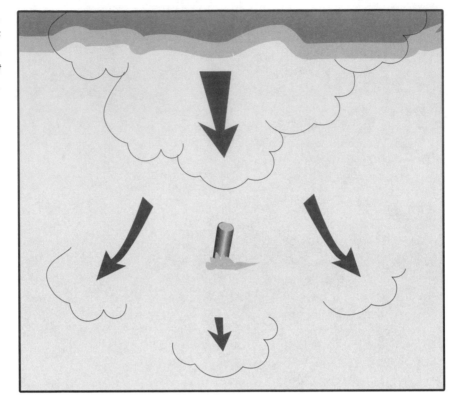

Close to the shoreline, where the marks are, puffs will usually spread out. Each edge is a significant windshift.

In conditions like these, we can exploit the fact that every sailor's natural inclination is to stop tacking once in the vicinity of the mark. Most of our competitors will decide they are close enough and move out to the layline to get their place in line. At that point they have put their fate in the hands of the wind. We, however, are taking a more active role, by working up to the mark from the middle and delaying our tack to the layline. A long lift on port tack may take us to the starboard tack layline a little earlier than ideal, but we don't want to tack away from it. We need to be alert to the wind swinging back, and we want to tack when starboard becomes advantaged, unless we are within a few boatlengths of the pin.

In the presence of a steadier wind, or when sailing to an offshore mark, things get a little tougher. There are still shifts, but they are slower. This means you have to be more aware of where you are in the cycle. Your approach to the mark has to be based on your anticipated course for going in. If you anticipate a lift on starboard tack, you can move toward the layline, tack well short, and ride the lift up to the mark.

As boats cross behind you or close in front, foot off so when the opposing skipper asks, "Are they making it?," the answer from his crew will be a resounding "No!" If you *are* making it, or will eventually, every foot they sail beyond you is one more in the bank for you.

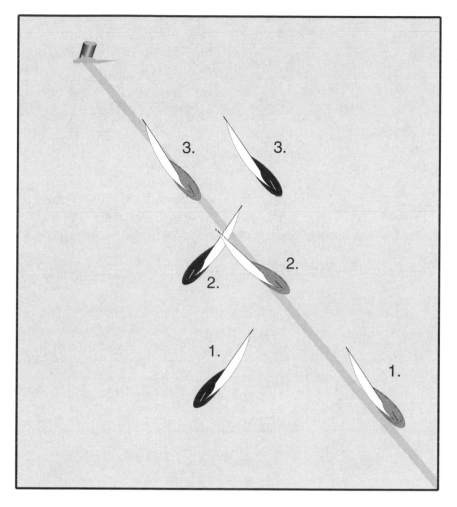

Footing as a boat crosses
in front of you may delay
his tack to the mark.

If the wind direction is favoring port tack, try to arrive at the starboard tack layline no more than five boatlengths from the mark. This should give you some time to find a gap in the parade of starboard tackers, but also sufficient time on the lifted port tack to get above the boats that hit the starboard layline early. Shooting for a five-boatlength gap at the mark will leave you some room if the lift on port is larger than you expected and takes you to the mark.

At the Mark

Now that you have worked two extra shifts and placed yourself a little farther up in the fleet, you take one last tack over to port—and are confronted by a mass of white sails. Boats are lined up heel to toe to go around the buoy, and you feel

RULES 41, 42, 43.3

These rules determine how and when an inside yacht shall be given room to pass an obstruction—in this case the weather mark. Complications arise when a port tacker tacks to starboard inside the two-boatlength circle, creating a new overlap. The tacking yacht is entitled to luff in order to round the mark if he has completed his tack without interfering with the yacht on a tack (Rule 41). A windward yacht must permit this (Rule 42.1). If the port tacker crosses in front of a boat on starboard before tacking, the starboard tack boat must be given room to round the mark if a late overlap is established (Rule 42.3). If the boat approaching on port tacks so short of the mark that he has to tack again to clear it, he is not entitled to room to do so (Rule 43.3).

A critical situation typically occurs when a port tack yacht tacks in front of an oncoming starboard tack boat and tries to carry the tack to windward to round the mark. This forces the starboard tack boat to alter course to stay clear; the situation counts as a foul for the tacking boat because it did not keep clear of another boat that was on a tack (Rule 41). With the new rules, which only require a 360-degree penalty turn after touching a mark (as opposed to a 720 for fouling another boat), you are better off hitting the mark than fouling an oncoming boat.

like a pool player who has to jump the cue to avoid an opponent's ball.

Fear not—you have two things working in your favor. If the line is in fact that dense, the boats in it have been working each other up to try and stop those who have overstood from grinding over the top. More than likely they are beyond the layline. If they are down from the layline, they are pinching for clear air and moving relatively slowly. There are probably gaps to shoot across, and because of the slow speed of the boats, these gaps can be narrower. The small amount you lose by overstanding will pale beside the number of boats you passed by taking advantage of the last two shifts, not to mention sailing that much longer in clear air.

You may find a gap large enough to consider tacking in rather than shooting through, but it had better be a good tack. If you are going to tack into a gap, tack early. The air through the gap should be fairly clean, and a smooth tack will allow you to maintain your speed. If you are near the mark, it is unlikely that another boat will get into the gap and close off your air. You can then quickly get rolling and shift into pointing mode if needed. A crash tack directly in front of someone puts

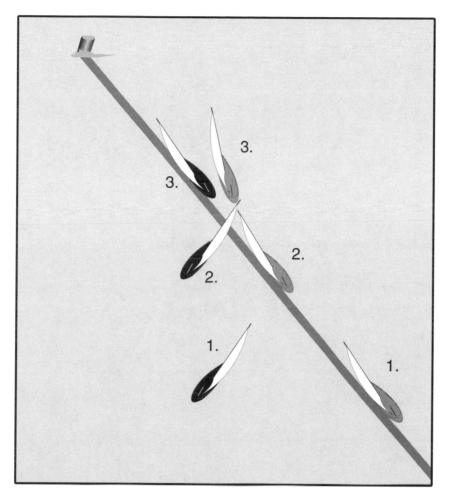

A tack through a larger-than-normal angle will leave you slow, and vulnerable to protest.

you at risk of being protested for tacking too close. The burden of proof would be on you here, and yours would be a hard case to make. Quick turns also eat up boat-speed, which would force you to spend that early part of the reach trying to rebuild speed. Worse yet, you may have to squeeze for the mark and just not have the speed to do it. This is where those tacking drills come in handy.

If you are extremely close to the mark, make sure you have at least enough room to complete your tack before you start a luff to squeeze around the mark. If another boat has to avoid you while you carry your tack through the wind, you have tacked too close. According to Rule 41, a tack is considered to be complete when the boat tacking resumes his normal close-hauled course on the new tack. Your sails do not have to be full, but you must come down to course before you can start back up to initiate a luff. In heavy boats there is a tendency to use the momentum of the boat

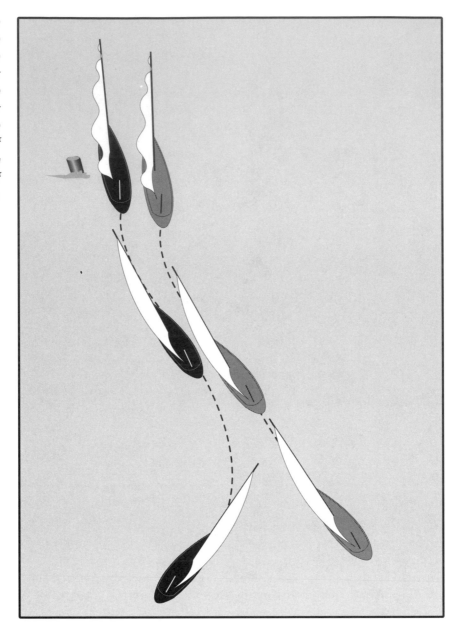

to try and get around the mark. If you do so while tacking—that is, if you dig straight to windward—any boat on a tack has rights over you. If you find that you need to incorporate this kind of move into your rounding, causing other boats to alter course, you have chosen the wrong gap; another space farther down the line would have been preferable. The proper sequence of events requires that you allow enough room to tack to starboard and time to rebuild speed before initiating a luff.

In some boats, it just doesn't pay to try to come up from underneath. A catamaran or light planing monohull accelerates dramatically when cracked off just slightly. If the gap you aim for looks too small for a clean tack, shooting through it and then tacking later may be the ticket. This virtually guarantees you the windward position on the reach and gives you a lot of speed when other boats are slow. Up, around, and down—the other boats will have to stay high to rebuild the speed they've bled off getting to the mark, while you might carry yours right back down to their course. The only caveat here is that there may be boats already lurking to windward of the line. They will be hard to see, and can be dangerous if they force you into an emergency tack to avoid a collision before you've cleared the other starboard tackers.

What can go wrong at the mark? Most anything. This is a classic high-risk, high-reward situation. Let me illustrate.

I was sailing an MC-scow midwinter regatta in Tampa Bay. I had gone to the left and had sailed over with just one other boat. We were working the left side together. Realizing that it was early in the race and the first race of the series, we left each other alone for the most part and concentrated on sailing the leg fast.

We finally tacked to the mark from the left side together. I had tacked first, and we were about even. Now, the thought of rounding that mark first started to look rather attractive. Our side had been favored and we were going to be comfortably in front of the boats coming in from the right. My plan was to cut the starboard tack layline razor sharp and force my buddy either to cross behind me or tack too soon.

Well, that part worked like a charm. He tacked, faced the mark, looked back, said "uh oh," and bailed out. Unfortunately, I was not going to make the mark either. I tried to pinch up and over, but I was moving too slowly and hit the mark just as the thundering herd arrived on starboard tack. This was before the rule change, so around we went, waiting for an adequate hole to reround.

Even the best approach will sometimes result in a situation such as this. When you find yourself just short of the mark, you cannot allow yourself to panic. If you've gotten out there early and are still some distance from the mark, you have to avoid starting to pinch your boat. Pointing too high will only slow you to the point where your leeway will definitely take you below the mark. Keep the boat moving; you can put it into a high-pointing mode by pulling the traveler up, easing the cunningham and vang, and straightening the mast. Check around for escape routes if you have to tack. Keep in mind that the closer you get to the mark, the denser the crowd will become. If you elect to try punching up around the mark, the last few yards should be sailed to build speed. If you have been pinching, or are receiving a great deal of bad air, let the boat start to roll here. Foot off and get ready to turn smoothly up to the mark.

Proper boat trim will get you around some marks you thought were impossible to make. As you start to foot, ease the sails slightly to accelerate the boat. Initiate the

*Get a good head of
steam before you surge
up around the mark.
If you have been
pinching, start to foot
to build boatspeed. Heel
the boat to start the turn,
and let it slide on up.*

turn up to the mark the same way you would start a roll tack—let the boat heel to trigger the turn to windward, and retrim the sails. Try to avoid using the rudder to jam the boat to weather, because the drag will rob you of the speed you need to carry into the wind.

Once you get over the mark, try to pull the boat over to windward as you head down. This is similar to roll tacking, except that you're not actually going through the wind. You want the boat to turn itself up and back down with as little rudder input as possible. As the boat approaches head-to-wind, ease the sails to keep the jib from backing. Then when you turn the boat down around the mark, the heel to weather plus the quick trimming of the sails will give you a boost around, not unlike the kick of a high jumper's legs that lifts him over the bar. In a dinghy, you have to be careful not to pull the rig so far to windward that it tangles with a boat above you.

When I am in this situation, I have the crew delay their preparations for the spinnaker because I need their weight on the rail to keep the boat flat and assist in pointing. Keeping movement to a minimum at this point also helps maintain boatspeed when we need it. Most of the time the crew are ready with the set by now, and it is merely a matter of keeping them on the rail a bit longer.

The rounding sequence is not complete until you are moving at top speed toward the jibing mark. If you have had to "stuff" around the mark, you really have no other option than to hold high to rebuild speed. If a faster boat goes by, let him get around and head up sharply after his transom. This may allow you to escape the parade of boats coming in at top speed above you.

The approach to the weather mark is another opportunity to consolidate a good start or atone for a bad one. By keeping your options open right up to the mark, you can get in and out of it smoothly. Do not allow yourself to be backed into a position where other boats control what you do, and never stop looking for situations you can exploit.

Now that we have arrived at the reaches, we need to concentrate on benefiting from the tendency of the fleet to spread out. The boats that led at the first mark have a chance to greatly increase their lead at this point. We want to make this happen if we are fortunate enough to be in that position, or prevent it from happening if we are behind.

Questions

Q What if I have followed a lift well out to one side of the course, and I only seem to be a hundred yards or so from the layline? Should I continue out, given that I have committed myself to that side anyway?

A In short, no. Anytime you get to the layline well away from the mark, you are placing your fate in the hands of luck. If the lift that has taken you out to the side is a persistent shift, by allowing yourself to be driven to the layline you concede to the rest of the fleet the inside position on the shift. If it is simply a big oscillation, tacking short will probably find you lifted to the mark when the wind eventually shifts back. If you are way out there, you'll likely be over the mark by the time the shift has taken full effect.

As you get to the extreme left- or right-hand side of the course, start looking a little harder for opportunities to dig back in. Recognize that you might have to take some small shifts that didn't seem worth the trouble earlier.

Even if you do end up taking a long tack in just short of the mark, you can still take advantage of changes that occur later in the leg.

Q Is there buoy room at the windward mark?

A The windward mark qualifies as an obstruction, so a boat is entitled to room to avoid hitting it. Rule 42.3 states that if a late overlap (i.e., inside the two-boatlength circle) has been established due to a tack by the windward boat, the leeward boat may luff the windward boat as needed to round the mark. The important thing to remember is that the tack must have been legal—that is, not too close to the oncoming boat. If the inside boat has just tacked, it must come to a close-hauled course on the new tack before it can proceed to luff. It doesn't matter where the two boats are in relation to each other. If there is any overlap at all, the outside boat has to yield the inside boat the room necessary to round. (See illustration on page 84.)

Q How can I pick a hole when I am coming into the mark on port tack?

A You have to hope that there will be one when you get there. If the whole starboard layline seems stacked up, find a gap that might yield some clearer air (there won't be any really clean air) and tack underneath into it. If the whole line has overstood, you might make it in. If the air is strong enough, you might be able to luff the boat above you and get around that way. If the worst happens and you get squeezed out entirely, you are still not much worse off than if you had reached down the line until you found a hole.

Q If I am on starboard tack and on the layline, how can I defend against boats crossing me and tacking on my wind?

A We discussed how you can fool boats into passing farther beyond you before tacking. Another tactic is to hold higher than normal and make them go underneath you. Then you can foot to them and try to beat them on the set at the mark or down the reach.

Chapter 8

The First Reach

The reaching legs present an interesting problem. All the boats are headed in the same direction, and there is no tacking going on to separate them. Everyone sails the leg in more or less the same wind. So why is it that some people are able to pass other boats or extend their lead so consistently?

The answer is that they approach the reaches on the offense.

They don't waste time trying to sort out where they ended up after the beat. Instead, they immediately start attacking other boats, setting themselves up for a successful leg even before they go around the weather mark.

Success on the reaches is a matter of aggressive positioning and the ability to keep your boat moving at all times. Most offensive and defensive tactics on reaching legs are essentially straightforward. If anyone tries to go over you, take him head-to-wind until he desists. Do this often enough, and no one will want to be caught near you. If you are going to pass someone, break out over his wake, blanket him, and take a puff back down in front of him.

That is not the whole story though. A simplistic view of reaching has led some to advocate the elimination of the reaches in favor of straight windward-leeward courses. But good reaching sailors know there is more to these segments of the race than just getting in line and sailing down to the jibe mark.

Sail Trim on the Reach

Let us first consider how to set up the rig for fast reaching. On the reach, the sails are eased and the forces they develop are more in line with the direction of travel than on windward legs. Easing the cunningham and outhaul will deepen the sail and make it more powerful. Allowing the mast to straighten by releasing the backstay will also push more draft into the sail. We need the power produced by this draft to accelerate the boat. The fuller sails will generate more drag, but the

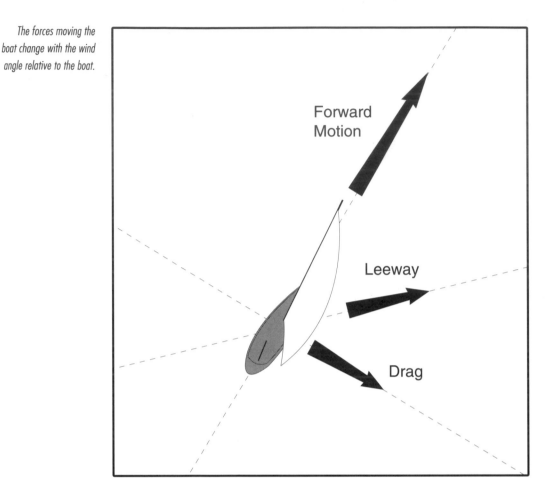

Forward Motion

Leeway

Drag

induced drag of the sails will affect the forward motion of the boat very little.

Besides increasing the power produced by the sails, we need to encourage the highest possible volume of air to flow through the sails at the highest speed possible. We will ease the boom vang slightly to produce a fair curve and an even flow of air over the leech of the mainsail, and we will ease out the traveler and move the jib leads outboard as far as we can. Changing the angle of attack in the sails shifts the lift vector more into line with the boat's direction, so that the extra drag induced by fuller sails becomes tolerable because it does not act directly against the forward motion of the boat.

This setup will ease pressure on the helm and underwater foils; they need not produce as much lift to keep the boat moving in a straight line. As a result the underwater foils will create less drag, so we can achieve greater speeds than we would upwind. Indeed, in centerboard boats we reduce the area of the underwater foils by lifting the board, and the boat then produces more speed with less leeway.

This is another instance where the location of the sail controls is important. A boat can easily go out of trim while the crew sets up the sails for the reach. This usually happens at the worst possible time—right next to the mark, say, while boats at close quarters are jockeying for position. In heavy air, it doesn't matter as much; any sail configuration will produce enough power to accelerate the boat, and we will be trying to depower in any case. In light air, though, it's a different story. As we are trying to coax our boat away from the fleet, every movement counts. If we are on the low side, trying to heel the boat, we want the relevant controls to be with us. Rocking the boat around to get something that's out of reach will certainly not help us accelerate, and may kill whatever speed we carried around the mark. Movements associated with getting the spinnaker up can be just as detrimental. Setting up the chute is important, but so is maintaining clear air ahead of another boat. If our boat is stopped by crew movement, the other boat will be on our air before we can get the chute full and drawing.

The boom vang is critical to reaching trim. The rule of thumb is to tighten it so that the leech of the main forms a shallow, fair curve all the way up to the masthead. A telltale attached to the top batten will fly straight off the sail when the vang is adjusted correctly. This indicates that there is attached airflow on both sides of the sail, and the breeze is exiting smoothly from the leech. If the vang is overtightened, the air will stall on the upper leech and the upper telltale will curl around the sail.

In light air, we want an open leech. The wind may not have enough energy to flow all the way through the sail, and if we force it to follow the curve to a tight leech, it may just start spinning in the sail and provide no thrust at all. The vang should be eased, and boats with an adjustable topping lift will want to use this control to support the weight of the boom, since even the modest tension caused by the boom would pull the leech too tight in these conditions.

As the wind increases, the vang can be applied more tightly, for the wind now has power enough to follow the curve of the sail out to and past the leech. But when weather helm becomes a problem, you will want to ease the vang again to open up, or release, the top of the sail. In essence, you are trading the power developed by the top of the sail for the reduced drag of a lesser helm pressure. In broaching conditions, the vang may need to be eased completely when the boat attempts to spin out, but it will need to be reapplied as soon as the boat is back under control. To facilitate all this easing and retrimming, the vang must have enough mechanical advantage and be located conveniently.

In light air, if your speed seems somewhat slower than desired, try less vang in order to open the top of the sail. In medium to heavy air, more vang may be the answer to speed problems.

Spinnaker trim on the reaches works on the same principle as trimming the other sails. For spherical sails, encouraging air flow through the sail means raising the pole to open the top of the sail. Opening the leeches will also flatten the sail, so we

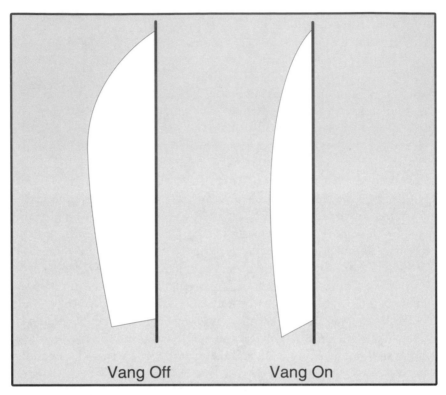

The vang removes the twist in the sail when the sheet is eased and makes the top of the sail more effective.

Vang Off   Vang On

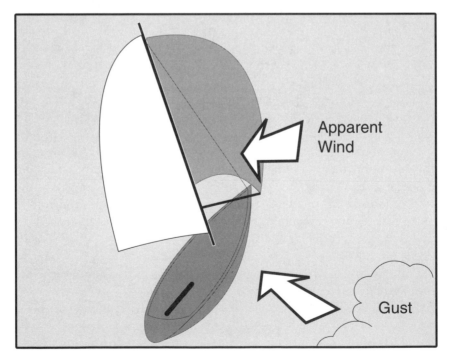

As a puff enters the sail, the true wind momentarily makes up a larger portion of the apparent wind. This swings the wind aft until the boat accelerates.

Apparent Wind

Gust

The masthead wind indicator is useful on the reaches. It will point farther aft at the onset of a puff. The helmsman should use minor shifts in the apparent wind as steering cues.

can carry it in higher winds. For radially cut sails, the pole needs to be moved lower. This opens the trailing edge of the sail and pulls the draft forward, reducing the chute's tendency to cause broaching.

Trimming the spinnaker requires an appreciation of the apparent wind. The increased velocity of a puff moves the apparent wind farther aft, so the spinnaker sheet needs to be eased into the puff. This will prevent the puff from simply causing the boat to heel. It is important, though, to keep the sail full; otherwise, a drastic course change may be required to reinflate it. So ease gradually until the boat accelerates.

As the puff lets up, the apparent wind will swing forward. The chute may have to be trimmed quickly, then eased again as boat and wind speeds reach a new equilibrium. Trimmers will often pull in the sheet as the boat slows, but then neglect to ease it. This leaves the chute stalled, creating excessive helm and not much thrust. Active trimming is the key to maximum speed when sailing with the spinnaker. Rotate people on the sheet if fresh hands are necessary to keep the trimming aggressive.

Spinnaker trim is also influenced by the fore-and-aft position of the pole. Unless you have to let the pole all the way to the headstay, its optimum position will move with the gusts. Nevertheless, you want to avoid fooling too much with the pole on a reach. The object is to keep the apparent wind at a fairly constant angle. The small changes in apparent wind direction caused by the onset of gusts and lulls shouldn't require adjustments in the pole; instead, they should be used as steering cues for the helmsman, as we will discuss in a moment.

The pole should be moved far enough forward that the leading edge of the spinnaker extends vertically up from its end. If the trimmer has to sheet hard enough to pull the luff to leeward of the pole, either the helmsman is steering too high or the pole needs to go forward. In either case, the trimmer should alert the helmsman.

If the pole is positioned too far forward, the luff will swing to windward. This means that the chute is not projecting its full area and consequently is not contributing to the speed of the boat as much as it could. The helm should either steer higher or call for the pole to come back.

Boatspeed on the Reaches

Fore-and-aft hull trim is one of the major factors determining your speed on the reaches. In most cases, your job is to put the boat in the ideal trim as envisaged by the designer, to allow it to pass through the water as easily as possible. If the bow is too far down, the boat will have to push aside too much water. If the crew weight is too far back, the stern will be dragging. As a rule, a quiet boat is a fast boat; if the wake is gurgling merrily as it leaves the transom, the stern is probably too low in the water.

The heel of the boat is likewise important. Most boats are fastest when flat: resistance decreases and efficiency increases. When a boat heels too much, the keel starts to drag through the water, the rudder starts to cavitate, and the boat will make noise like a banshee. We can confirm this by looking at the knotmeter: the highest speeds frequently are attained not when a puff first hits, but after its leading edge has passed and the boat is back on its feet. Then the acceleration seems effortless. All you need to do is expend the vigilance and effort to keep the boat level *throughout* the puff. Even forgoing some of the initial impact by easing the sails is advantageous if it serves this purpose.

There are times, though, when some heel is desirable. In a planing boat, in light air, heeling reduces the wetted surface and thus the resistance of the hull. On the other hand, placing the boat flat on its planing lines when a puff hits will pop it onto plane. Most displacement boats also have less wetted surface when heeled, and when the wind is light enough, the reduced friction produced by the heel outweighs the added drag produced in the foils or hull sections. In real blasting conditions, of course, proper trim may consist simply of keeping the boat underneath you.

In conditions other than extremely light air, crew movement is necessary to get the most out of the reaches. As a puff approaches, have the crew move to the rail. This momentarily causes windward heel, inducing the boat to turn downwind. When

the puff hits, the crew are already in position and the boat accelerates. Even if they cannot actually heel the boat into the puff, the crew's weight keeping the boat flat makes it possible to steer lower. As the puff passes and the boat begins to decelerate, you want to turn higher to keep the apparent wind forward. The crew should move back in, heeling the boat slightly. This will induce a slow turn to weather, keeping the apparent wind forward and taking you up to the next shot, where the process is repeated.

Notice that we are not rocking here. This type of weight shift is not rhythmic, nor is it repeated willy-nilly. It is a response to the wind encountered. A common criticism of someone sailing off the wind is that his masthead seems fixed in one spot, indicating either that the helmsman is not steering through the puffs or that he is using too much rudder to do it. In executing the described weight shift, by contrast, we are not forcing the sail through the air; rather, we are using the shape of the boat to aid in steering.

In larger keelboats, crew movement is not as often involved. But though the effects of shifting weight are less dramatic in bigger boats, they are still important. It's odd that people will go to great lengths to save a few ounces of weight aloft, yet not train their crew to respond to wind changes. I like to have my crew surge outboard if they are already on the rail, and move to the rail if they are inboard. I don't like to have them flopped all over the deck where they will have to roll around to move. They should have their feet underneath them so they can move swiftly when needed.

To head up:	**To head lower:**
Trim mainsail	Ease mainsail
Ease headsail	Trim headsail
Heel to leeward	Heel to windward
Crew weight aft	Crew weight forward

Steering on the reach involves much more than just using the tiller to point the boat where you want it to go. Anytime you move the rudder you are slowing the boat, and the moment of greatest drag is when you initiate the turn. You want to use the rudder to control the speed and duration of the course change, but you want to use the sails and the hull shape to start the turn.

Of course, this piece of advice should not be taken to extremes. When I was growing up, I had a friend who was learning to drive. Her father had taken her out and was trying to teach her some good defensive driving techniques. He mentioned to her that a good driver rarely uses the brakes. That must have been all she heard, because the next time she was out, she drove right into a ditch in her effort to be a "good driver" and stay off the brakes.

Steering the reaches should be routine. It requires practice because it involves every force on the boat. Sail trim has to be coordinated with boat heel and helm movements. If you are sailing along and a monster puff announces itself, you'll want to head off and go with it. If it hits and you just try to pull the boat off with the tiller, there's a good chance you'll lose control. As the wind builds, the apparent wind will swing aft, the boat will heel, and the forces in the sail will try to pivot the boat around the board until it points straight into the wind. Trying to overcome all this with just the rudder will cause it to stall; if that happens you can put the tiller in your pocket, because you are just riding the boat.

When you see heavy air coming, flatten the boat and head off, then ease the sail rapidly as the puff hits. This is called a *reverse pump*. The boat will quickly accelerate, which will move the apparent wind forward again and allow for the sails to be retrimmed. At this point, if you're lucky, one of those pesky waves you couldn't catch before may come along; you can put the boat right on the crest and ride it down all the way to the trough.

The quick ease of the reverse pump breaks the equilibrium of forces that had been moving the boat in a straight line. The maneuver allows the boat to be turned off the wind and then accelerate without being overpowered. It also accommodates the fact that the velocity of the puff swings the apparent wind aft. If the puff is coming in hard enough, the boat will jump on plane. If it does not, the boat can be allowed to roll up a bit later in the puff to decrease the wetted surface. In either case, the reverse pumping allows you to maintain control and accelerate faster. This will give you a higher top speed.

A quick ease is necessary even in a heavy displacement boat. The aft movement

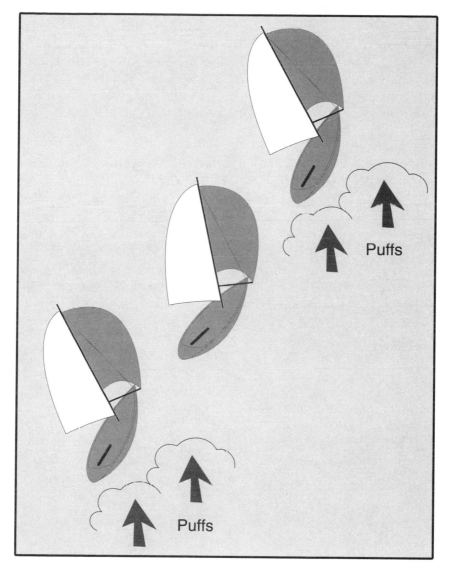

Heading down in a puff prolongs its effect. You sail longer at a higher speed.

of the apparent wind is going to create a lot of yawing moment in the sail plan. The boat will want to pivot around the keel, and you will have to counter this force with the rudder. If the sails are eased, the force won't be as large, keeping the boat on course will require less input from the rudder, and consequently you will create less drag. Again the final result is a higher top speed.

Steering down in a puff accomplishes two things. First, as the puff comes in and the boat accelerates, the apparent wind initially swings aft, then forward. Heading off allows you to maintain the increased apparent wind farther aft, thereby reducing the energy it takes to keep the boat headed in a straight line. As stated earlier, the less energy spent on holding course, the more energy is available for acceleration.

Second, by sailing down in the puff you increase its duration. Puffs move across the water in rough bands of fixed width. In the reach you are sailing across them, but when you pull the boat off, you start moving diagonally across the gust. Your actual course in the area of increased wind is longer, and you spend more time at a higher speed.

When the puff begins to tail off, steering higher can maintain your speed and move you toward the next puff. Why? Because turning toward the wind adds a component of the boat's speed to the apparent wind speed. Until drag catches up with you, you can fool the boat into believing the puff is still with you. Start to turn up as the velocity starts to flag. At that point the apparent wind will creep back, so mind your sail trim. You don't want to be caught overtrimmed when the next shot arrives.

Your course down the leg should take you above and below the rhumb line (on this leg, the straight-line course from the windward mark to the jibe mark). You can't control the wind, of course, and in the early part of the leg it is more important to go with the flow, so to speak, milking those puffs for all they are worth. If you end up below the rhumb line late in the leg, you can head up and thereby maintain a higher speed approaching the jibe mark.

Success on the reaches is a matter of boatspeed. The same rules apply as on the beat—keep the boat on its lines, use the crew weight before the boat heels, and use the sails and the boat's shape to steer. Alertness and quick reactions are crucial here. You'll find that little advances will add up by the time you turn upwind again after the leeward mark.

Traffic will affect the way you use the gusts. You may not want to let a puff take you too far down on the course if, as a result, a batch of boats move to a position to roll over you in the lulls. They can use the lighter air to go high and block the next shot for you. If you dive low and they don't, make sure you can swing back up into clear air. You might want to turn up earlier than you otherwise would, using your greater speed to maintain clear air.

High or Low?

The first decision facing you after rounding the weather mark is which side of the rhumb line to sail. Rarely is the straight course to the next mark the fastest. You always have to make a commitment to one side or the other. In doing so, you need to consider the spacing of the other boats, the anticipated direction of the wind, and the length of the leg. There are decided advantages to going either high or low.

Sailing high places you above everyone's bad air. You get first crack at the puffs coming through, and you can blanket the boats below you. If the leg gets tighter (that is, if the wind shifts farther forward) as you progress, you have the option of heading off to the mark. You are also sailing above the wakes of the boats immediately ahead.

A skilled, relatively heavy crew works to your advantage here. If your people can handle the adjustments needed to avoid a competitor's quick luff, then you can probably work past other boats with a minimum of fuss. Practicing tight reaching will give you the skills you need to build the windward separation that will discourage other boats from attacking you in the first place. The ability to accelerate rather than heel is key here; knowing how to keep the boat driving will move you over your competitors. The challenge consists in applying what we said earlier about acceleration without having the luxury of bearing away in the puff.

What goes up must come down. In the later stages of the leg, the boat that has worked above the fleet has got to start looking for opportunities to sail lower, in order to come down to the mark. This is easy if the wind has been building, or if it has shifted toward the jibe mark; it takes more care if the wind is steady or dying. The idea is to prolong the effects of the gusts to compensate for having to sail a lower course. Anytime you have passed one clump of boats and see a gap before the next one, you should work as low as the puffs allow. You don't want to turn down just for the sake of getting lower, though, since you need to keep the apparent wind in the same place. This means you have to steer down in the puffs, with higher boatspeed. Pick out the gusts and use them; otherwise, have patience.

Sailing low on the reach also has its advantages. The boats above you are restricted in how far down they can sail. Once you get below their disturbed air, you can basically follow your own course and concentrate on sailing as fast as possible. The boats above you may choose to ignore you altogether, most times at their peril.

You can also count on having a boatspeed advantage as you approach the jibe mark. You are sailing higher to get to the mark, you are moving faster, and you are on the inside. The extra speed will provide you with an edge as the competition clumps together and slows down at the mark. It gives you a better chance to spot an opening and get to it.

Later in the leg, the factors that work to the advantage of the boat that went high will work against the boat that is low, and vice versa. If the reach gets tight, the boat on the low side of the leg may have to struggle up to the mark. As the fleet congregates on the rhumb line close to the mark, the disturbed air may make it difficult to get in position for rounding. Although success in the early part of the leg depends on getting below the disturbed air of the other boats, the end of the leg requires that we come back up to the rest of the fleet.

In most races, the choice of high or low has to be made right at the windward mark. The entire reach is needed to make either strategy work well. If you have rounded the first mark at the top of the fleet, you can probably work your way straight down the rhumb line, following the lulls up and the gusts down. You can also probably pass a couple of boats by working above them late in the leg, but you absolutely cannot work low unless you work with a large part of the leg or find a major puff to take you down.

As a rule of thumb, the looser the leg (the farther off the wind it is), the more likely I am to take the low route. There are two reasons for this. First, I like the added speed I will carry into the jibe mark, because of the tactical possibilities it opens up. Second, if the first reach is loose, the next is likely to be tight, and I want to be on the inside at the jibe mark and high on that second reach.

If the legs are switched and the second reach is the loose one, I don't mind so much working from the outside. In that case, I can stay low on the second reach or work high across the fleet if necessary. Later we will discuss where we want to exit the jibe mark, and how we need to sail that second reach.

Dealing with Other Boats

As I mentioned earlier, there has been talk of eliminating reaches because of their "follow-the-leader" nature. The criticism is that the leaders get to stretch out while the rest of the fleet is left with the small chance of catching a boat here or there. There is a certain amount of truth to this, but the ability to marry strong boat-speed with an aggressive sailing style can still make the reaches an area of opportunity. There *must* be opportunities here, given the predominance of defensive tactics on the course and the slant of the rules. These make it all the more important that a boat seeking to improve his position plan things well and keep alert for sudden openings.

You need to have made an assessment of the tactical situation in the early part of the reaching leg before you round the windward mark. Is the crowd ahead, behind, or all around? On the first reach the answer is, most likely, all around. The key factor in evaluating your position will be clear air. In light planing boats, you can get pretty far down below the pack in just one good puff; all you need is a small gap to let that puff through. Once you are below the disturbed air of the other boats, you can sail quite cleanly. If you are in a heavier boat, you need to find a larger area of clear air to go low or, failing that, to make a quick move to start high. This may mean merely holding high momentarily after rounding the mark, or it may require sharply luffing the boats above you to break out on top of the pack.

To be effective on the reach, you have to be aware of the offensive and defensive weapons at your disposal. A boat sailing on a free leg of the course can work with four zones of influence: the area directly to leeward of the sail, the area to leeward and behind the sail, and each of the two trailing wakes.

The first is the area commonly referred to as the *blanket*. The sail of the windward boat stops the wind, so that any boat in its blanket is not going to feel it. This area of blocked wind directly to leeward changes in size and location with the wind angle.

RULES 35, 37, 39, 40, 54

The rules covering the reaching legs define the process of establishing an overlap and the restrictions placed on the leeward boat. Rules 35 and 39 make clear that after starting, when a yacht has the right to luff, the luff need not be slow and deliberate. This gives a leeward, overtaken yacht a powerful weapon with which to defend himself. Of particular interest to the tactician are the limitations on sailing below a proper course and the application of the principle of mast-abeam.

To take a puff down or ride a wave below the direct line to the next mark is, arguably, to follow one's proper course. It is the path I would take in the absence of other boats, which is how the rules define "proper course." It is also a chance to close on a boat to leeward and throw some bad air and water his way. Heading below the mark solely for that purpose is illegal, however, and when you are within three boatlengths of a boat to leeward or a boat astern aiming to pass you to leeward, you should not head below your course to the mark (Rule 39.3).

Mast-abeam has occurred when the helmsman of the windward boat, sighting directly across at a boat overlapped to leeward, is ahead of that boat's mast. The leeward boat must then fall to his proper course to the mark (Rule 39.1). If the two boats are not on parallel courses, the helmsman of the windward boat may call "mast-abeam" when he passes the line drawn directly abeam from the other boat's mast. The leeward boat must respond to a hail of mast-abeam, but may protest if he thinks the hail was made improperly.

Another consideration is that the leeward boat may luff more than one other boat only when he has the ability to luff all affected boats individually (Rule 40.3). If two boats have established an overlap to leeward of a third boat from astern, the boat farthest to leeward may not luff the middle boat when that luff would affect the windward boat, since it could not luff the windward boat in the absence of the middle boat.

Rule 54 governs the means of propulsion. It defines and limits the type of "body English" sailors may use to assist the boat through waves or to induce it to plane. Class rules may vary here, but the intent is to ensure that the boat is propelled by wind and water, not by a series of crew movements. Good steering incorporates a number of movements that might be construed as violations of this rule; if you start to hear complaints, be prepared to explain what you are trying to accomplish. (See also Chapter 12.)

If there is a gap in the boats immediately behind, you can be assured of continued clear air when heading low.

On a broad reach, boats in front can be slowed by placing them in this area. When the wind is forward of the beam, the blanket angles aft and can be used to prevent boats from coming up and passing to leeward.

The fact that the blanket area moves as the wind shifts is important; it affects the timing of both offensive and defensive tactics. When a puff moves in, the first thing to happen is that the component of the apparent wind not generated by the forward motion of the boat increases, and this moves the effective wind aft. It shifts the area of your blanket forward and momentarily places it on a boat to leeward and ahead. We will discuss how to exploit this effect later.

The second area to be concerned with is the *backwind* of your sail, which extends to leeward and behind. As the air exits the sail, it trips off the leech and wants to start spinning. Since it alters the normal wind flow, it will affect any boat trying to sail through it. This area of disturbed air extends the effective area of your blanket. At

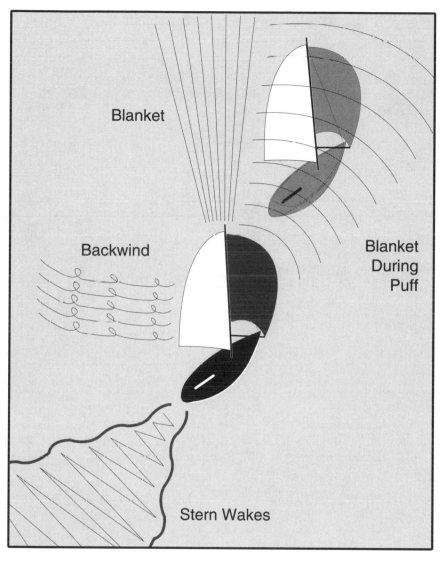

Blanket

Backwind

Blanket During Puff

Stern Wakes

times, you can even direct the backwind, using your leech like a spray hose.

The effective ranges of the backwind and blanket vary with the wind speed. As a rule of thumb, their effects are significant out to the mast height of the boat throwing the shadow. A boat may seem to be throwing a blanket from farther to windward, but the observed effect is the result of a puff hitting them first.

The wake extending from your transom can be a double-edged sword. Keeping a boat in your disturbed water will generally slow him down, but if he is slower to begin with, the wake may help him keep up. In one-design racing, a faster boat approaching from astern has got to break through the windward wake before he can mount any serious attempt to pass. Keeping him in the wake, or to the inside of it, should slow him. While he stays back there, he can't mount much of a threat.

The same can be said for a boat trying to break through to leeward. If he is always running up to your wake and then bouncing around, eventually he will have to force himself lower to a less disturbed area. You can't sail below your course to the next mark to keep him in your wake (according to Rule 39.3, a windward yacht cannot sail below his proper course to block a yacht passing to leeward when that yacht is within three overall boatlengths of him), but you will want to make sure he travels far in his effort to get through. You can feel comfortable taking puffs down as they come along until you are within three boatlengths of the other boat. That is the fastest, and therefore the proper, course to the next rounding. Once you reach that three-boatlength area, you have to keep your course at least as high as the mark.

If you are sailing in a handicap fleet and the boat immediately behind is slower, you have to be aware that your wake can be used against you. Many times I've started down the reach happy with the prospect of increasing my lead, only to find that boats I had thought to lose were still there at the jibe mark. In this situation, your job is to deny the boat behind you the opportunity to latch onto a tow, without jeopardizing your overall position.

Let's look at the application of these tools. You've just rounded the windward mark in light air, which you expect to build as the day progresses. As a matter of fact, some stronger puffs are starting to move across the course, a prelude to the full arrival of the sea breeze. As you round the mark, keep the boat heeled to reduce wetted surface, and perform your sail adjustments from the low side. In this light air, your only adjustment may be to ease the outhaul, since everything was fairly loose already for the upwind leg. There are several overlapped boats about a boatlength behind you, and the boat in front of you is clear ahead and overlapped on the boat ahead of him.

A puff moves in that will hit the boats behind first, then you, then the other boats. It is an isolated patch of wind, but relatively strong. As the boats behind start to accelerate, put your leeward wake on them. This will give them some added resistance to overcome, buying you time to get up to speed. You also want your backwind to affect them as you accelerate. Conversely, you need to get below the boats ahead and move outside their area of influence (their wake zone), while giving yourself room to turn up in the lull. As long as the boat ahead is overlapped with another, he cannot move down with you, giving you a clear lane to head off. Keep the boats behind you in your wake zone as you go down, and make them pay for that little bit of early acceleration.

If the trailing boats are sufficiently spread out, it makes sense to milk the energy in the puff. Make sure that the wind you are going to take low will be strong enough to carry you below the disturbed air of the boats in front of you. If you get caught in their bad air, the boats behind will start a parade over you. You'll have to bite the bullet, head up and force your way into line wherever you can break through.

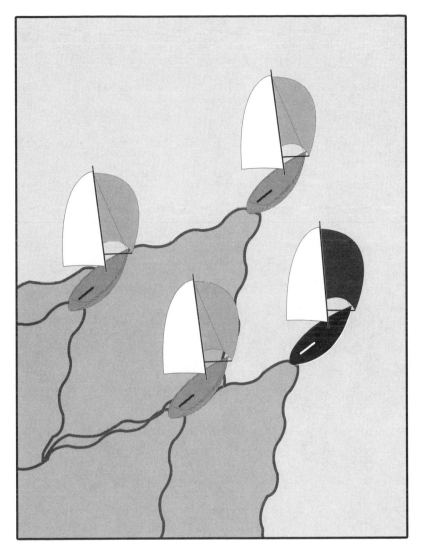

Place your wake on the boats below you, and try to get by the wake of the boats ahead.

In a building wind, it will be hard to get enough separation without giving up access to the stronger air.

In keelboats, the best place in the leg to go low is immediately after the weather mark; you are likely to get enough separation there to continue working up and down without interference from the boats above. As the boats higher up jockey with each other, you are free to use the wind to develop your best speed down the course.

The key in any boat is to maintain your ability to sail at a relatively high speed below your competitors, which means you have to have room below the blanket of

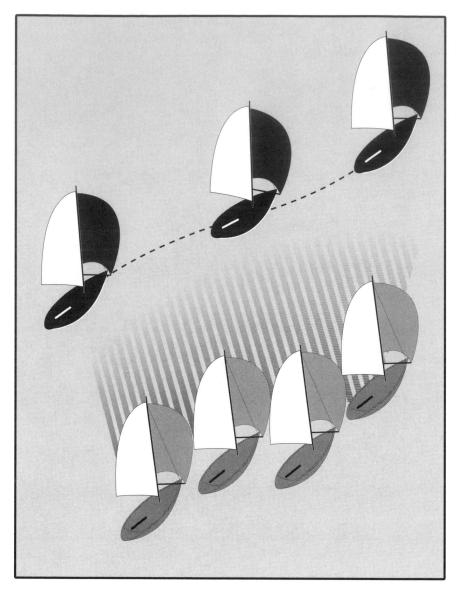

boats to windward to work up in the lulls as they occur. By working up while you
still have good boatspeed, you may be able to pull the apparent wind right through
the other boats. In other words, if your boat is moving fast enough, a change in heading will "fool" your sails into thinking the wind is coming from in front of the
windward boats. This effect can only be sustained if their blanket is fairly narrow—
that is, if you are already pretty far below them. If your higher course takes you
into the bad air of a bunch of boats, you might as well stay down. Unfortunately, this

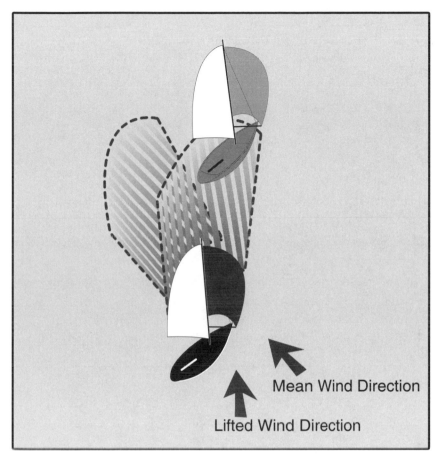

Mean Wind Direction

Lifted Wind Direction

means the next puff will get to them first, and you will be stymied in your attempt to get by them. Then you have to use this puff to build more separation for your next attempt.

What of the other route? Let's round the mark and be right on the boat in front of us, with the rest of the pack equally close. There is only one way to pass: up and over. You have to get over the forward boat's wake as soon as possible, which calls for a quick move to windward. If you can time this move to coincide with a puff, so much the better, and if that puff is a lift—well, excellent! The lift will swing your blanket area forward toward the boat ahead. You and your crew hit the straps, give the sails a quick ease to allow the boatspeed to catch up with the greater wind strength, and boom! you roll right over him.

For this maneuver to succeed, you need to be able to get the boat accelerated as quickly as possible without losing control, by shifting crew weight and easing sails as necessary. Here is where a lot of novice crews fall short. They have the right idea, but when the puff hits, they try to use it all. Even in moderate wind they will end up rolling the boat up, stalling the rudder, and creating a lot of drag as they struggle to bring things under control. That drag prevents them from reaching the speed they need to get above the other boat and stay in position. A well-sailed boat won't even come up after them, but will merely accelerate away.

Once you are above the other boat, it is simply a matter of paralleling his course until the next puff. As soon as you are clear of his weather wake, you can use the puffs to come down slightly, then turn up in the lulls. You need to get by this competitor relatively quickly, but you don't want to provoke him into a protracted luffing battle by coming too close.

This leads to two rules: Don't try to pass six inches away, and make your move when the wind is changing. The first is just common sense. If the boat ahead is truly slower, you don't want to dilly-dally with him as the rest of the fleet catches up or pulls away. A close pass will simply force him to try holding you up. If you are a larger, faster boat, it is tempting to pass close by because you are moving at a higher speed and could just roll over him. This isn't NASCAR, however; they don't wave the slower cars aside. Save yourself some trouble by acknowledging the fact that your competitor got in front of you at some point, and give him some space as you go over him. Separation will also make it more difficult for him to pick up a ride on your stern wake and add insult to injury.

Sometimes you have to be content just to survive the reaches. If the wind is blowing hard and you are on a tight spinnaker reach, merely keeping the boat underneath the sail may well gain you some places. I remember a race in the MORC Midwinters in a Wavelength 24, in which we rounded about five boatlengths ahead of a Lindenberg 28. Once both boats had their chutes up, the Lindenberg 28 quickly started to gain ground, but every time he tried to punch through our wake he would round up and lose all he had gained. Had he gone lower to maintain control, at the very least he would have had an inside overlap for the jibe.

Keeping the boat going is primarily a matter of anticipation. One of the crew has got to spot the big blasts far enough away to allow everyone on the boat to prepare. Now, you may ask what the crew, who are already sitting on the rail, can do to prepare for a puff other than grab a stanchion and hang on? Well, they can "surge" to windward as the puff hits, and if they can surge on the spinnaker guy at the same time, so much the better. Even if they do not actually move it, pressurizing it helps pull the bow down and prevent a broach. If this surge is timed with the helmsman's turn off the wind, the boat can accelerate cleanly. Besides, anything that contributes to keeping the boat flat is useful. Once the keel deviates from the vertical position, its drag increases immensely, giving the boat a pivot point to spin around.

This is an area for potential improvement in most PHRF crews. They tend not to move around the way a dinghy crew does, because they don't get that big feedback from that big displacement hull. But if you compare the intervals between boats in most PHRF fleets with the time gaps in high-performance one-design fleets, you'll see that the differences are not as great in the former, which makes each technical detail that much more important. A hundred yards is not a big gap in an E-scow or catamaran race, but in a keelboat race it is a small horizon job. So an energetic crew can help, even if the boat doesn't seem to be responding. A small weight shift at the right time can make the difference, especially when the goal may just be an overlap approaching the jibe mark.

In summary, since all the boats are headed in the same direction and on the same tack, gaining advantage on the reach is a matter of sheer boatspeed—both straight-line velocity and rapid acceleration.

I've said that reaching is a game of positioning. You want to get yourself in a position where you can develop your speed without interference from other boats, be it aggressive luffs or merely areas of disturbed air. The ability to run at a fractionally higher top speed, and to get to that speed just a little quicker, can put you outside the range of such influences.

Conversely, the defense against other boats building speed on the reaches is to keep them within your "zones" of influence. Keeping them in your wake or forcing them to go far afield to avoid the bad air from your sails will cause your opponents to waste their speed.

People have a tendency to arrive at the weather mark and occupy themselves with the mechanics of getting the boat set up for the reach or raising the spinnaker. This distracts the helmsman and tactician precisely at the point where the opportunities for good positioning abound. Take advantage of this tendency in others: anything done when the boats are close together can save a lot of time trying to grind through them later in the leg. And it is easier to climb over someone who is busy with a spinnaker set than it will be even seconds later, when his chute is full.

Later in the leg, when the choices of high, low, or in between have been made and there is more separation between boats, we have to devote some thought to our position at the jibe mark. The combination of specific rules, varying boatspeeds, and course considerations always makes this an interesting place. We will discuss it in the next chapter.

Questions

Q How do you keep your speed up when reaching in extremely light air?

A You simply have to go as high as necessary to keep the sails drawing and the boat moving. Keep going even if this takes you well above the mark. If the jibe mark suddenly ends up downwind or you get too high to bear off for the buoy, you just shift into downwind mode and keep moving as best you can.

It is important not to head off when you do get some wind until the boat has accelerated to the fastest speed it will achieve. In a light boat this won't be very long, but in a heavier boat it could take some time. Allow the boat-speed to wind up, then bear off.

Q How can I avoid getting stuck under a parade just after the weather mark? It seems that I never have any clear air there.

A You have to take a higher line out of the mark to prevent the parade from forming above you. It sounds as if you are watching your crew set the spinnaker and are consciously or unconsciously heading lower to make the job easier for them. This would give the boats behind you a chance to get on your air.

You have to allow the crew to do their job, and if they need practice, you need to supply the opportunity and motivation for that. During the race, though, your job is to place the boat where it will do the most good, not where the spinnaker set might be easiest.

Q Late in the leg, after I've gone low on the reach and started to work back up, how can I prevent boats from sailing down on me and stopping me?

A If these boats were ahead at the beginning of the leg, I wouldn't worry too much about them. The decision you have to make is whether there is enough time for you to mount an offensive move to windward or whether you should just maintain position and keep an inside overlap for the mark.

If you decide to go over the other boats, try and take a shot at it just as they have turned down. They will have to make an abrupt turn in order to counter you, and that may slow them down enough for you to break through. By contrast, if you want to maintain the overlap, try to stay outside their blanket as long as possible, then tuck into them when you are near the two-boatlength circle. More on this in the next chapter.

Q How can I tell when I am about to broach, and how can I prevent it?

A Broaching is caused when the boat rotates around the keel; it is usually the result of the boat heeling too far. When the boat heels, the foils—the rudder and keel—stall, losing their lift and causing a lot of drag. The center of effort in the sail plan shifts to one side of this drag and rotates the boat around it. The hull also tries to force the boat to windward, due to the shape it presents to the water as the boat heels. Since the rudder is stalling, it won't generate any force to turn the boat back down.

The solution is to reduce the force trying to turn the boat. We do this by easing the vang, which releases some of the force on the main, easing the spinnaker sheet, and pulling on the guy. Easing the chute and pulling the guy places more of the effort forward, thereby assisting in holding the bow down.

If you feel the rudder start to lose effectiveness, you can neutralize the helm (center the rudder briefly, then turn it again) to try to reestablish flow around the blade. This might restore some control.

The key to a broaching problem is prevention. If you have a tendency to broach, head down a little sooner in the puffs. Anticipate them by releasing the vang as they hit, rather than after the boat is heeled too far over and the broach is imminent. When the boat accelerates and the pressures are reduced, crank the vang back on and go with the speed. See Chapter 10 for more discussion of broaching.

Chapter 9

The Jibe Mark

T he jibe mark is a place where no one wants to spend much time; a high-speed approach followed by a good rounding leaves it quickly behind. A well-executed jibe should make the rounding feel like a mere change in course, but a poorly executed jibe will lose boats and might even leave the crew in the water.

Approaching the Mark

Having decided to sail high or low in the early part of the reaching leg, our path into the jibe mark will be determined by what other boats are doing. If we have gone high, we will continue to sail high enough to be above them. If they come up after us, we will go higher. We have to keep playing this game until they make their break for the mark, or until we have passed them and are clear ahead.

If our first move was low, our need for separation keeps us down there. We take our turn up toward the mark only when we can be relatively sure of clear air up to and around it.

These two scenarios obviously differ in the opportunities they offer. I like to put pressure on the other boats at this point. If I am moving fast coming up from the low side with clear air, it's time to force the inside overlap on a boat ahead. If I am coming in from above the rhumb line, I want to look for a chance to take advantage of someone else's mistake, either by passing over him or by sweeping in behind him to establish an inside overlap. I may even want to hold back to allow a stack of boats ahead of me to create an opening.

The angle of the next leg determines whether you want to come out of the mark high or low, and the boats around you determine how you get there. Before we look at some of the tactical problems involved, let's consider the rounding in the absence of other boats.

On a well-set course, you will be sailing a fairly tight reach into the mark, then turning onto another fairly high course. That kind of jibe is called a *reach-to-reach jibe*. In spinnaker boats, it means moving the chute from one side of the boat way over to the other. The sail thus moves across a considerable distance, but more important, it moves from one highly loaded condition to another. Assuming the pole is double-ended and will be jibed end for end, this loading controls the timing of the maneuver. Good or bad coordination between the helmsman, the spinnaker trimmer, and the foredeck crew can make the jibe a study in grace or a grunting, shoving, swearing ordeal.

Let us look at the mechanics of the jibe—including the many things that can go wrong. Initially the pole is forward and loaded by compression. Because the spinnaker guy is trying to thrust the pole aft through the mast, it is next to impossible to remove the pole from the mast fitting. If the foredeck crew does manage to jerk it off, the pole will pivot on the headstay, and the end formerly attached to the mast will head for the teeth of the unlucky person on the bow.

It is far better to unload the pole before disconnecting it; this is accomplished when the bow starts to swing down. At this point the trimmer can give a good ease on the sheet, then start the guy aft. The ease should alleviate the pressure on the pole, which then must be taken off the mast and released from the old guy nearly simultaneously.

Releasing the old guy from the pole allows the sail to blow out from the boat, making the chute easier to keep full. As the boat turns underneath the sail, the sail has to be brought around the forestay still inflated. It will have a tendency to fold upon itself, because the new spinnaker tack has to go from the center of the boat all the way to the headstay in the time it takes the boat to turn. If the old tack (new clew) doesn't move away from the boat, the chute will start to collapse under the blanket of the main. The trimmer will usually react by pulling both the sheet and the guy, but this will only pull the sail deeper into the blanket and prevent the foredeck man from pushing the pole forward.

At this point the errors often start to build upon themselves. If the pole is late getting forward as the boat continues turning, it will have to be pushed forward against the full backward thrust of the newly loaded chute in an attempt to attach it to the mast. This usually requires another person or a collapse of the spinnaker; even with the spinnaker collapsed, the shaking of the sail will make that last inch hard to get. Needless to say, the position and maneuvers of other boats will go unnoticed in the course of this mess.

The key to getting the sequence right is the role of the trimmer. He has to be able to isolate the sides of the chute, and he must resist the tendency to trim both lines at once. On larger boats, where his duties may be split between two people, they must coordinate their moves so that they are bringing the chute around together. Ideally the chute won't be eased an inch more than necessary, but will allow the foredeck crew to take the new guy with the end of the pole and move it forward as he clips the pole onto the mast. The pole needs to go forward with the guy and clip to the mast fitting before the hard trimming sets up the compression loads. The fore-deck crew has to be quick in securing the new guy to the pole, but then must have enough slack in the guy to push the pole forward. This slack does not necessarily mean that the new sheet has to be hauled in. The wind is behind the boat at this point, and the chute doesn't have to be trimmed as hard. When the foredeck crew locks the pole on the mast, it should be almost in position for the new leg.

The helmsman facilitates all this by setting up a consistent rate of turn. It can be fast or slow, but it is important that it remain as constant as possible. In the absence of other boats, there is no reason why the jibe has to be a snap roll. Any extra distance sailed to make the turn easier will be more than compensated for by the increased speed produced by a good jibe, and by not shedding speed with a sharp turn. At the end of the jibe, the helmsman should modulate the rate of turn to correspond with the progress made by the foredeck crew. In general, it is the helmsman and tactician's job to place the boat where this kind of smooth turn can be made.

The harder it is blowing, the more interesting the jibe can be. The chute generates so much lift that it is difficult to keep the pole level. The solution here is to hold the chute down with *twings,* which are lines well forward holding the guy and sheet near the deck, or to choke the chute and collapse it behind the main while the pole is being attached. Given sufficient wind, it should be no problem to reinflate the sail.

In boats without chutes, the key is to prevent the momentum transfer when the mainsail swings over from taking over the boat. The sail will snap over and transfer its momentum to the rig, causing immediate excessive heel and, again, stalling of the foils. In small keelboats this can produce a quick roundup, whereas in small dinghies it can produce a quick bath. You will find that control over the last few feet of mainsheet will make the difference. You can let the sail out a full arm's length too far while slowing it after the jibe, and then take that arm's length back in a pump to get back to speed. In moderate and light air you can make this work for you by executing a roll jibe. As the boat rocks, it forces air through the sail plan much like a roll tack. This helps you accelerate.

No matter what kind of boat I'm sailing, I like to get the main across quickly. Then the rest of the crew can see what is happening on the foredeck, and I can absorb the shock of the main loading with the rudder by turning the boat back underneath the main as it fills on the new tack. I help the main come over by either sheeting rapidly or just grabbing the boom and tossing it across the centerline.

One trick that makes the job a little easier in puffy conditions is not to jibe until the boat has reached maximum speed inside the puff. As the wind abates, the boat is going relatively fast and the sails have a minimum load. This is somewhat tough on the crew psychologically, but the results are always better. Planing boats really benefit from the delay. They are sitting ducks if the jibe is completed just before the puff and the full brunt of the wind hits the boat when it is moving slowly. In a puff,

RULE 42

The "buoy room rule" discusses when and how inside overlaps must be established in order to gain room to round a mark. The rule spells out the proper moves and options of the inside boat, including when and how it must round the mark, and defines at what point the boat attains inside status.

In a dispute, the burden of proof will depend on who is the injured party. If the outside yacht claims there was no overlap, or claims to have broken the overlap, he must satisfy the protest committee that the overlap was indeed nonexistent, or that it was broken outside the two-boatlength circle. If the inside yacht is claiming room which was denied, he has the responsibility of proving that he did in fact acquire the overlap, or that it existed at the all-important two-boatlength circle. If both boats agree that an overlap did exist at some point, the burden of proof is on the outside boat. However, if the inside boat established the overlap at the last moment, he must prove he was still outside the circle.

This is an important provision that should govern some of the decisions we make entering the mark. If we are the burdened boat, we have to either accede to the other boat's requests or gather witnesses and other evidence that we were in fact correct. This is a judgment call, so we need to give some thought to the costs and benefits involved. The facts may well be fluid, and as is the case in most courts, the outcome of a protest hearing is unpredictable. The speed at which overlaps are established and broken, as well as the differences in perception between individuals, can make it very difficult for the burdened boat to defend itself.

We have now introduced all of the important rules covering the start and certain typical situations during the first few segments of the race. The rest of the race is merely a succession of more such segments—windward legs, leeward legs, and marks. Some attention must be paid to the role of obstructions that are not marks; these are covered in Rule 43.

Never forget that races should be won on the water, not in the protest room. You must know your rights in order to make sound tactical decisions, but in certain situations, the smartest tactic may be not to press these rights.

by contrast, they accelerate quickly enough for the loads to virtually disappear, making the jibe relatively painless. The boat is also much more stable when it is up on a plane.

The complex nature of the jibe makes practice imperative. Rounding the mark is one of those situations in the race where you can put maximum pressure on the competition simply by executing your moves well. Knowing that you can place your boat where you will have the advantage coming out of the mark gives you the confidence to force another skipper into a mistake. Someone who has gone wide around the mark has to come up sharply to prevent you from rounding inside. This will throw his foredeck-trimmer combination off stride and may ruin his jibe. He will have to pull off while the crew puts the boat back together, and you can sail merrily on by.

Sizing Up the Tactical Situation: Before the Mark

As we discussed in the last chapter, the reach is a difficult leg for passing other boats. It is much easier to grab the advantaged position at a mark and use your boat handling skills to exploit it. Identifying the advantaged position is the first step. Usually you will be approaching the jibe mark from one side or the other of the rhumb line. You need to start thinking about the rounding 10 to 20 boatlengths out. The primary question is whether you will have the inside overlap as you cross the two-boatlength circle, but that's difficult to call from this far out. The corollary question is whether establishing the overlap is going to give you a sizable advantage.

An inside overlap is important if there are going to be several boats wheeling around the mark at the same time. Getting caught on the outside of a large group of boats is like taking a number at the bakery: you might as well sit down while the rest of the boats clear out. In fact, if you cannot establish an overlap, it makes a great deal of sense to trail the pack into the mark in order to preserve the windward position on the next leg.

While it may be hard to tell from a distance whether you will have the inside overlap, an early assessment of the situation will at least permit you to recognize if other boats are coming up below you and are about to establish an overlap on you—a hazardous position to be in. You can slow down if there are boats below you that are ahead even though you've overlapped them. But what about boats that come up from below and behind to establish an overlap on you? They are too far back to let by. You have to begin the approach into the mark by trying to prevent them from getting that overlap.

The mechanics of working back down to the rhumb line from a position above it are fairly simple: you have to milk the wind you are given. Ride each puff down and extend it as far as you can. You can even sail below the mark if there are no boats immediately overlapped. Since you are the windward boat, you will get first crack at the wind coming down the course. As you accelerate and turn off, place your wake where it can do the most good—right on the bow of the boats working up.

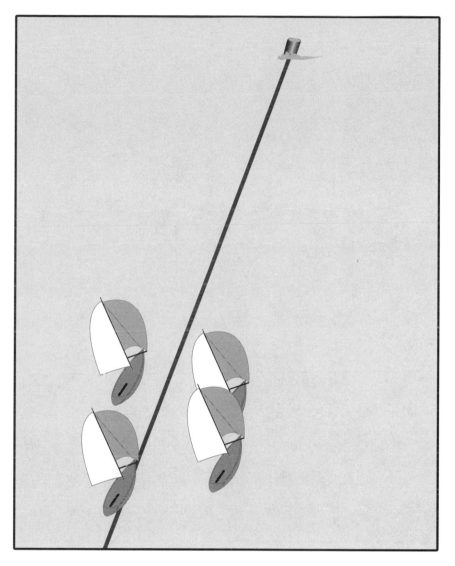

At about ten boatlengths out, you should start to formulate your game plan for the mark and angle toward establishing the necessary overlaps.

When the boats below you get close, control your course by trying to match or exceed their speed. Use the early part of any puff you get first to go down, then stay parallel to the course of the other boats as they get it. That way you will avoid conceding the overlap and will achieve a position where your backwind and wake can affect those boats. In light air, you may be able to take the leading edge of a puff right down to their course line, but resist the temptation to continue below them. If the wind is that spotty, they might get the next puff and simply roll over you. When you reach their course, parallel them or at least head for the mark. Once you get to the two-boatlength circle, you're in free.

Slide down to the path of the boats below you, then turn up to parallel their course. This should equalize boat-speeds and hold the other boats behind you.

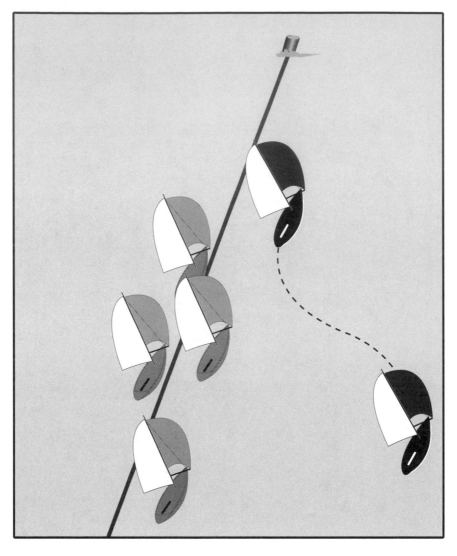

As discussed in Chapter 8, Rule 39 controls how aggressive you can be in steering down toward boats that are trying to establish an overlap to leeward. You need to stay on your proper course to the mark when these boats are within three boatlengths of you. If there are well-defined puffs, steer toward the mark in them. This will allow you to converge with the other boats without being accused of sailing down on them. In the lulls, steer a course roughly parallel with your opponents, and try to keep them under the influence of your wake and backwind. If the wind is steady, steer a course that keeps them in your disturbed air and water with the course toward the mark as your lower boundary. Try to converge on them slowly, and be aware of their position. If they drop back past three boatlengths or steer a course which would not lead to an overlap, descend like a vulture.

This has got to take place well before the two-boatlength circle. While you are working your boat low, the boats behind and to leeward are trying to come up. Their apparent wind will be ahead of yours, so they will be reaching higher speeds. After you have come down to the rhumb line, you can turn back up and achieve those same speeds. This is essential when preventing the other boats from getting an overlap on you. People tend to be somewhat subjective when judging the actual distance covered by those two boatlengths, so you need to be secure in your call when denying room. I like to call out when I've broken the overlap. I also call out when the overlap is established early. "You've got it now, but we're not in yet!" This will strengthen your credibility when you declare that you've broken the overlap, a boatlength or so later.

It is easy to get into extended conversations at this point. Don't—one wave can make the difference here. If you catch this wave, solidify your position by sinking to the other boat's line, or below it if the mark is down there. This will prevent the dangerous situation of having the boat behind establish a late overlap, which forces you to avoid hitting him and then drag him to a protest hearing after the race.

If the boat coming in from behind moves to the outside of you, you can drift out to the line you would take around the mark in the absence of other boats. If he stays on your transom, or keeps probing inside, you need to take care not to open a large enough gap there for him to jibe to the inside and roll right over you on the next reach.

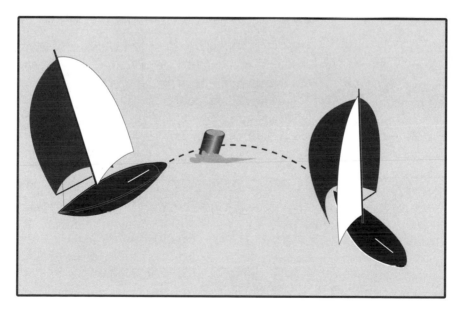

Start your rounding wide so that it will finish tight to the mark.

You have to balance the need for a smooth turn with the need to take up a lot of space here. The key is to extend the turn to windward of the rhumb line to the next mark. This will shut off the windward side without requiring a two-stage turn. Making the jibe, stabilizing the boat, then heading higher takes too much time and rudder input, and will slow the boat unnecessarily. Tell the crew you are going to shut the door on the other boat or boats; they should then be able to keep up with the bow swinging, and won't be surprised when the spinnaker guy has to go farther forward than the leg would seem to require.

This can be devastating for the boats behind you. It pushes the apparent wind forward, accelerates you out of the turn, and puts them right in your exhaust at a time when they may be having difficulty flying their spinnakers anyway.

Rounding in a Pack

Trying to get around the mark when surrounded by other boats is one of those situations where boldness can be rewarded and failure severely penalized. Attaining an overlap may put you on the inside of the wheel, but if you miss, you are on a long trip to the outside.

Flexibility is important, as is a willingness to make the most of a situation gone bad. I like to use a technique I call "the wedge," which is simply an attempt to split the pack around the boat. A gradual luff as you approach the mark may force the boats above you to turn up, while the boats ahead, unaffected by the luff, will pull farther ahead. The resulting gap gives you some room to work around the mark.

As the wheel turns around the mark, the boats on the outside are going to lag behind. Maintaining the room and opportunity to slip inside them will put you around the mark and in the weather position before they can close on you. Their efforts at avoiding the other boats rounding with them will often carry them out and beyond the mark. They will be sailing in disturbed air, unable to come up and close off the gap on the leeward side of the mark. By splitting the pack you reduce the chance of another boat occupying that inside opening.

A clean exit is crucial. You have to have the ability to sail extremely high at the outset if necessary, to avoid boats coming up from outside and ahead. They will have to wait for overlaps on boats inside of them to break, and when the overlaps do break, they will have to head high for clear air.

One danger here will be the boats that are so far on the outside of that first group that they've jibed before the mark and are knifing in on port tack. They may start around the mark from outside the two-boatlength circle. Those behind but on the inside—which is where you will end up after you've split the pack—will already have an overlap as these boats start to come through. Assert yourself early if possible. The boats from the outside will try to exploit their speed advantage while you jibe. They know they are trying to make the best of

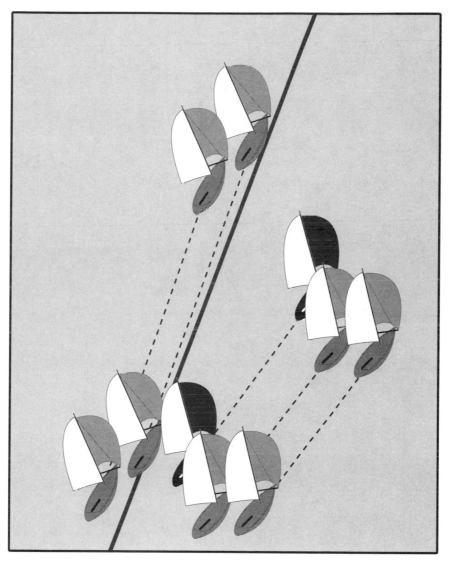

a bad situation and you have to let them know that it's not even that good.

In the worst-case scenario, if they are already inside the circle, you've got to bite the bullet and swing out behind them, thereby allowing one of the trailing boats to grab the hole you are leaving. You can avoid this by slowing down to let these competitors pass. By slowing rather than turning out, you preserve your place on the inside. Frequently you can jibe right behind one of the boats and follow him through the gap. Again, try not to let a boat establish an overlap on you from behind. If you are inside the circle, the other boat will have no legal way of doing this, but sorting

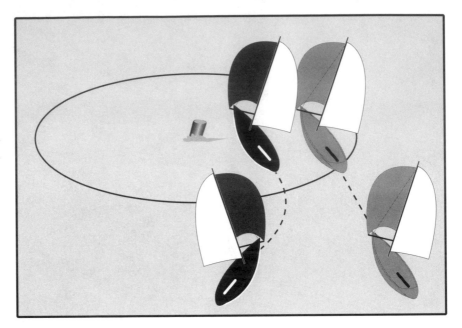

Boats coming into the circle from outside on port tack have few rights. You need to turn on their inside so that they are forced to the outside of you. They will carry greater speed as you jibe, so you don't want to allow them to get over you. If they are able to cross, make them cross ahead of you.

it all out will cost you. A cautionary hail will let the boats behind know that you are intent on protecting your rights.

Approaching the mark on the outside of a large pack is a losing position, but one that is all too easy to fall into. If you have been staying high on the reach, you may not be able to get back down to the rhumb line before the mark. If so, you may have to consider jibing well outside the mark, then trying to find a gap inside some of the boats rounding. You might be better served by three jibes—one back to the rhumb line before the circle, another to approach the mark on starboard, and finally the jibe around it.

Assuming you are sailing a boat that accelerates quickly and your crew is up to it, the three-jibe scenario creates an opportunity to establish an inside position at the mark. But the reach must be fairly loose for this, so that the extra distance sailed on port tack isn't too great. The boats bunching ahead of you at the mark will be moving fairly slowly. If the leg being completed is sufficiently broad, those boats ahead will be in the blanket of those trailing, and some defense is going to be played. This will give you the opportunity and the clear air to cross behind them all on port jibe. The correct timing will have you jibing back to the mark in time to have regained full speed just as you enter the two-boatlength circle. Grabbing a puff as you jibe, or just before, should help. Crossing angles will be wide, and it should be easy to find a gap to get across on port tack.

There is one potential hazard: after the jibe back onto starboard, you may be confronted with a wall of boats and nowhere to go. If that is the case, you may have to

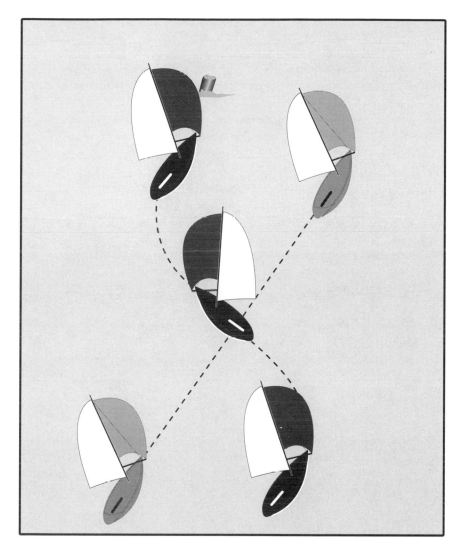

If you end up high on the first reach, consider two extra jibes into the mark.

resort to a couple of S-turns until a gap opens up. Once it does, though, you can get around the mark and head up and over the boats trying to claw their way up from the outside.

If the conditions don't permit this maneuver—if the wind is so light that the extra jibes aren't possible—try to enter the two-boatlength circle on port with speed. As the inside boats slow in their jibe, gaps will open for you to go through and get on the new windward side of the crowd. The important thing is to reach that windward side as close as possible to the mark, so that you can work the new reach with clear air.

Exiting the Mark

The effects of the jibe mark rounding will be noticeable well into the second reach. As the boats are spit out of the mark, they are sailing from positions on either side of the rhumb line. This is where the *passing lane*—the area to windward of the general mass of boats—really comes into its own. It offers a chance to build speed in clear air while passing over boats that are in dirty air.

In the simplest case, imagine three boats going into the mark abreast. As the boats make the turn, the inside boat gains by virtue of his position. He moves to blanket the middle boat, who in turn is hammering the outside boat. The outside boat slows and takes the transom of the middle boat, thereby moving into the passing lane. As the inside boat accelerates away, the middle boat tries to come up but isn't yet up to

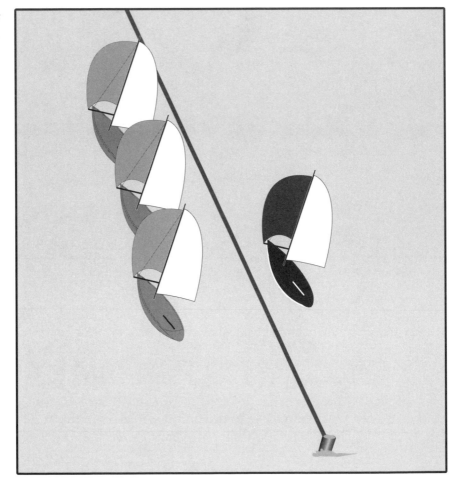

The passing lane forms quickly after the mark.

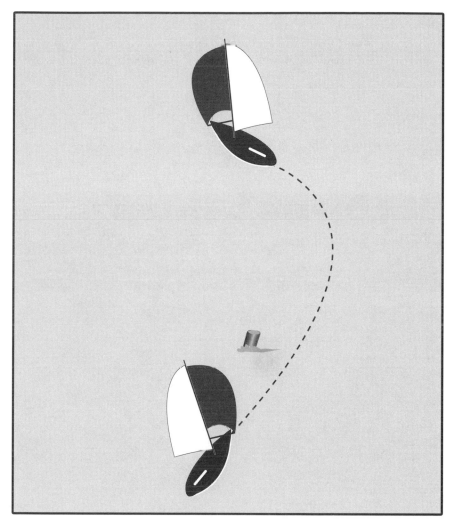

You can delay your jibe and set up the low route for the next leg. This works well in light air or when the second reach is loose.

speed; the outside boat, enjoying clear air and greater speed, roars by and starts blanketing him before he can mount an effective defense.

This can be repeated as many times as there are boats immediately behind you, so you've got to come out of the mark high and hot. The greater your boatspeed, the lower you can go, but if you were slowed down by some drastic moves in your fight for position around the mark, you've got to get up in clear air right now just to rebuild speed.

This maneuvering can go on for quite some time. The boats that struggle high to get clear air will have to sail lower late in the leg to get to the downwind mark. This creates the only other way out of the dilemma of being outside at the mark: not jibing at all at the mark. If the pack is rounding tightly and you are already stuck on the outside, you can carry the first reach beyond the mark and jibe late. This sets you up for the low route to the next mark.

Just as in the first reach, it will take patience to make this tactic pay off. Resisting the temptation to close with the other boats during the light spots, and taking the shots down instead, requires intestinal fortitude. The essence of the strategy is not to come up until everyone else has to head straight downwind to get to the mark. There is always the possibility that the leg will be so loose it becomes a downwind leg. If this happens, you will have gained substantially by sailing a course that has given you maximum velocity downwind, rather than wasting time heading too high like your opponents. If you catch sight of some boats jibing early toward the mark, you can pop the bubbly!

Jibing late provides you with a good deal of separation. To maintain this separation you need to steer toward the mark in the lulls and well below it in the puffs. After the first half of the leg, any logjam above you should be broken. Since the boats to windward have spread out, they will no longer present an impenetrable wind block, and you can start to move back toward the rhumb line. Slowly, gently, close with the fleet. If you have been successful going low, you would needlessly limit your gain now by closing with the other boats too soon. As a rule, try to stay low and out of the way as long as possible. Once you reach the boats that have sailed down the rhumb line, you will need to react to them and cross their blanket areas; that will slow you down by either driving you higher or forcing you to sail lower.

General Thoughts on the Jibe Mark

Sailing into the jibe mark (or *any* mark, for that matter) requires great anticipation, but that anticipation must be tempered by a healthy dose of opportunism. Maintaining flexibility without losing sight of your strategy is what makes the mark so difficult.

Your plan may be to go in conservatively and only to look for the high lane coming out of the mark if the boats immediately in front of you slow and swing wide. If they do, you'll have to change the entire timing of your rounding, sacrifice boatspeed for position, and then hold that position. Your crew has got to keep up with the boat. It can be a thrill.

Try to avoid dithering until it is too late to move, or until the wind swings behind you and you can't reach your spot through the shadows of boats behind. Rather than accept being locked in, keep your eyes open for marginal improvements, those openings that can move you toward the inside coming out of the mark. Remember that what's critical is not where you are *at* the mark but where you are when you exit the two-boatlength circle.

Access to the passing lane is the important goal, because getting on top early in the second reach gives you the best shot at a successful leg. You can achieve this by being the inside boat—turning wide initially and taking transoms immediately after the mark—or, if you are forced to the outside, by waiting for the boats inside to pass and then heading up for the passing lane. Clearly the last alternative is the least desirable.

The rules governing the rounding determine the techniques available and the risk involved. They force the situation to reveal itself somewhat earlier, allow the boats with rights to solidify their spots, and let the burdened yachts start immediate damage control. Damage control here involves a crew ready to jibe, an examination of the competition for spaces to shoot through, and warnings to the boats behind not to try any funny stuff.

The potential for collisions between boats is probably greater at the jibe mark than anywhere else on the course, as the rewards for violating the rules are immediate and sizable. Since your planning must rely on the predictable actions of others based on those rules, it is important to communicate that you expect everyone in your area to abide by them. Your hails must be timely and clear. You don't have to recite the rules and list the appropriate appeal numbers, but the other boats should get the notion that you have firm knowledge of your rights and intend to enforce them.

Once I was sailing toward a mark with another boat overlapped and nearly parallel on my inside. We were about ten boatlengths away, and I was briefing my crew on my intentions for the rounding, when the other boat blew out his chute. We were moving fairly quickly and broke his overlap about five boatlengths from the mark. I hailed him to that effect, upon which he correctly pointed out that we were still outside the circle. But I wanted him to realize that we were clear ahead already, so that when I swung down there would be no question in his mind. Also, we would have to make a tight turn, and I wanted his bow safely on our outside as we slowed in the turn. I had been telling my crew that we would swing wide initially, aiming to end up above the other boat coming out of the mark. Fate had other plans, and we responded accordingly.

This experience is typical of the kind of action that occurs around the jibe mark. You can't be juking the boat all around trying to create that overwhelming advantage. Rather, you've got to be smooth and make the most of the opportunities that come your way. If you and your crew are up to speed when it comes to jibing, you will have a tremendous advantage over 90 percent of the other boats. Using this advantage to ensure consistent speed through the rounding will take you around and over less skilled crews.

Questions

Q How wide can I force outside boats if I have rights at the buoy?

A According to Rule 42, you can force them to give you room to make a "sea-manlike" rounding. That is one of those beautifully undefined quantities in the rules. Ideally, you want to jibe without making an excessively sharp turn, and to exit with the mark close aboard to prevent boats behind you from ending up higher. That goal provides a practical guideline which there is no need to exceed. If you go too far outside, not only will the boats you've forced outside want to skin you, but some boats behind will sneak into the gap you've left. They are perfectly free to do this as long as they don't interfere with your rounding.

Q When should I release the old guy from the pole during a jibe?

A This needs to be done as soon as possible. In light air, the key to keeping the chute flying around the jibe is to have it as far away from the main as possible. If you keep the guy in the pole end, you will pull the chute under the main when you reach for the new guy.

Release the old guy by triggering the pole end and tilting the pole so the guy lifts out. If the wind isn't strong enough to lift the guy out of the pole, rotate the pole one half turn and shut the end. It will be free of the guy even if the guy is still lying on it.

Q What should I do if I've tried for an inside overlap approaching the mark and failed to get it?

A The first thing you have to do at that point is make sure you do not foul the boat you've tried to overlap. If there are boats to the outside over which you do have rights, slow down to avoid the boat ahead but preserve your inside position. Recognize that you will have to make a tight turn and will need to accelerate quickly after the mark. If the boat ahead messes up his jibe, an opening may appear to windward of him.

If you have no rights over anyone, you'll have to move to the outside. Chances are you'll find several boats stacked up out there; somewhere there will be room for you to jibe without risking a foul. So move to the outside, but be prepared to turn when you see your opening.

Q How can I recognize the two-boatlength circle?

A This is quite difficult. All you can do is estimate the circle, establish your overlap, and hail for room. The outside yacht is responsible for determining where he is in relation to the mark, whereas the inside yacht must ensure that all the other conditions of Rule 42—the overlap, the hail, and the existence of rights over the other boats to windward—are met. If the outside yacht declines room and causes a collision, he will have a tough time winning his case. When you find yourself on the outside, it is best to give the benefit of the doubt to the inside yacht.

Chapter 10

The Second Reach

After the jibe mark, the character of the race changes. By this time, disturbed air from the leaders and disturbed water from their wakes, as well as differences in raw boatspeed, have caused the fleet to spread out. Whereas success during the start and the first two legs depended primarily on gaining a strategic position superior to the rest of the fleet, the latter part of the race becomes more of a battle between individual boats. With the fleet spread out, the advantaged positions on the racecourse are available to more boats. At this point, too, most people have gotten the message and will be heading for the same spots or sailing according to the same strategy.

After rounding, the leaders will try to extend their lead, and everyone else will try to pass the boat immediately in front or fight off the boat storming up from behind. Once the overlaps after the mark are sorted out, the search for clear air and the universal temptation to try to climb into the passing lane brings the boats into a line. It becomes extremely difficult to pass, as a move to windward will bring a response from the boat ahead, which will bring a response from the boat ahead of him, and so on. The typical parade is the result.

Unless you are recovering from a nasty first leg or were over at the start, the second reach usually finds you with boats sailing at about your speed. Any technical advantage you may have had will have been evident on the first reach, but unless you are leading, this advantage will slowly disappear as you move farther up the fleet. It gets more difficult to pass as you draw closer to the guys who are leading the race.

Hard Defense, Opportunistic Offense

Holding position is the goal of this approach. You don't want to have a slew of boats jumping over you, and you don't want to engage in an extended luffing match with the boat ahead. If you are near the front of the pack, you've worked hard to get where you are. The odds run in favor of maintaining the status quo.

This leg is an opportunity to extend your lead over the pack. Sailing fast is more important than passing any particular boat—at this instant. The extra lead you build here is capital you can spend later in an aggressive maneuver against a boat ahead, at a time when the odds of success are much higher.

There are two things you need to accomplish: you need to hang on to the boats in front of you, and lose the boats behind you. I would consider hanging on to the boats ahead my first priority.

I like to try to find a spot inside the wake of the boat ahead. This gives me good flat water to work. If a gust moves through, I will pull off in it to accelerate toward the transom of the boat ahead. He should get the wind before I get too far along. If I move right up to him, I will turn up slowly so he realizes that I am not trying to climb over him. This leaves him free to turn off with the puff as well, and we will both make tracks down the leg.

The idea is not to threaten but to extend. Some shouted encouragement may also help prevent your opponent from feeling challenged. You want to avoid trig-

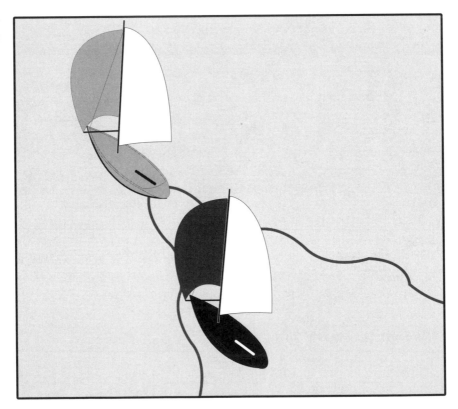

Ride on the smooth water just inside the leading boat's wake.

gering a defensive response because it would only slow you both down or force you to attempt the pass before you are ready. You can take a puff across from the windward wake to the leeward wake without stirring up too much trouble. If you have broken outside the windward wake, try to ride the quarter wave and stay high.

Of course, as you are laying off the boat ahead, you have to keep the boats behind from jumping on you. You need to defend your position hard on this leg to stop a single pass from becoming a parade as you lose your clear air. Steely eyes and a strong move to windward should keep the dogs at bay. Use the weapons at your disposal, and keep the boats behind inside your wake. Try not to let someone break through to the point where they might start to ride your wake up and over.

The single most important element to your defense is to be moving too fast to be caught. You have to get the jump on any puffs that are coming down. It is imperative in planing conditions that you get up and on your way. Keep your focus on the wind and waves, and assign a crewmember to keep track of what the boats behind are doing. In lighter air, milking the end of a puff will also make a difference. Keeping your speed up and making a smooth turn back to windward using as little rudder input as possible will stretch your advantage.

Another technique to use on the boats immediately behind you involves the boats behind *them*. If you are aware of the situation of the boat behind, you may induce him to lock up with a boat following him. If you see someone creeping up on the outside two or three boats back, a move to windward by you should trigger a corresponding move by the boat right behind you, who then suddenly needs to deal with this third boat and can no longer concentrate on tracking you down. I love this. The situation gets better if a series of gusts rolls down as the two of them hook up, because you can head low and fast while they are occupied with each other.

So much for the hard defense. Now what does opportunistic offense mean? It means that if the boat ahead makes a mistake, pass him. This is still a skill leg. Lightsails are up, the boats are reaching, and the reach may be tight.

In light air, the boats in front may sail into a hole. The wind may lift over an obstruction, or there may be a dead spot as a precursor to a shift. In any case, you need to make an attempt to preserve your speed and use it to place you in a better position relative to the other boats. Having an idea of what will happen next is critical to choosing the most promising approach. If the wind is going to come back from the same direction, heading higher places you closer to it. If it is going to resume from a new direction, as in the case of a sea breeze coming in, heading toward the new wind becomes the priority, and may require a jibe.

As the wind lightens, the optimum jibe angle for a downwind leg or a very loose reach will take you above the actual sailing angle to the next mark. In other words, achieving your highest *velocity made good* (VMG) to the mark requires that you head above it and jibe back later. You'll sail farther but get there faster. (The concept of VMG is described more fully in Chapters 11 and 12.) It also helps to maintain enough boatspeed to head toward an area of new wind, and heading

Try and get the
boat behind you
tangled with another
boat behind him. Once
they are involved with
each other, you can
concentrate on
speeding away.

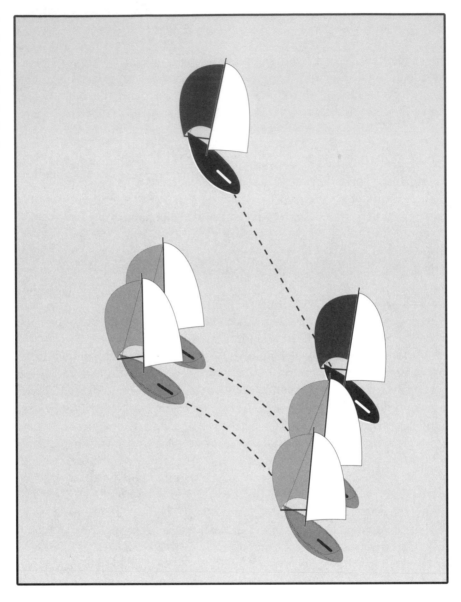

up will enable you to preserve what might become a scarce commodity.

The wind shadow thrown by a windward boat in light air is a formidable obstacle. If your course to the new wind takes you below the boats ahead, you must aim for as much separation as possible and consider jibing. If you are to continue below them, you'll need to be at least one mast length away.

As soon as you notice the boats ahead dropping into a hole, start reviewing what you know about the weather and make an attempt to go around the dead spot. If

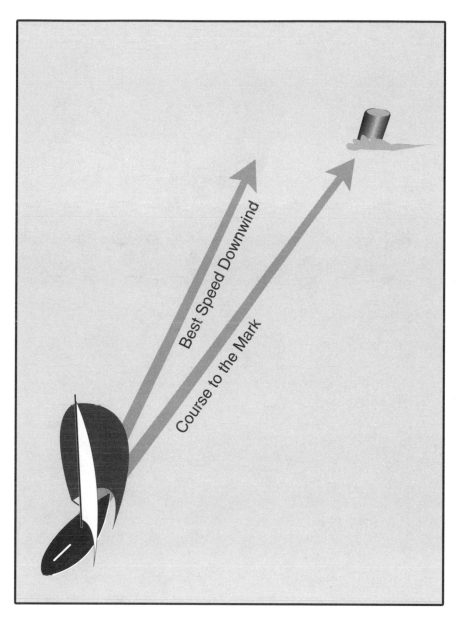

Best Speed Downwind

Course to the Mark

Sometimes the optimum course downwind ends up being higher than the course to the mark. The leg then plays like a run, and opportunities to exploit shifts and jibing angles appear.

necessary, jibe toward the expected new air and get comfortable; hopefully you won't have a long wait.

If the winds are heavy, boats may be rolling out all around you. If they are close and one broaches right in front of you, you need to be ready to make a split-second call—up or down. The rule of thumb is to go down in heavy air except when close to the mark. A boat with its rig in the water doesn't cause much wind shadow.

If a boat rolls out in front of you, pass below him; if his spinnaker develops problems, pass above him.

Going down with the wind allows you to keep your own boat under control.

When someone in front of you develops a problem and slows abruptly, he becomes more of an obstacle than anything else. If he is broaching, he doesn't have any control; if his spinnaker has blown, his crew will be occupied cleaning up the mess and trying to get a new one up. In any case, he will have slowed dramatically and will be unable to move against you or take any action to defend himself.

In strong air, the best route is down to pass him and then, once you are by, up to bring the apparent wind forward. As you head off, the apparent wind swings aft, giving you a few extra boatlengths before the other boat starts to interfere with the air reaching your sails. When you notice the disturbed air, you can turn up and pull the apparent wind forward of it. This will get you through the region of disturbed air quickly, and will set up your defensive position after the other boat has recovered.

How do you keep from broaching when all those around you seem to be heading back upwind? A combination of three techniques will help keep the boat underneath you. The key is anticipation: the entire boat must know the puff is coming. Again, the crew and the helmsman can reduce the chances of broaching by trimming the boat for the puff *as* it arrives. Not before—that would slow the boat unnecessarily—and not after—that is too late, because the first indication that you are in trouble will be the boom hitting the water.

The first technique is the reverse pump. As we discussed in Chapter 8, this technique will reduce the impact of the leading edge of the puff on the mainsail. A reverse pump consists simply of letting the mainsheet out when the puff first hits. Although this reduces its impact, it still feeds more power into the sail. This gives the boat some time to accelerate and lets the keel or board stay vertical. If the underwater foils remain close to vertical, they are not going to develop as much drag; this in turn will allow the boat to speed up rather than load up. Then the main can be retrimmed.

The second technique requires steering the boat low while executing the reverse pump, so that the rudder can do its work before it gets highly loaded. When a helmsman tries to turn a boat down *after* the rudder is loaded, he or she can do little more than keep the boat moving in a straight line. The additional angle of attack of the rudder may cause it to stall, and then the boat simply turns around its keel and the game is over. If your rudder does stall, pumping it by centering it briefly, then again trying to turn down, may reattach the flow and bring the boat back under control.

On smaller boats, pumping the spinnaker guy is the third method to avoid a broach. Repeated pumping is generally prohibited by the rules except when planing, or trying to plane; however, pumping once in a puff to discourage a broach falls into the legal range of action. If the wind is blowing hard enough to cause broaching, it is difficult anyway to imagine the size of the person necessary to effectively haul the guy aft. But moving the guy is not necessary; all that is needed is to translate some extra force forward. Keeping your boat on course during a heavy-air reach is a balancing act, and it never takes much to alter the balance of forces. If you pressurize the guy, you take a little bit of force off the rudder, which then may not stall and can guide the bow down.

Continuously monitoring the vang tension is critical here. More than anything else, the vang is the throttle on the main. If you need to depower in a puff, throwing off the vang will release the top of the main and help bring the boat back under control. The vang needs to be reapplied as soon as possible though. Resist the temptation to throw it off and forget it until things have settled down. The power of the main, if properly controlled, will keep the boat moving and balanced.

One other mistake commonly made by boats on this second reach is to break low for the mark too early. They start out high on the leg and get weary two-thirds of the way down. So they pull the pole back and head for the mark. It is very easy, however, to go from a course that is too high to one that is too low. After a certain point, the fastest course to the mark is to carry the height you've acquired on the early part of the leg farther and jibe back for the mark. You need to know the optimum jibe angle for your boat to make this approach successful. To achieve your best speed downwind you may not want to continue as high as you have been sailing, but you still need to stay above the mark.

Most boats can gain a significant amount of speed by heading on a course higher than dead downwind. This is especially noticeable in light air. If the bearing to the mark is less than this "ideal" heading, you must continue until the bearing to the mark matches your ideal bearing on the other tack. Then you can jibe over to starboard tack and shoot into the mark with rights and boatspeed. The boats that have gone for the mark too early will either still be on port tack or be sailing too low on starboard. If they carry their starboard jibe high enough to reach their optimum speed, they will have to jibe again before the mark and will approach it from the outside. At best for them, this is a neutral outcome. They will have to do their jibing outside the two-boatlength circle, and that may slow them enough for you to get in ahead of them.

Opportunities to pass may or may not occur. The object of the strategy of opportunistic offense and hard defense is to avoid directly challenging the boat or boats immediately ahead, while sailing fast and pulling away from the rest of the pack. There will be more effective opportunities to pass boats later in the race, and we may need the cushion behind us to utilize them. If you have a real speed advantage on the reach, however, you may not be able to avoid tangling with slower boats ahead. In that case, take them on and get it over quickly so there will be plenty of leg left to exploit that speed advantage. Get outside the other boat's wake, and start to roll.

Charge!

If you've been buried on the first leg and haven't fully recovered by the end of the first reach, you really have but one option. The race is rapidly running out, and you have to stay on the offensive. Passing boats on this second leg is difficult, but it can be done, and if done, t'were best done quickly.

You need to avoid any direct confrontation early in the leg. This requires that you build separation between yourself and the other boats as soon as you can. If the boats in front are having trouble completing their jibes, grab the advantage by

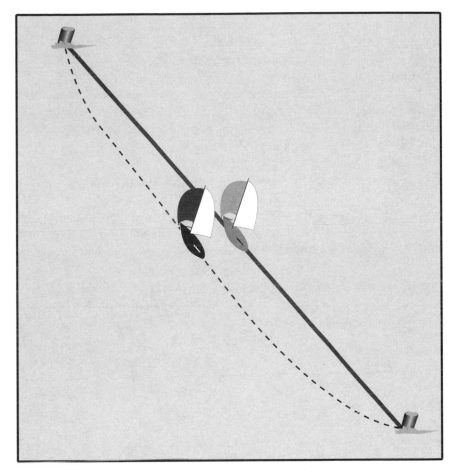

Mentally move the rhumb line up with you and play the puffs to either side of it.

heading sharply above them. In medium and light air, take the first puff up to accelerate rather than down to extend.

As on the first reach, you have to break through the wake of the boat ahead. By staying clear of his defensive weapons, you are free to develop your own boatspeed. If you are successful at attaining this windward position, move the rhumb line up to your course. In other words, don't worry about getting back down to the mark right away; play the leg as if the mark had been moved in front of you.

As the boats around you start working on each other, they will climb up to your line. In the early part of the leg, the passing lane will determine where the fleet goes, because eventually everyone will have to head up to get into that line in the never-ending search for clear air. If you are the first one up there, you can control how far the fleet will go.

After the mark has been left behind and the fleet has lined up, the easy passes are over. Your situation should be somewhat improved. The boat ahead of you has probably edged up close enough to feel he can cut you off if you try to sail down on him in a puff or over him in a lull. Your only task here is to make sure you are still outside his wake, so you can accelerate fully in a gust and won't have to waste time or energy breaking through the wake.

The boats behind you cannot be ignored, but they are not the focus of your strategy for this leg: you are trying to get by the boats ahead. Nevertheless, the move up into the passing lane should also help you break out of any threatening situation. In this case, the best defense is a good offense.

Eventually you will end up going against a boat that won't let you pass. Either he will be moving at about your speed or he will not let you get high enough to pass him without sailing right off the course. This situation is particularly difficult when the wind is slightly aft of the beam and you are getting the puffs first. You accelerate in the puff, roar up to your competitor—and he goes head-to-wind to cut you off. As you slow down, you interrupt the flow of obscenities in your thoughts

Take the puff you want to pass with up instead of down. This will give you good separation quickly.

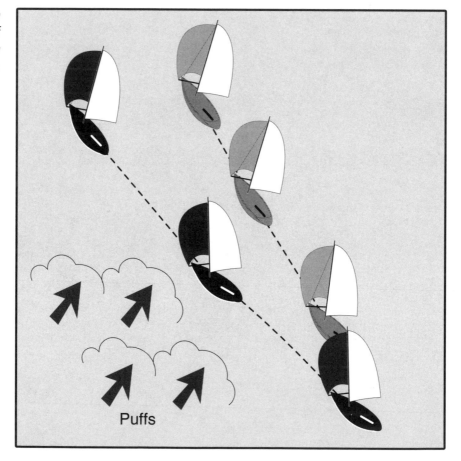

Puffs

to realize that he is only doing what you would do in his position and probably doesn't want to go any higher than you do.

It is time to work on setting up a more sophisticated pass. You can initiate the maneuver by now dropping inside the wake of the boat ahead. Since you are getting the wind first and are moving in relatively smooth water, you should sail right up to his transom. This bit of provocation is going to leave his team a little jumpy. You should try the high side, just in case they are sleepy and don't respond, but chances are the other boat will immediately turn up to give you a strong signal. When he does, pull off and slide below him slightly. Your speed will carry you to an overlap to leeward, but that won't last. As he breaks the overlap, slide up to his transom and repeat the process.

After a few repetitions, your opponent should decide that you are some kind of wimp and cease to worry much about your plans. Maybe he will even start to fix his greedy eyes on a boat ahead. In the meantime, you spot a puff moving down and edge a little farther to windward. When the puff is about to hit, you strike. Take the puff up and over the other boat. Rapid acceleration is the key here: the bigger the jump you get the less chance the other boat will have to move against you. This works even better if the puff is a lift, because the wind will swing farther aft, projecting the blanket from your sails forward and onto your opponent earlier. Make it fast and sweet, and don't provoke him by hooting and hollering. Hold your higher line slightly longer than necessary, in order to leave your leeward wake on him after you are by.

If you are in a mixed, or handicap, fleet and have a definite speed advantage over the boat in front of you, simple courtesy may get you by. Inform your friendly competitor that you will go quite high to pass him, minimizing the impact on him, if he will allow you to get up there. Otherwise, you will just have to go close by and let him take you both out of the race. He may see the wisdom of this approach if there are no other boats immediately behind you, so that there isn't the disagreeable prospect of letting one by and opening the door to others.

As you work by him, don't return the favor by letting him ride your stern wave. If he is allowed to be drawn along by your wake, essentially he will be building his lead over you, taking time corrections into account.

To the observer, passing on a reach, particularly in planing boats, seems to occur very quickly and with an overwhelming advantage to the boat doing the passing. This impression is rarely accurate. Attaining the advantaged position can be a slow process, and the difference between having it and not having it is very small. The challenge involved in crossing the wake of the opposing boat is a case in point. Punching through requires rapid response to a puff, grabbing a ride from a passing wave, or a combination of the two. If you can't get up to speed quickly, both of these assists are going to pass you by; you will slog up to windward, and the other boat can easily counter. But if you do achieve the necessary speed quickly and attain a position to windward, the other boat may concede without much effort to stop you.

Taking the Low Route

The second reaching leg is the leg most likely to turn into a run before it is over. After the first reach has stretched the fleet and all the boats have struggled for the inside at the jibe mark, they will move to windward to maintain clear air and pass each other. The entire line of boats will move in more or less identical fashion.

The fleet will eventually have to turn down to get to the mark, and whereas it was spread out heel to toe before, it will now start to form clumps again. Boats that have worked far to windward may have to jibe to get back to the mark. Indeed, if the second reach is fairly broad, you can count on this happening in a fleet of any size. So why not take that jibe at the beginning of the leg instead of the end? By continuing past the jibe mark without jibing, you can do just that, and reduce the number of jibes in the leg by two.

This is less risky than it sounds, but it does take commitment to keep going when all those around you are jibing tightly around the mark and heading upwind in their quest for the passing lane. You need several pieces of information before you decide to take this route.

First, you have to know where that downwind mark is. In most courses it will be either the starting mark or a mark close by. On those occasions when the starting area is in the middle of the upwind leg, knowing how far below the line the mark is gives you a tremendous advantage. Those who don't know will have to jibe and sail for a while until they spot it. They will inevitably edge over toward the starting line and end up well high of the mark. Part of your prerace preparation should include sailing over to the rhumb line of this leg and getting some accurate bearings for later use.

The second piece of information is an accurate estimate of the jibing angle for your boat in the prevailing breeze. Remember that in lighter winds the best speed downwind is usually delivered by reaching and tacking downwind. If the rhumb line to the mark is already below this best course, you don't risk much by continuing past the jibe mark. The more likely location of the rhumb line will be at or above the best jibing angle, but the fleet will probably sail well above the rhumb line after the jibe mark, opening up room below. The earlier in the leg this happens, the better the course to leeward looks. You can't predict exactly what the fleet will do, but the broader the reach to the mark, the more likely this situation will develop.

The last piece of information you need is an informed guess on the next windshift. If a backing, or counterclockwise, shift is likely, the leg will loosen up at the end, favoring the low course. If the wind is going to veer, however, and the leg tightens up, you may not be able to get back to the mark from a leeward position. Taking down your spinnaker early to beat up to a leeward mark is not fast.

If all of these considerations favor the leeward course, you will probably realize big gains with it. The low route is the best way to pass boats in a wholesale fashion on the reach. It can also save a poor rounding at the jibe mark by allowing you to simply bypass the crowd at the buoy.

Sailing fast below the fleet takes concentration. There aren't a lot of visual cues to tell you how you are doing. Crew and helmsman must be willing to work every wave, every puff, and squeeze out the last little bit of boatspeed in anticipation of a reward to come later in the leg. Moving the rhumb line mentally, ideally with the help of a spot picked on the shoreline, is a good technique here as well. The important point to remember is that you need to either steer low or stay on starboard tack long enough to ensure clear air below the line of boats to windward.

Once the required separation is attained, you want to go right to your best speed made good downwind toward the leeward mark. If this course is still above the mark—certainly a possibility with some race committees—then you've jibed to port too early. You can stay on port jibe as long as none of the other boats falls out of line to threaten your wind, but unfortunately, this will probably happen fairly soon. Adjusting your tactical frame of mind from reach to downwind leg will allow you to execute the maneuvers necessary to protect yourself.

Approaching the Downwind Mark

Even if the fleet was still packed fairly closely after the jibe mark, it will surely have spread out by now. For most boats the race has turned into an effort to improve their position by leapfrogging lone competitors or small packs. We approach the leeward mark trying to secure a position at the head of one of these clusters.

Once again, we need to focus on the conditions we expect early in the next leg and how we plan to exploit them. If we are going to harden up on port tack as we tackle the upwind leg, approaching the mark below other boats but with clear air will give us the ability to set up for maximum boatspeed while they may be pinching each other off. If we intend to flop over to starboard and head for the left side, we need to be on the inside of the pack so that we can tack at will.

This kind of tactical consideration will be a recurring theme throughout the rest of the race. No matter where you are in the fleet, you have to start fighting for the ability to do what you think is necessary. Other boats will interfere with your air and get in your way. There is no worse feeling than wanting to tack and finding yourself pinned by another boat. You may be able to work yourself out of the position, but it will delay you.

Unless you are one of the top two or three boats, you will be approaching the mark from either side of the rhumb line. When you are above the line, working down becomes a challenge, and choosing the right moment to break toward the mark is critical. You want to keep your boatspeed up as much as you can. This means working the puffs down and the lulls up, even if the lulls take you back above the mark. The apparent wind has to be kept forward, so that the blankets of the boats behind will not affect you. You need to be on the lookout for waves, small puffs, anything that will give you a little more speed when trying to make distance to leeward.

The importance of speed here is illustrated by the fate of those boats who decide they can't pass any more boats by going over them and end up heading for the mark too early. They become locked on course, and the boats behind either camp on their air or carry past them higher on the course, winding up inside at the mark.

Knowing when to head down for the mark or jibe to starboard tack is a matter of recognizing the proper conditions for the maneuver. Do not start heading low unless you get some windshift forward to do it. Failing that, wait for a particularly long and deep puff that will carry you well down toward the rhumb line.

If you approach the point where you want to jibe and you are next to another boat, the question becomes, who will jibe first? If the mark is fairly close—five or six lengths away—it may be wise to let the boat ahead jibe away. The reason is that if you jibe first from behind, the other boat has you on the outside; he will hold you away from the mark, and it is unlikely that you will have enough time to pass him and reach a position clear ahead before you get to the two-boatlength circle. By hanging back and following him into the mark you gain two advantages. First, if there are other boats around, your opponent's entry into the immediate area of the mark is going to cause them to back away. This may leave room for you to swing around on the inside. Second, your opponent may develop some crew problems in trying to get the chute down, set up for the weather leg, and jibe again to round the mark. While you have to do these same things, you don't have the added pressure of another boat right at your heels. (If you do, you will of course ignore it!)

By contrast, if both boats have jibed over to starboard but will have to jibe back to port to get to the mark, your jibe to port should be first, or at least simultaneous with his. This will get you into the circle with an overlap, shifting control to you at the mark; it is a risky, aggressive maneuver, though. If there are a lot of boats overlapped at the mark, sorting out who has rights and who doesn't may take some work, and there is little time for that in a rapidly developing situation. Being the trailing boat, you need to plan your escape route well. This is most difficult in light air.

Finally, if the mark is some distance away and a prolonged sail on starboard tack is anticipated, you as the trailing boat want your competitor to jibe first. This is difficult because, although you need to make the jibe late enough to carry a high angle into the mark, you don't want to allow the other boat to wait so long that you can only trail him to the mark. If you can be particularly aggressive here, you may distract the other boat and induce him to jibe away. Making a series of moves to weather may keep him distracted, and eventually he will want to get back to the middle of the course. Executing your jibe after his will place you on the inside should a further jibe back to port be necessary.

Resist the temptation to avoid a second jibe by fading down to the mark. Keep up a good speed, and be ready to jibe inside the other boat. If the second jibe isn't needed and your competitor sails directly to the mark on starboard, he may leave the mark wide and give you the opportunity to end up on his hip once you've turned upwind.

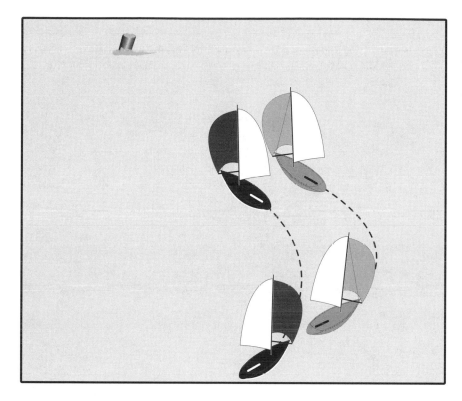

From this position, jibe back to port before the boat ahead. This will give you a shot at an overlap at the mark.

As we said earlier, the fleet will start to clump up again near the mark; boats sailing lower angles will slow down, and other boats will get on their air. The effect of these clumps on your upwind leg is what we have to consider next. The object of your tactics is to leave you free to do what you want immediately after the mark. Depending on your strategy, you'll need either room to tack to starboard, or clear air and water to continue close-hauled on port.

If you want to continue on port tack, you can approach the mark fairly close aboard and leave it wider but fast. If you want to tack to starboard, you can approach the mark wide to leave it tight, swinging up behind some transoms and shedding boats that might otherwise have pinned you on port tack. How to choose between these two options will be covered in the next chapter.

Questions

Q When the conditions are marginal—when the reach is fairly close or the wind fairly strong—how can I decide whether or not to put up, or keep up, my spinnaker?

A This is a highly subjective question, and the answer assumes a couple of things. First, we assume that you are very familiar with the capabilities of your boat with the spinnaker up. In other words, your assessment of marginal conditions is accurate. Second, we have to believe that the crew on the boat is up to the task of tight spinnaker reaching, and that the action of setting the chute and taking it down won't be costly.

Given these two premises, I would say that anytime the wind has been dying, you should put up the chute. If you expect a shift behind you, put up the chute. If you need to gamble a bit to improve your position, put it up. Should things work out the wrong way and you end up below the mark, a smooth takedown may turn the situation to your advantage. In general, putting the chute up early will give you clear air by keeping you out in front of other boats.

Conversely, if you know that the mark is considerably higher than the other boats are heading, leave the chute down. If the wind is building and the situation is already marginal, leave it down. And if there is an advantage on the high side of the course—new wind or an expected shift—again, leave the chute down.

To remove some of the anxiety from this decision, you and your crew need to be prepared to set the chute from any position, at any time, with minimal loss of boatspeed. As always, the issue comes down to practice.

Q How can I work back down to the mark after being forced high by other boats?

A If the course is not going to require a jibe, you need to start from a position that will guarantee you clear air. You cannot just head lower if there is another boat ready to slide onto your air. If that is a danger, keep scalloping up in the lulls and down in the puffs; just take the puffs lower. Your course should still angle back and forth below and above the mark.

Try to make the most of every opportunity to sink lower. If a wave wants to take you well low of the rhumb line, go with it. The extra distance to leeward may allow you to hold higher through a light spot later on.

Q What if I start to converge on another boat to leeward while I am going down?

A The rules don't allow you to sail below a rhumb line course to the mark if another boat is within three boatlengths of you to leeward. If this is the case, curtail your scallops below the mark, and concentrate on using the puffs, which you will get first, to extend beyond the three-boatlength area. Then you can continue making your fastest overall course toward the mark.

Q Suppose I am the low boat coming up from leeward of the rhumb line. I've caught up with some of the boats who went high, but now they are coming down to the mark and interfering with my air. How can I continue to work by them?

A There are no restrictions on the leeward boat's heading. You will want to work the puffs down and try to come up enough in the lulls to break through the narrow part of the windward boat's blanket. If you can build sufficient speed, take a path that will lead you to a position clear ahead of the other boat, then go to the mark. If you can't escape before the mark, stay wide so you can start the weather leg on his hip.

Chapter 11

The Second Beat

The character of the race changes once again on the second upwind leg. There are more lanes of clear air. The fleet has spread out, and the race may become a battle for the lead within the groups of boats sailing together. Applying the lessons learned from the first leg, these groups will head toward what has been the favored side of the course. Some boats will gamble by heading deep to one side or the other.

If we can accept that such strategic factors as the favored side and the influence of current are more widely known after some time on the course, we can see that tactics become more important on the later legs. With the fleet dispersed, there is more freedom to maneuver. The focus shifts from finding clear air and the correct side of the course to developing and exploiting advantages over specific boats. Relative advantage replaces absolute advantage in most cases.

As the wind shifts, so does the relative advantage. It will change in degree, and may flash in and out of existence altogether. The second beat is a time to be alert to instances of relative advantage and prepared to exploit and consolidate them. These instances will develop predictably. A knock may bring a boat that is on your hip and to weather closer, and may even give you a chance to cross him. When the chance comes, it must be taken regardless of how long ago you last tacked or how close you are to the layline.

The second beat highlights the importance of good tacking skills. Most of the offensive maneuvers used in this leg depend on a tack to initiate or complete them. The larger the boat, the more complicated this becomes, but the greater the gains to be realized. A defending boat also depends on good tacks, and they are just as difficult for him. Whichever position you're in—whether you recognize possibilities for closing the gap on a boat ahead or for building a stronger defensive position against a boat behind—you need to overcome your natural reluctance to making what seems like an excessive number of tacks.

Dividing the Leg

The second beat can be viewed as consisting of three distinct segments: clearing out of the downwind mark, sailing the middle portion of the leg, and making the approach to the weather mark. The strategy for each segment can be summed up in a few words:

- Exiting the downwind mark requires that you stay clear of traffic, quickly determine the favored tack, and get onto it.
- Sailing the middle of the course requires that you stay in phase with the windshifts, try to knock your competition out of phase, and cut corners wherever possible.
- Finally, approaching the mark requires that you stay off the laylines, sail on the favored tack, and keep clear air all the way to the mark.

It is all fairly simple in concept, though somewhat more difficult in execution. These instructions take for granted that you are in complete control of sail handling, trim, and the myriad other details involved in reorienting the rig to upwind sailing. Below, we will examine each segment of the leg in more depth.

Exiting the Downwind Mark

Our major concern when starting the new upwind leg is to ensure that we are on the favored tack. The time to choose which tack is favored is before we have actually rounded the mark. Since we have come from a reaching leg, we don't have the direct experience of windshifts that a downwind leg offers, and it is more difficult to determine where we are in the wind-directional range. A simple increase in velocity will masquerade as a shift by bringing the apparent wind aft, and a decrease in wind speed will bring it forward.

The proper course of action is to have the reference headings from the earlier upwind leg handy (see Chapter 6) and confirm any initial impression by examining them. A good rounding can be followed closely by a tack, and coming hard on the wind will confirm or negate any impression of a shift. If the boat has an instrument array, of course, the true wind speed and direction should be known well before the mark.

Deciding which tack to pursue and being able to take it with clear air are two different things. Quite possibly the fleet is approaching the mark in a line, and the actual rounding could be a matter of merely dropping the spinnaker and hardening up. Unless the leg was so loose that boats have jibed to get back to the mark, there will be a minimum of jockeying for position before the rounding. The easiest way to get into an advantaged position is to enter the rounding wide and exit near the

As the boats try to
pinch above each other,
only the first one gets
away cleanly.

mark. This will accomplish two things. On the one hand, the wide approach will
take some of the pressure off the chute and make it easier for the crew to gather it in.
On the other, the swing up and to the mark will place you at least on the same line as
the boats ahead of you, allowing you to continue in clear air if that is the favored
direction.

As boats line up leaving the mark, the boats ahead will start squeezing the boats
behind. Only the first few boats will be able to continue on port tack making their
best speed, and it may be necessary for you to take a quick clearing tack to avoid this
problem. You won't be alone: other boats will break out of line, too, as soon as
they feel they can. The first boat out has an advantage, and those who can tack
cleanly will also gain.

This leads us to several conclusions. The worst spot to be in is low in line with
another boat on your hip pinning you on port tack. Once again the fundamental
skills of sail handling and tacking make their importance felt. A late spinnaker douse
will force you to the outside rounding the mark, and foredeck problems may prevent
you from tacking as effectively as a boat on your hip. By the time things have been
pulled together, half the fleet has split, and your choices are to continue in bad air
or tack into bad air. Waiting until the situation improves would only concede a
greater margin to the boats that were able to get in and out of the mark unscathed.

In a scenario where port tack is favored and most of the fleet is heading right, a
quick evaluation of your speed relative to the boats around you will provide the
cue for your next move. If the boat immediately in front of you is pointing higher,
then you must take a clearing tack. Even if the boat is pointing so high that he has
slowed considerably, continuing will only take you to his bad air. If there is a stack

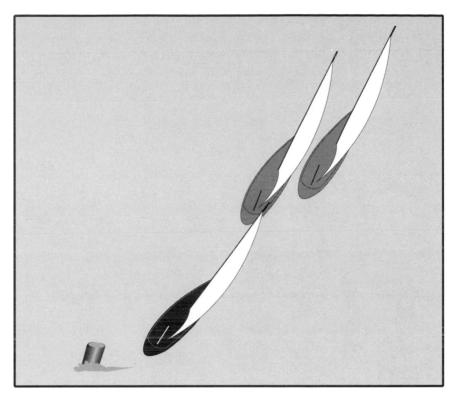

If you plan to tack but can't do so right away, sail toward tho transom of the boat that is pinching up. You'll close a lot of distance by footing while he is slow.

of boats ahead of him, rest assured your situation will deteriorate. Check your hip and tack—if you wait, the boat ahead may tack first and continue to plague you with dirty air.

In contrast, if the traffic ahead is thin or making good time, by all means continue on the favored tack. Your only consideration must be the wind: if it is oscillating, you will reach the veering shift first, or at any rate sooner than the boats that have tacked behind you, and you'll get a chance to leverage your position. If the backing phase lasts the length of the leg, however, the boats to the inside of the course will carry the day. The information you have gathered before the race and confirmed on the earlier legs should allow you to make an educated guess.

If the favored side is to the left, clean up the lightsails and tack over there as quickly as possible. Try to find yourself a lane of clear air. If you have to wait for boats who were able to tack immediately, make sure you sail at a high speed leaving the mark; pointing high at the expense of boatspeed will just keep you on the wrong side of the course longer. Since you are planning to tack, you do not need to worry about sailing into the backwind of a boat ahead. If the boat tries to squeeze up to attack you, steer toward it, close the distance, and either tack away when the lane is available or tack after the other boat does. If you can sail up to your com-

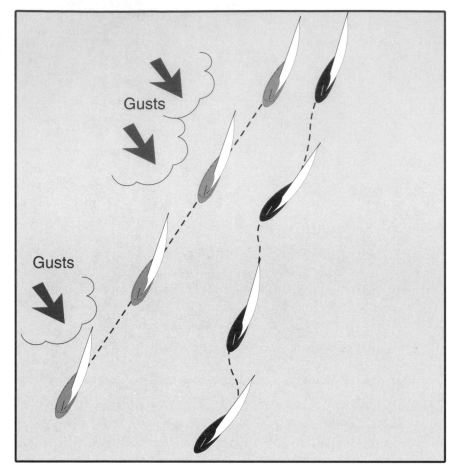

Work up on a boat by scalloping. Come up in flat water and use puffs to accelerate.

Gusts

Gusts

petitor while he pinches, you may be able to force him to stay until you want to tack. Either way, closing the distance will pay dividends farther up the course.

Even if we are pinned by a boat behind when leaving the mark, the game is not up. We have a choice of options to rid ourselves of this pest, but all of them require good steering skills. Eventually, of course, the problem will take care of itself, as the other boat will either tack away or roll over us. But we want to force the issue in order to regain our freedom to maneuver as quickly as possible. The situation is similar to being pinned on the starting line, and the same responses are needed.

We want to either force the other boat to tack away or sail faster than he to give ourselves room to tack. If we're too close merely to tack over to starboard and start hailing, we will be affecting his wind, or close to doing so. A scalloping course will build speed for us, then allow us to point higher and bleed the speed off. The timing of the scallops is critical: we need to use flat water to steer higher and gusts to build speed.

It is important that the sails be properly managed during this maneuvering. Building speed through the gusts instead of just feathering up is difficult. We have to keep the boat on its feet by dropping the traveler, tightening the vang and cunningham, and keeping the headsail well ventilated. Once the speed comes up, it can be translated into pointing, or distance to windward. Merely holding the bow up into a puff or big seas may stop one boat from rolling over you, but it lets others close up from behind or sail away ahead.

By not squeezing up in the puffs you will throw your opponent off balance. When he comes back down in the lull, he'll find you carrying a great deal of speed up high and right onto his nose, and he won't have enough boatspeed himself to do anything about it. Knocking the other boat off stride in this way will hasten his decision to get the heck out of there, and may even send him to the wrong side of the course. None of this will take much time, and the confusion accompanying the mark rounding will soon give way to the more orderly environment of the middle of the leg.

If we are the boat doing the pinning and we want to hold the other boat, we need to work high so that he will not persist in coming up at us and instead will simply continue down the course. Again, we should look for flat water before trying to pinch up. A big wave would simply stop our forward progress and force our boat to slip sideways, besides slowing us. This would move the boat in front closer to windward and farther ahead; we could only tack away at that point.

We should also shift into pointing gear. The traveler should be brought up, sail controls and backstay eased, and the sails allowed to twist slightly. As the airfoils generate more power and lift, the boat must be kept flat so that the underwater foils generate maximum lift. Keeping our boat flat relative to the competition will give us an effective pointing advantage, since they will generate greater leeway and less boatspeed.

We are not truly clear of the downwind mark until we are sailing upwind with clear air on the tack we prefer. Only then does our focus change, and we start to make decisions based on the mechanics of the beat itself.

Working the Center of the Leg

In many instances, the second beat will be the longest of the day. In the widely used Gold Cup–type courses the beat from the downwind mark all the way to the upwind mark occurs only once during the race. Depending on the location of the race, this leg may feature anything from the smoothly shifting winds of coastal waters to the choppy air of a small lake with an irregular shoreline.

Once again, getting on the right side of the shifts is the most critical factor in the upwind leg. On lakes, this consideration may lead to frequent tacks and rapidly changing positions as the advantage shifts from one location to another. On the ocean, or in coastal waters, the wind may be steadier and the advantaged side more clearly evident. Sailing the second beat under these two sets of conditions certainly offers some similarities, but in order to race effectively in each setting, the differences between them must also be taken into account.

Lake Sailing

As we discussed in the context of prerace strategy (Chapter 3), the topography of the land surrounding the sailing area is very important. This is especially true for lake races. On the windward shore the wind will simply flow around obstacles, whereas it will start to respond to them as it approaches the lee shore. There will be great variation in wind direction due to this phenomenon alone. For the most part this variation will be consistent, taking the same form each time it occurs. The vexing thing is that it may not be there all the time.

The lake sailor has to be constantly scanning the water ahead of the boat to be sure he or she is sailing toward more wind with a favorable slant. The gusts and puffs are visible on the water, but they may shift locations. Accordingly, the favored side may shift without warning or visible reason. The crew must be able to feel the boat moving through the water as their eyes are directed up the course.

The benefit of a favorable shift far outweighs most other considerations, so the lake sailor must be able to concentrate on getting the most out of wind changes. The boat has got to be positioned to take advantage of each shift; this may mean sailing higher than normal to pick up a favorable puff, or footing off to get into a heading shift sooner and tack earlier than others.

Thus the seasoned lake sailor's first priority is to look for the wind and, anticipating its arrival, do what is necessary to get the boat into it. Shifting gears is the name of the game; boatspeed and pointing become cards to be played at the appropriate times. Going slow to squeeze up into a new wind may be appropriate at one place up the leg, whereas trying to stretch out with boatspeed may be the key elsewhere. Some of these techniques would be anathema, no doubt, to someone sailing in the open ocean or a large coastal embayment.

Ocean and Coastal Sailing

Coastal waters are subject to more regular wind conditions. As the day wears on, the sea breeze component of the wind will roll in, causing it to shift ever farther in one direction. Inside that shift may be small, regular oscillations worth catching, but in general, the name of the game is to hit the favored side of the course and work it to the mark.

The concept of VMG, or velocity made good, is useful here. Specifically, VMG is the velocity made good toward the next mark; maximum VMG on this leg results from the optimal compromise between pointing and boatspeed. On a lake, VMG is often sacrificed to pinch or foot off to a shift; on the ocean it should usually be maximized.

Steering for maximum VMG requires that the heading and boatspeed be closely coordinated. If an incoming gust lifts the boat slightly, the boat should be allowed to accelerate first, then brought up to a new heading. Conversely, if the puff is a header, the boat should be held up until some speed is bled off before coming down to the new course.

Raw boatspeed becomes a tactical instrument in its own right here. It is used to obtain or preserve clear air and to build apparent wind if conditions are light. The object is to be faster upwind than the competition, to hit the favored side of the course first, and to exploit speed advantages. Steering precision, proper sail selection and setup, and clear air make the difference.

To be sure, boatspeed is not your only effective tactical weapon in open waters. Positioning yourself favorably relative to your competition matters as well, and the ability to recognize when opportunities present themselves becomes more important because of their subtlety. Finally, since engaging your opponents will require a light hand, the skill to get other boats tangled up with each other may be the best weapon of all.

Tactics for the Beat

If we are fortunate enough to be in the lead after the first triangle, we will want to protect that lead, and extend it if possible. We can start to apply a loose cover on the fleet and practice herding them in the direction we wish to go. At the same time, though, we mustn't lose sight of where we want to be on the course, because the fleet is generally going to split. Other boats will seek to pass by splitting tacks, and the farther down the line they are, the more desperate will be their search for a flyer.

At this point we have to look at the larger picture. Where are we in the series? Are there many boats to worry about, or has the competition been reduced to just two or three other boats, and if so, where are they? These questions will have been answered before the start, but now the information must be applied. For the moment we will assume that it is early in the series, so everybody is a potential threat. This is the most challenging scenario tactically; it provides the framework for tactics dealing with more specialized cases in which we ignore the boats closest to us to concentrate on those we need to beat in the series.

We want to encourage the boats immediately behind us to follow us to the favored side. This can be done simply by allowing them clear air when they are headed in the right direction. The most straightforward course of action is to emerge from the mark on port tack, continue on until the other boats are approaching the rounding, then tack over to starboard. This places you in the center of the course, free to go in either direction with the other boats. Unless there is a large advantage toward the right, you should be able to hang up there and sail with them. The drawback to this tactic is that if the wind does move toward the right, your competitors may reach the shift before you.

The safest policy is to place the boats close to you under your direct control. The farther other boats are behind you, the greater the distance they will have to make up

Sail one-half the distance to the next boat out, then tack. This places you directly to windward when he gets to the mark.

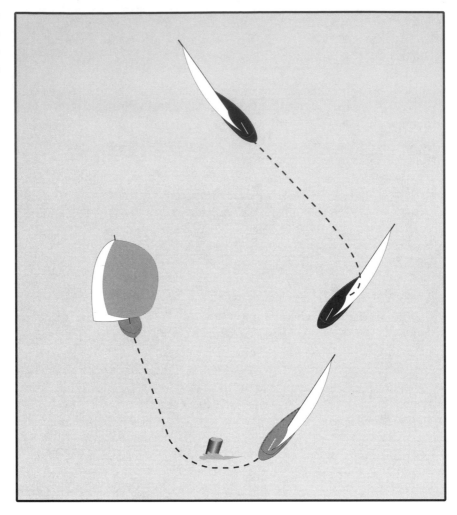

on an unexpected shift. You can deal with someone who emerges from a distant pack and suddenly appears right behind you, but it's tough to watch a boat that was right behind you break away from its pack to come in a couple of hundred yards ahead at the windward mark.

If the shifts are regular or there is one obviously favored side, the game changes. Rather than just sailing with your opponents, you want to force them away from the advantaged side as much as possible. When they head toward it, force them to sail in your backwind by tacking right on their air, so that they will have to tack away to clear their air. After they have tacked back, be alert for any small shift that will allow you to sail over and camp on them again. Pushing them continually away from the good side may even make them decide to try the opposite side, just to get away from you.

Keep the other boat's air clear when he is heading where you want him to go. This preserves your advantage relative to the fleet and keeps the other boat under your control.

This is the occasion when a hard cover is really appropriate, even early in the series. As elsewhere, we can only carry on until boats farther back start getting deeper into the advantage than we are. Still, those boats will have a longer distance to make up, and if we parallel them on the inside we can offset most of their leverage.

On a lake, the most prudent course is to head for velocity. Look for an area of higher wind, move into it, and get on the favored tack. If you can recognize which tack that is—great; if not, the increased pressure will take you where you want to go. I sometimes announce to my crew that if the telltales lift on the jib, we're tacking. That gives them a little warning. The magnitude of the shifts makes it all the more important to get in phase with them. They will be heralded by an increase in wind, and your prerace preparations should give you a pretty good idea of their direction. You can't ignore new wind on the course. Sail to it, and treat it as a favorable shift.

In lake sailing, meet the
puffs whenever possible,
tacking on headers.

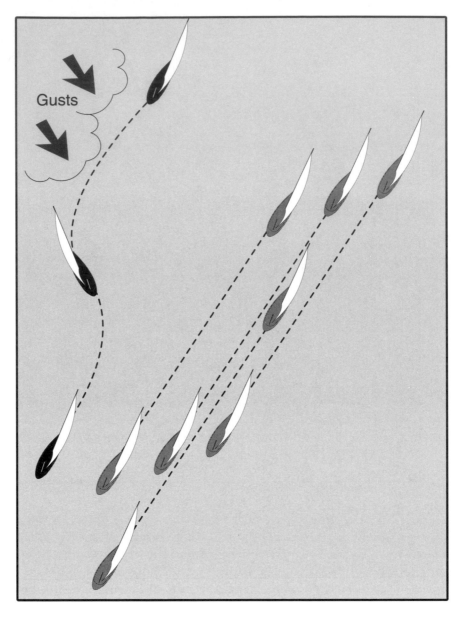

Gusts

If it lifts you, continue, and if it is a knock, tack. Take the lift even if it arrives when
you are already out on the side of the course; the rapid shifts on a lake will probably present you with an opportunity to get back. If it is a header, don't wait: tack and
take it as far as it will go, then come back to the rest of the fleet. They will either tack
with you as they get it, or miss it entirely. If you wait on the header until boats behind
you start to tack, you've just given up the distance that you've sailed away from the

favored course. This is not good. Since the shifts on a lake are often isolated and compact, one may come in behind you and give your competition the means to close with you or even pass you. A shift that is missed is gone forever.

This scenario highlights again the importance of good tacks, executed in as smooth a manner as possible. The ability to make two quick tacks—one to grab the lift and the other to come back—gives you the means to insert huge blocks of space between you and the rest of the fleet. When trying to catch up, you can reel in a boat ahead that is not tacking well simply by accelerating out of the tacks more effectively. As we will discuss momentarily, the boat behind has at least one advantage in this situation, in that the boat ahead is telegraphing information about the magnitude and duration of shifts.

Passing Upwind

Rounding the mark in a pack often causes the early part of the leg to be a blur. You round and tack. Someone tacks on top of you, so you tack back. Then another boat tacks on you. You tack once more and find clear air, but you are heading in the wrong direction. Do you shrug and say, "Well, you can't win by following"?

Sometimes that's true, but it is a sentiment much more suited for the last leg. The battle for clear air after the mark can be won with a few simple techniques.

If you have to tack right away, do so. If you still want to work the right side, travel a couple of boatlengths up, then tack back. As other boats take these clearing tacks, do all you can to have them either tack well below you or continue well past you.

It is more important that you proceed upwind on this leg on the correct tack than it is to clear your air by splitting from other boats. You can live in slightly disturbed air, and may even be able to work your way into free air by taking a lower or higher line. Unless someone really plants himself just above you and ahead or on your lee bow, spend your time on the tack that gives you the greatest advantage.

You can coax another boat into tacking before interfering with your air by making your course seem lower than it is. You do this by footing slightly, so that when your competitor looks up to spot you, he thinks you're sailing lower and are going to cross sooner. He will then tack earlier to cover you. If he's tried to tack directly in front of you, you can resume your normal course, carry the extra speed higher, and build some separation. If he is going to cross, then tack, you can delay his tack by pinching slightly. As a result, he will carry farther than he might have otherwise. When you come back down to course, you probably will have broken through his lee and might even be able to carry through to a safe leeward position. Of course, that will make his day.

Let's imagine we round the leeward mark in a pack and want to continue to the right until we get the veering shift we expect. We see the boats ahead of us start to fall off in the initial stages of the shift, then tack over to starboard and head back into the middle of the course. If possible, we should evaluate the shift using these boats as markers.

Cut the corners in an
oscillating wind. The
indecision of the boat
ahead can be your gain.

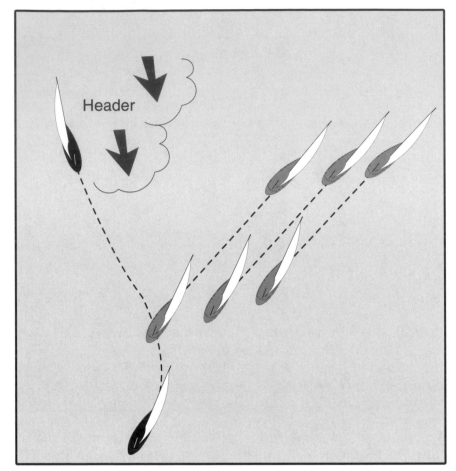

Header

A boat in the lead should sail well into the shift before tacking. The shift will not occur all at once, and the leader may well want to confirm that this new wind is for real and requires a tack. This tack will take him away from the boats behind, so he needs good reasons for it.

The boats right behind will not want to have the leader cross them and will jump on the shift sooner. That allows them to close on the leader initially. We can watch this process and judge for ourselves the extent, strength, and duration of the wind change. If it looks like a deep, long-lasting change, we will want to tack as close as possible to the leading edge. If the shift is coming in unevenly instead, we might cross behind the initial tackers, sink deeper into the new wind, and then tack over, so we will be on the inside of the wheel as the shift continues.

We should be cutting corners as the shifts come in. The boats ahead of us have to sail farther to one side of the course to get the new wind, while we want to tack as it reaches us. If the shifts are such that we will get an odd number of cycles before

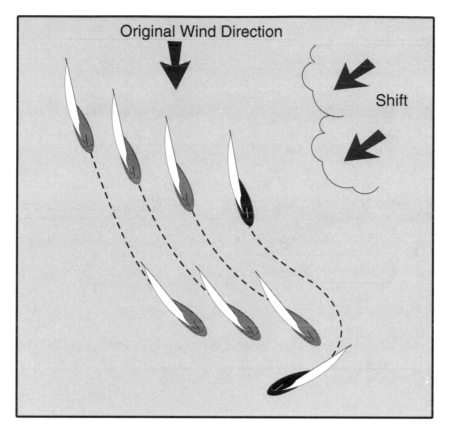

If you are sailing into
a persistent shift, take
some transoms to get
on the inside.

the next weather mark, we will gain. If the number of cycles is even, then we should still come out a little ahead. We should gain the distance the lead boat sails into the shift to confirm its existence each time we tack.

If we think we are sailing into a persistent shift, or that no more than one oscillation cycle will occur during the upwind leg, we need to cross behind the boats ahead of us as they tack on the shift. We want to attain the position farthest toward the new wind, so that we'll be on the inside of the shift and be carried toward the weather mark.

We have to be careful, though, not to go so far that the shift carries us above the layline. In the case of a long oscillation, this can be a problem. If the leg is short enough to be sailed within one oscillation, it is probably only 20 minutes long, and 8 minutes on one tack may be too much. When in doubt, tack short of the layline. If the shift puts you on the layline, you will at least gain on the boats that continued and on all the boats that have tried the other side.

Underlying this moderate approach to the leg is the idea that every piece of information you can gain from the boats ahead of you about the wind moving down the course allows you to make your response to a wind change more efficient. Equipped with this kind of advance notice, you should be able to accelerate your boat faster, jump on the shift a little sooner, and work up to the boats ahead of you.

Protecting a Lead

The second upwind leg is not the time to devote yourself slavishly to preventing the boat immediately behind you from passing. Indeed, if it is late enough in the series to focus your attention on just one or two boats to the exclusion of others, they may not be the ones immediately behind you.

It is more likely that there will be a group of boats behind you presenting an equal threat. These boats will round the mark and split up. How far apart they travel will depend on their perception of the shifts. If the favored side is evident, they will merely take some clearing tacks and resume heading in your direction. Utilize any small shift against the grain to consolidate your lead by reestablishing a controlling position over the boats who are behind but to windward. You need to be ready to take advantage of what you most expect to happen, but you also want to protect yourself against potential hazards as much as feasible.

The best position is closest to the next header and at least as far to windward as the boat closest to you. This position will not encourage your competitor to go off

When the fleet starts splitting up behind you, encourage the boats closer to you to rejoin the pack by getting on their air when they are headed away and letting them sail freely when they are headed toward the fleet.

somewhere else, but it will give you time to react if the wind switches to the other side.

The boats immediately behind you and those to windward will benefit from a lift, since they are on the inside of the wheel. If that lift is persistent, or holds until you reach the layline, all of them are going to gain. At some point you have to bite the bullet and dig back in. The earlier this is done, the less you lose.

This is the chief rationale for the loose cover. If you don't give a nearby boat a reason to split, he will likely stay close by, which means that he will not gain too much on any adverse windshift. You can then employ the speed that got you to the front to keep you there.

Behind the four or five boats at the front of the pack, there will be boats that are ready to roll the dice. Some will undoubtedly have reached the opposite conclusion about the future of the wind and will head for the far side of the course. You can't be too worried about them. Their gamble could pay off, particularly when a wind that has been oscillating has now shifted decidedly in one direction. But in the absence of compelling evidence to the contrary, it is pointless to abandon your strategy and head over there to protect yourself against a long shot. If the main body of the fleet is going away, you might want to influence the boats around you to head over that way as well, by making sure they have clear air when moving back to the middle.

The simple strategy of getting and staying on the correct tack, keeping inside and to windward of the immediate competition, and staying away from the laylines should keep you pretty safe in the middle of this leg. The second beat is a leg where the differences in boatspeed are apparent, and there should be ample clear air. If you are patient, the windshifts will work for you. The key is to stay in phase and not to panic if things are not looking so good at any particular moment. Consolidate and cut corners whenever you can.

This really is the grind-it-out leg. There is plenty of racing left, and a losing gamble at this point could mean throwing a great deal away.

Approaching the Weather Mark

Approaching the second weather mark is much the same as approaching the first—in traffic, exactly the same. If you happen to be separated from other boats, approach from inside the laylines, sail the lifted tack into the mark, and allow yourself enough time to get a decent spinnaker set.

If there are boats rounding the mark ahead of you, be careful that you don't get held out by them when approaching on port. The boats rounding and heading off on starboard tack have rights and can force you to wait for a hole to pass through them. If you are short of the layline but coming in on port tack, these boats may also force you to sail through a large region of disturbed air and waves. This may cause you

to miss that opening you were going to tack into to round the mark.

The layline call can be critical here, which is another reason for avoiding the layline early: the closer you are to the mark, the easier it will be to call the layline spot on. If you are overlapped with another boat, holding him out beyond the layline will force him directly into your backwind, perhaps far enough back that he cannot interfere immediately with your spinnaker set. Conversely, if you are the leeward boat in a pair moving across on port tack, tacking to starboard first might give you the inside track at the mark and force your opponent to give you room to shoot the mark. You can beat him on the set and jibe away for clear air, or he may be so demoralized that he goes away.

The layline is also important due to the influence it gives you on boats coming in on the other tack. If you have overstood or are right on the line, boats crossing behind or ducking you can be fooled into thinking you are not going to make it. Simply by scalloping into the mark you may cause them to sail an extra boatlength or two.

If a boat looks as if he is going to tack underneath you to establish a lee-bow position, try to build some speed by footing. When he tacks, you can take this speed to windward to maintain clear air into the mark. If your opponent has tacked too soon, you may be able to drive over him as he pinches to make the mark. Alternatively, if he does succeed in lee-bowing you, and you are already pinching to make the mark, you might as well tack back immediately. Check for traffic and get out of that position if you have the chance.

When approaching the mark, be conservative with the layline if you have the competition below you or pinned, but be aggressive if everyone is free. Maintain a good head of steam coming into the mark, and scallop slightly to avoid letting everyone else know exactly where you stand. If other boats are filing in on port tack, head at each one to get them either to duck or to tack early, then take your speed up higher to escape their bad air. Always remember, it is going to be really tough to get in two tacks at the mark if you are short.

To summarize, the second beat is by necessity a tactical leg. Most of the advantages of strategy have been exposed earlier, and the objective now is to keep what you have or whittle away at what you want. The geometry of the race becomes very important, as does the ability to recognize changes early. If in front, the game is simply to place yourself in a position where you will gain as much as or more than other boats from the expected winds, while limiting as much as possible your exposure to being hurt by the unexpected.

If behind, use the indications given by the boats ahead to react more efficiently. You will know what is coming, whereas they can only suspect it. That should be good for a few feet here, a little quicker acceleration there, and an extra couple of boatlengths per shift, until you are the boat ahead while your demoralized competitor wonders what happened.

The mark, like all marks, is a chance to secure the gains made on the leg. As on the reaches, the fleet has to come together here, which allows you to move more effectively against other boats. Their freedom of movement is bounded on one side by the layline; you can hold them against this wall if ahead, and trick them into moving beyond it if behind.

After the weather mark, spinnakers fly—the end of the race looms near.

Questions

Q How can I know which side of the course I should head for when rounding the leeward mark?

A A quick glance at your compass should tell you whether you are being headed or lifted relative to the first upwind leg. If conditions haven't changed, you should be able to get on the lifted tack using that information. Conditions seldom stay exactly the same, however, and if your reading is off the scale one way or the other, you need to ask yourself whether you expect a persistent shift. If you do, sail into the header. If no shift seems near, climb onto the lifted tack and start taking cues from the boats around you or the differences in wind velocity that you may see. If you have instruments on your boat, the true wind indicator should give you some idea of the current trend before you get to the mark.

It is important that you integrate what the wind did near the end of the second reach with what you expect it to do during the beat. Don't get caught off guard; it is easy for the boats immediately behind to grab a quick advantage and control your position up the leg.

Q Should I remain in phase, or should I cover the boats going the wrong way?

A The answer depends on who these other boats are, how dramatic the shifts are, and how far the other boats will go to escape your presence. I would certainly not recommend tacking away from a good lift. When the wind starts to swing toward the median compass reading, perhaps you may tack over a little earlier. If the boats are close to you, placing a hard cover on them may drive them back to where you want them. They will probably be looking for an excuse to get back on the favored tack.

Boats that present no real threat and are heading away from the favored side should be left alone. But when there are boats for you to catch in a series, you cannot afford to let them go. This question becomes much harder during the last leg, to be discussed in Chapter 13.

Q What if my speed hasn't been good on the first upwind leg; do I need to gamble to try and get back into the race?

A If you are not up to par in boatspeed, you will probably do better defending yourself against boats coming up from behind. Gambling is just that, and the odds are pretty long. Try changing your controls to develop better speed while you are covering other boats. Change one thing at a time, and give it a chance to take effect. Adjust your sheet tension; move your jib leads one hole forward or aft; try to drop the traveler a bit and foot more; or ease the jib halyard tension to round the entry of the jib. Obviously, this type of tuning should be done before the race, but it oftentimes is not, and if this is what is slowing you, it can be fixed.

Q Should I tack a great deal on this leg?

A You need to tack to cover other boats, to consolidate a gain, and to get or keep in phase. Other than that, no. Seriously, you have to tack as often as is necessary, and that is about all one can say about it. There is no reason not to tack if it will accomplish something.

For example, imagine that you are sailing into a slight header and a boat that was ahead of you has sunk to the point where you can tack and cross him. You expect the shift to continue heading you. In the absence of other boats, the right tactic is to tack, sail up to the other boat, and tack back. This consolidates your gain in case things go the other way later in the leg. Avoiding the tack means that if you are wrong and the wind swings back, you've given up a potential gain.

Chapter 12

Downwind Sailing

The ride downhill is the best chance left to improve your position. It is not a time for relaxing, regrouping, or anything that takes your mind off the race. The downwind leg gives you a chance to exploit the same windshifts you utilized going upwind, with the possibility of more dramatic results.

The techniques of downwind sailing vary slightly from boats that will plane to those that do not. Planing and other high-performance boats respond to being sailed well by moving much faster than if they are sailed poorly. Displacement boats will not show such dramatic speed differences, but will benefit from picking the correct side of the course. A well-sailed high-performance boat may come out on top even if the crew heads the wrong way.

Our discussion of the downwind leg will cover three distinct topics: the techniques of achieving high speed through the water, the strategic principles underlying the selection of the side of the course to sail on, and the tactics for passing or defending against other boats.

Boatspeed Downwind

When sailing straight downwind, the sails of the boat do not produce any lift; it is their drag that moves the boat. Only when the heading of the boat varies appreciably from straight downwind will any flow develop across the sails to generate lift. This lift will combine with the drag to accelerate the boat, which moves the apparent wind forward, which further enhances the sail's power and the speed of the boat, and so on in a self-reinforcing cycle of cause and effect that will continue until the increasing resistance of the boat through the water reaches an equilibrium with the power produced in the sails.

The helmsman can initiate this cycle simply by heading up slightly. The boat will start to accelerate, but it won't be heading directly toward the downwind mark

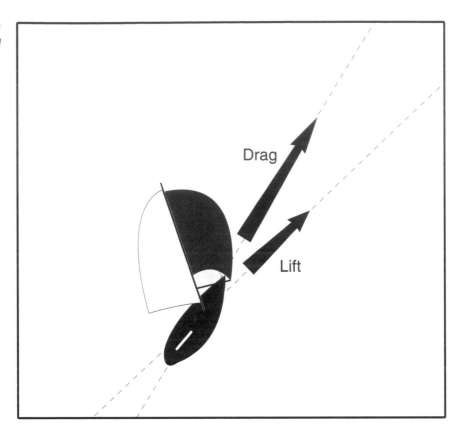

anymore. At some point an ideal trade-off is achieved between extra speed generated and extra distance sailed. Just as there is an optimum VMG upwind, so is there a best speed made good downwind. At times maintaining this speed will require a higher heading, and at times it will require you to dive to leeward; this is just a fancy way of saying "Up in the lulls, down in the puffs."

Above a certain wind speed, the heading that produces the best boatspeed downwind drops off dramatically. This point, which is referred to as the *cliff* and differs from boat to boat, can be derived from the polar diagrams of your boat. Basically, when the cliff is reached, you fall off—that is, you take the boat almost directly downwind to get the best speed down the course.

The question then becomes, how far up and how far down? There is an optimum interval of rapid acceleration with only a small change in wind angle; beyond this band lies a region of diminishing returns, where the boat will move faster through the water but also be taken farther from the mark. Steering below the optimum band moves the boat more directly toward the mark, but at a slower speed. We need to have determined where this band is for the boat we are sailing.

Simply put, we have to know what it will take to get our boat to move significantly faster. If we head up (away from the mark), will we be able to plane? Will we be able to surf on the waves? Either prospect provides ample justification for sailing the extra distance. The decrease in hull resistance when planing will allow us to maintain a high speed with less power input; we can head down once we make the transition. If we are able to surf, we can also head lower at a higher speed, averaging a much greater speed toward the mark over the entire leg.

A number of factors bear on the calculation. If the boat is heavy, it will take too much power to accelerate it. We would have to head too high for too long to get any significant speed increase. For example, in all but the lightest air, most PHRF boats make good a better speed when headed close to or directly at the mark. Some of the lighter PHRF boats may plane with enough encouragement, but they will do so only in fairly stiff breezes that would have us heading nearly straight down the course anyway.

In planing boats the same trade-off will have to be made. At higher wind speeds, a small alteration in course may suffice to get the boat to jump up onto plane. Once up on plane, the acceleration will take the apparent wind far enough forward to allow us to bear off to our original course or even lower. In light air, though, the light planing boats will accelerate enough with a small change in apparent wind to justify heading aggressively higher.

Heavy-air conditions are really no test; it doesn't take much of an alteration of course to get results. But in medium air and marginal planing conditions, experience and practice will make a difference. The trick is to get the boat up over the bow wave; if it is dancing right there, a little body English can put you over the top. Rule 54 specifies the type and amount of body movement and pumping you can use to promote planing. The rule prohibits the use of these techniques beyond what is necessary to trigger the initial surge, but it need not interfere with our effort to do everything we can, at the time when it will be most effective, to get up on plane.

The key word in the rule is "repeated." You aren't permitted to set up a pattern or rhythmic motion using your body, but you can hike abruptly and trim hard once to increase the initial impact of a puff or cause the bow to surge down the face of a wave. You wouldn't want to go into a full straight-leg hike on a run, but a quick lean to weather to induce a windward heel will help you steer the boat down the wave without moving the rudder.

It is also important, once planing, to head down to and if possible below your proper course to the downwind mark. This is simply a case of translating the higher velocity of the plane more directly into VMG downwind. If you can take the plane below the mark, you can maintain a greater velocity after the puff by heading up, just as you would on a reach.

In marginal planing conditions, maintaining the plane is critical. When the boat starts to slow, it is important to head up to keep the apparent wind forward. Should more wind be coming, the boat will accelerate much more quickly if it is still planing. Should the wind be letting up, the plane should be maintained even if that means

heading toward the side of the course. This will give you a higher, faster course to the mark on the other tack.

The overall result of this sailing technique is a course toward the downwind mark that snakes back and forth across the rhumb line. In terms of distance traveled, such a course may look inefficient, but it achieves the greatest average velocity toward the downwind mark—if you can muster the concentration required to sail the wind conditions well.

In a displacement boat, the consideration is not planing but surfing. The waves must be large enough for the boat to be able to catch them, and there must be sufficient wind to produce the requisite boatspeed. Being able to drive the boat downhill as much as possible is the key. The waves may not be moving straight down the course: if a ridable one comes along, point the boat into the trough in the direction the wave is going. This will accelerate the boat and may provide an extended ride. Waves that simply pass underneath the boat do not lead to any acceleration.

To catch a wave, you may have to increase your boatspeed by heading up. If your speed is good, a lookout can alert you to a wave, and you can peel off on top of it much like a surfer on a board. Once the hull is in the grip of the wave, center the rudder. The hull form should keep the boat moving down the wave, and the increased speed will reduce the pressure on the sails, so there won't be as much helm.

In heavy air, once you peel off the top of the wave, the boat is going to roll to windward. It is easy to overcorrect at this point. If you allow the boat to continue down, you run the risk of an all-standing jibe, which is messy at best. If you jerk the helm to stop the nose from swinging, you may pull the boat out of the wave.

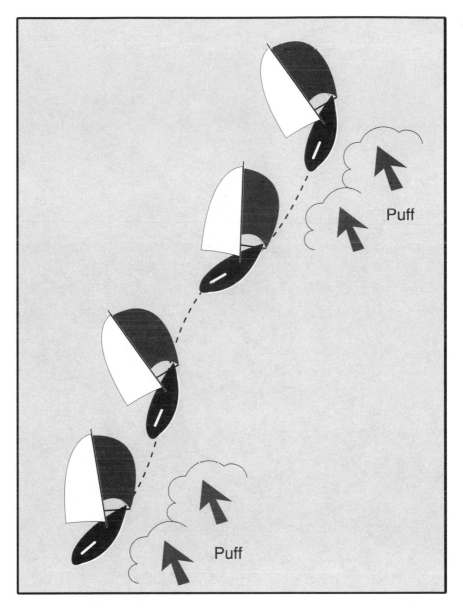

Jump from puff to puff when steering downwind. Stay in each one for as long as possible, but watch for the next one approaching so you can get to it quickly.

Puff

Puff

The rule of thumb is that the boat is going fastest at the scariest moment. With a little intestinal fortitude, you can hang on for the long ride.

As the boat slows in the trough, play the wave just like a puff and let the bow come up. This will keep the apparent wind forward and maintain your speed long enough to help you catch another wave. Each wave should be extended down as far as possible. Again, it is unlikely that the waves will be moving straight down the

Try to peel off the top of the wave with a little extra speed. Once you catch it, head the boat for the lowest point you see. If you start to run over the next wave, head up slightly to go over the back, then peel off again at the top.

course, but the speed boost you get will justify the extra distance you put in. After a series of waves, the course back to the mark will be higher and therefore faster than a course straight down in the absence of waves.

It is important for the crew to be mobile throughout these maneuvers. On PHRF boats, once the spinnaker is up, the nontrimming members of the crew have a tendency to settle down. They often sit with their legs spread out, making it difficult for them to move as required. An alert crew should have their feet underneath them so they can move from side to side or fore and aft easily. Shifting their weight forward as the stern rises with a wave may be the factor that sends the boat accelerating down the face of the wave rather than letting the wave pass underneath. Believe me, there is no worse feeling than to have the boat seemingly slide backwards down the back of a wave you should have caught.

Sail Trim off the Wind

Trimming the sails off the wind is a relatively simple process—so simple that people want to complicate it, and in doing so lose the basics.

The mainsail provides speed downwind primarily through its drag component. The mainsheet should be eased as far as possible to present the greatest surface area to the wind. At various times and in various parts of the sail there will be some airflow, and consequently some lift. The major variable in the setup of the main is the degree of twist allowed in the sail, which is controlled by the boom vang. A powerful vang, tightly applied, will completely straighten the leech of the main. This will

The wind will be blowing at a slightly different angle at the top of the mast. This may affect the amount of vang tension desirable.

eliminate most of the flow around the sail, but it will increase the drag; you will be fast if your course is taking you directly downwind. Some twist may be desirable, though, to account for wind shear—the fact that the wind direction at the top of the sail usually differs from the direction on deck.

If you do desire some flow, or you want to open up the top of the sail, you should ease the vang slightly and trim the main. Keep the top telltale flying off the leech. The advantage of this setup is that if the boat starts to get squirrelly, you can ease that two or three feet of mainsheet and dump wind out of the top of the sail. Since it is twisted, easing the mainsheet will turn the upper part of the sail inside out; this brings the thrust of the sail more in line with the center of the boat, which can restore control if the helm is not responding.

This setup is fast when sailing slightly above a straight downwind course. The apparent wind at the top of the spar will be farther aft than the wind on deck, and a small degree of twist will allow you to trim both parts of the sail correctly. If the boat accelerates, however, the overall increase in apparent wind may reduce the vertical variation in direction to negligible proportions; in that case, more vang can be applied to tighten the upper leech. This also has the effect of pumping the leech, which will add further acceleration.

The key requirement for effective main trim downwind is an understanding of how the main's thrust relates to the center of resistance of the boat. Since the main

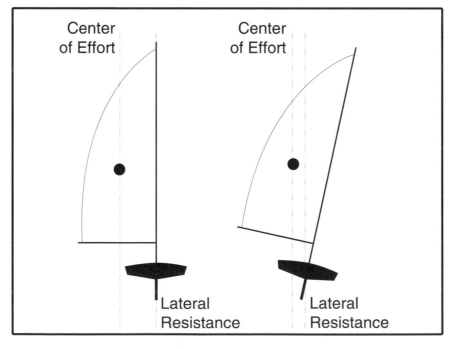

Windward heel can bring the center of effort more in line with the center of resistance. This will reduce the amount of helm input needed to steer a straight course. Less helm, less drag, more speed!

is hanging out over the side of the boat, its thrust attempts to turn the boat back into the wind. A spinnaker flying out to weather balances this, as does a jib flown wing-and-wing. If you have neither of these, you have to steer the boat in a straight line with the rudder. You can reduce the amount of rudder needed by pulling the rig over to weather, which will bring the center of effort more in line with the center of resistance.

If you want to make a course change, you can apply the thrust of the mainsail as a tool to break the equilibrium and turn the boat without using the rudder, which would slow you down. Heel the boat to leeward, and the main will push the nose up; heel farther to windward, and the center of effort in the sail will be pulled closer to the boat, making it possible for the hull form to turn the boat down.

Spinnaker trim is everyone's favorite topic when it comes to downwind sail trim. And no wonder, when you look at the size of the spinnaker and feel the acceleration once it is up. The spinnaker behaves much like any other sail, although it is not supported along any edge by a mast, boom, or stay. Like most sails, it does have a luff, a leech, and a foot, and we can influence its overall shape by applying tension to the leading edge, or luff (the one edge we have some control over), and altering the sheet lead on the leeward clew.

The spinnaker pole allows us to move the windward clew of the spinnaker, thus making this corner analogous to the tack on a jib or mainsail. If we move this point up or down by raising or lowering the pole, we are essentially adding or subtract-

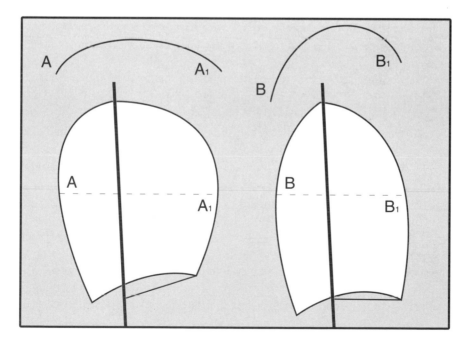

We can change the shape of the spinnaker with the pole placement. Generally, a fuller shape with draft farther aft is better downwind.

ing halyard tension. We know from our discussion of the cunningham that adding tension to the luff of the mainsail pulls the draft forward. The same holds for spinnakers.

Pulling the draft forward by lowering the pole will be good for reaching, when we have air flow through the spinnaker. The spinnaker will act more like an airfoil than a parachute, and we want it to have an efficient shape. Conversely, raising the pole to move the draft aft will increase the drag produced by the chute and make it a better downwind sail.

When we are reaching with the spinnaker in light air, we are trying to use the sail as a foil. We want the apparent wind to pass through the sail, generating lift. In heavier air, the drag of the spinnaker is itself sufficient to move us at or near hull speed, and we can maximize drag by projecting as large an area as possible.

The projected area must be balanced with pole height, however. If the pole is raised too high, the top, or head, of the spinnaker will fly straight out from the sheave. This area will be ineffective, and we will need to drop the pole to pull it down. At this point we may also have to adjust the lead on the clew to keep it at the same height as the tack.

Our control of the clew is provided by the *twings,* which are free-floating blocks or snaps attached to the spinnaker sheets. They are moved up and down from the rail to provide some control over the angle of the spinnaker sheets. The windward twing is usually kept tight, to take some pressure off the foreguy and help keep the pole in place. The leeward twing can be used to adjust the sheeting angle of the spinnaker. Easing the twing moves the sheet lead aft; pulling it down moves the lead forward. The overall effect is very similar to that of moving the jib lead. If we want a flatter shape to the spinnaker, during a reach for example, we sheet as far aft as possible. This opens up the leech and the top of the sail, which allows the air inside a clean exit.

When sailing downwind, we may want to use the twing to move the lead forward; this keeps the clews level and maximizes the projected area of the sail. Usually the spinnaker sheet runs underneath the main boom, which is sufficient to hold the clew down, but there are times when the twing should be used to pull the lead farther forward. In heavy air this will also stabilize the sail and make it easier to fly.

The first rule of spinnaker trimming is to play the sheet so that the luff is forever lazily folding back on itself, or *breaking.* If you ease the sheet too far, the chute will collapse—a major faux pas, and an occasion for much ridicule from callous fellow crewmembers. But if you overtrim, so that the chute is too flat and the luff never breaks, you are just as surely if more subtly slowing down the boat. The position of the break provides a general guide to the correct height for the pole and position of the sheet lead. If the spinnaker breaks high on the luff, you should raise the pole; if it breaks low, you should lower the pole. An even break all along the luff puts you in the ballpark, and you can then adjust the other parameters of the sail to fine-tune.

What makes the act of flying the spinnaker complex is the ability to move its effective attachment point fore and aft. We want to position the sail at the most effective angle to the wind; since this keeps changing, we must keep moving the pole to adjust. The rule of thumb is to have the pole at 90 degrees to the wind, or "square." Pulling the pole farther aft than this is desirable when reaching, and acceptable in a puff. The pole is "oversquared" when the spinnaker is being used as a foil. When the boat is oscillating back and forth and threatening to broach, on the other hand, easing the pole forward will stabilize things by moving the center of effort of the spinnaker out in front and toward the centerline of the boat.

In theory, the guy should be moved whenever the sheet is trimmed, but because of the loads involved it is often left stationary for some period of time. The pole should always be placed as far aft as possible downwind, so when in doubt, pull it back. On a well-flown spinnaker the luff tape will appear to leave the pole vertically. When it bows to leeward, the pole is too far aft and the chute is being overtrimmed to keep it full. When the pole is too far forward, the luff will curve to windward, but too little and too late to be used as a reliable indicator. The bias should simply be to keep the pole working aft.

Getting the most out of the leading edge of a puff is the bugaboo of all chute trimmers. When sailing downwind, the pole is pulled fairly far back and the chute is drawing well. Then the puff arrives, pulling the apparent wind farther aft. Immediately the main starts to dump some air into the chute and destabilize it. An inexperienced trimmer will usually trim hard at this point, which brings the chute into the backwind of the main and worsens the situation. The helmsman, seeing all this going on, may try to help by heading down, which also throws more of the main's bad air into the chute. He or she finally heads up to get some flow going, and bang!—the chute fills. Everyone breathes a sigh of relief, and the boat takes off.

If the trimmer had realized that the apparent wind always swings aft as the true wind increases, the pole could have been moved back, the sheet eased into the puff, and this wondrous acceleration could have taken place many seconds earlier. The pole will be slightly oversquare after the boat has built some speed and the apparent wind shifted back forward, so the helmsman can steer down with it. The entire crew needs to be alerted when this is about to occur.

The interplay between the trimmers and the helmsman is difficult. In planing boats, where the apparent wind builds and shifts rapidly, the helmsman makes the trimmer's job easier by steering to the apparent wind, and the trimmer makes the helmsman's job easier by realizing that the apparent wind will swing aft in a puff, necessitating an ease to avoid the buildup of large forces on the rudder.

In displacement boats, this last point is critical. An overtrimmed chute may cripple the helmsman's actions and cause the boat to steer itself into a broach. One can only hope it broaches to windward.

Tactics off the Wind

Sailing downwind is one of the rare situations when the advantage is with the boat behind: he gets the wind first, he can move freely to areas of increased wind, and his wind shadow extends forward to the boat ahead. As the wind shifts, the boat behind can jibe first and cut the corners so that the boat ahead never really escapes from the area of disturbed air.

It is worth keeping in mind, though, that the area of disturbed air breaks down fairly quickly after passing by the boat behind, and the disturbed air is harder to direct than one would imagine. The boat ahead also has several of the racing rules working for him, and this advantage offsets a great deal of the wind advantage. The boat behind must come to the boat ahead if he is going to pass. Even if he sails up on a puff, the overtaking boat must keep clear, whereas the boat ahead simply has to maintain a position between the threatening boat and the mark.

The trailing boat must react to what the leading boat does. He cannot just blithely sail down on his opponent and pass him. If he tries to pass to leeward, he will run into the other boat's wind shadow, slow down, and not be able to use any of the apparent advantage in speed he had.

Trickery and misdirection have a place in the tactical arsenal of a boat trying to pass downwind. If the attempt to pass takes place slowly and predictably, the leading boat will have plenty of time to marshal his defense. In the case of a dramatic speed difference, the pass may take place no matter what, but the accompanying skirmish will waste precious time with respect to other boats. Time is getting short at this point in the race: if the trailing boat has worked up through the fleet, he doesn't want the boats ahead to gain too much while he works around slower boats.

Rounding the windward mark presents us with the first opportunity to achieve a tactically superior position. The type of set we choose—either a straight bear-away or a jibe set—should depend primarily on the angle of the wind to the rhumb line. We want to sail away from the mark on the tack that points us closest to the rhumb line while allowing us to make the best speed—that is, the headed tack. In the absence of other boats, we would simply set and go. With other boats around, though, we have to be very sure we can start on the favored tack or get onto it first.

Many times the type of takedown used at the end of the reaching legs will determine how the set is done at the windward mark. This is not the best practice but common; it takes a large shift before people will abandon the set they are ready for and run the spinnaker sheets around to prepare for a set on the other tack. Opportunity knocks if you bite the bullet and make the change before the others. If you can accomplish this without disrupting your weather leg, you may have an option not available to less skilled crews. The problem is that the shift that determines which set you want may not reveal itself until late in the leg. I've had crews gather the spinnaker in their arms and run around the bow on the last tack into the mark. That is recommended only as a last resort, but it has worked pretty well on occasion.

New Wind Direction

We need to leave the windward mark on the favored jibe, just as we need to leave the leeward mark on the favored tack.

In any case, as we said, the goal is to get on that favored tack first. This may mean jibing right after the set, before the headsail is down. The quick jibe onto the favored tack is just as important as getting onto the right side of a shift sailing upwind. If you can fight the tendency to get the chute up, sort out the deck, and only then take a look around, you'll probably find an opening to jump right by boats who lose themselves at this point. Even if you are set up on the wrong side, making a definite decision before the weather mark to jibe as soon as possible will give you an advantage.

The decision to jibe away at the mark may lead to some excitement of its own. Jibing onto port tack in the face of an oncoming horde of starboard tack close-hauled boats can be tricky. Not only do they chop up the air, but any advantage you hoped to gain may be lost in evasive action. If there is a hole, however, a quick jibe and then

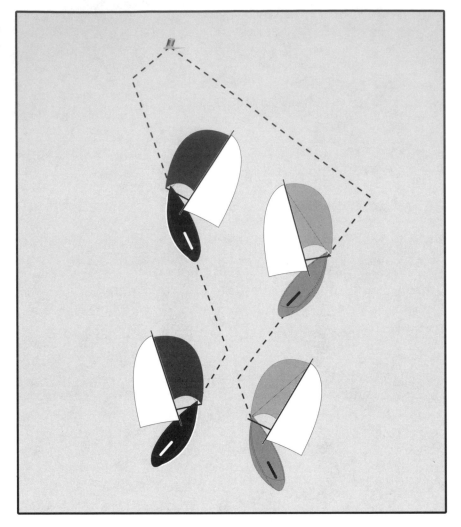

maybe a quick jibe back will put a great deal of pressure on the boats ahead. If they jibe to cover you, you will be on starboard while they come across on port. Also, they may be forced to avoid some starboard tack boats themselves. You can wait for them to jibe with you, then jibe away. If you've gained on the left side and they have to jibe to keep clear of you, an immediate jibe back to port may be in order. This forces them back to the unfavored right side while you continue left.

A series of jibes can also be the best way to work around a competitor. You have to be close to initiate this, and the other boat has to feel compelled to respond in kind to what you are doing. For one thing, this tactic allows you both to be sailing at your best speed without stepping on each other's wind. Then too, a number of jibes opens the door for your opponent's crew to make an error—not a possibility with your

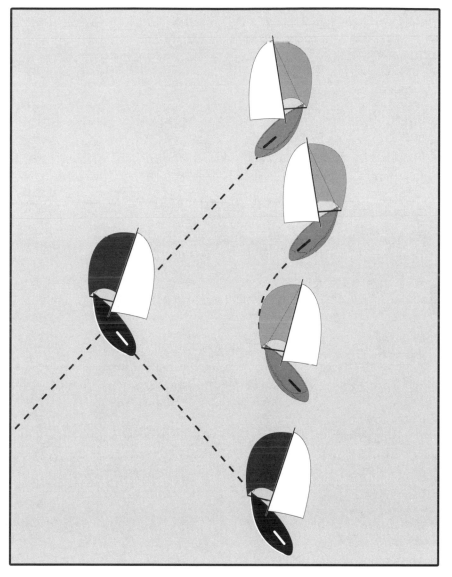

crew, of course—and allows you as the trailing boat to control the timing of the jibes. If you've established yourself on the favored side first, you will either be even or ahead, and you can keep bouncing the other boat to the unfavored side.

The timing of the jibes in this type of tacking duel is critical. You want to jibe with maximum boatspeed, and you want your opponent to jibe in a hole. Jibing at speed is easier on your crew because the sails are loaded as lightly as they will ever be when the boat is moving forward at its greatest speed. When you pull the helm over, the velocity of the boat opposes the true wind and then pulls the apparent wind forward on the new tack. You won't have to sail as high to reaccelerate. Your opponent, on the other hand, may be dealing with a highly loaded sail plan, which will wreak havoc with his steering, or he may have relatively little wind and will need to come up toward you to get in gear.

Incidentally, the worst time to jibe is just before a big puff. It invariably is coming faster than you think, and if you can't snap off a smooth jibe, the puff will hit you at your most vulnerable point. The major shift in the apparent wind may pull the chute over to one side or make it oscillate as it loses stability. The chute will quickly be followed by the rig as the boat broaches, and you will be riding your boat rather than sailing it.

The downwind leg is a good time to employ blockers as well. If there is a starboard tack boat coming across that will pass just in front of you, try and direct your opponent to the crossing boat. If he locks up with the crossing boat and jibes over, you may want to continue a bit and jibe with them, so that anyone else jibing ahead to cover you will fall into the blanket of these two. A lot depends on the characteristics of the crossing boat. You can't afford to get mixed up with a slow boat, nor do you want your opponent hopping onto the wake of a faster one. In general, as you get your opponent tangled with another boat, have your next move planned.

The toughest situation arises when one side is decidedly favored because of a current or a windshift. You have to line up with the other boats and sail to the mark. The downwind leg actually becomes more like a reach in this case. Getting clear air and setting up the boat for its best speed will get you down the course, but the only way to pass is to have a significant boatspeed advantage.

In a mixed fleet, this advantage can come from hooking a ride with a faster boat. Inevitably there will be a boat behind that just hasn't been able to get it together. On this relatively simple leg, he pulls up his chute, spreads his acres of nylon, grabs a path slightly to weather, and motors on down the leg. To hitch a ride with this behemoth, you need to let him pass fairly close by. You then grab his stern wave where it is fairly steep and you can nose right in. As he goes by, head up to build some speed, then stick your bow right in the trough of the wave. Do not come so far to weather that you will blanket him; that would be counterproductive. Be sure to smile whenever his crew look back at you: if they feel threatened, they can shake you off, and you'll find yourself too far to weather with nowhere to go.

Grabbing a tow, as this is called, will bring you up to the faster boat's speed and carry you past rivals who have not been able to hitch rides themselves. You need to be close to the towing boat so that no one tries to get between you and him. This requires alert steering: it is extremely embarrassing to accelerate into the other boat's transom as the result of an errant puff. Be prepared at all times to dive low and then quickly get back on his stern wave. The other boat may use the puff to steer higher momentarily, leaving you farther away from the tow and perhaps forcing you back a wave. The farther you fall back, the harder it will be to hold the tow—

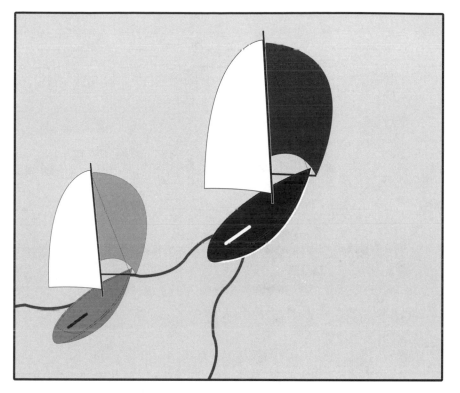

In a handicap fleet, use the wake of a faster boat to pull you along.

something to keep in mind if you are the boat doing the towing and you want to throw off a hitchhiker.

As a general rule, the way to take advantage of the downwind leg is to use it to close on the boats ahead. You need to hit the shifts first; to make the boats ahead of you jibe at inopportune times; and to maintain clear air while spilling dirty air on whomever you can reach ahead of you. If you can round the bottom mark bow-to-stern with the boat ahead of you, you are essentially even at that point: he can't tack away, and you can. You have to get out of there quickly, though, since your opponent's backwind will move you back in short order.

Defense off the Wind

Staying ahead off the wind is mostly a matter of maintaining clear air and positioning yourself between the other boats and the mark. If a group of boats are favoring one side of the course over another, place yourself between them and the mark. This will take you over to that favored side and will ensure that the other boats have to come to you when they head back to the rhumb line. In most cases it will also give you clear air to sail down the course.

If there is a boat right on your heels, the same general principles apply as on the reach. You have to recognize, though, that it is easier for the other boat to blanket you on the run, and position yourself accordingly.

Luffing to enforce your position is largely counterproductive until you are close to the mark. The best place to hold an opponent who is sailing down on more breeze or who has that significant boatspeed advantage is to leeward. Since the wind is directly behind you, this other boat will be able to pull parallel to you and perhaps even slightly ahead; but he won't get very far, because of the blanket from your sail. Make sure that he doesn't move too far below you in the process, or your blanket will be ineffective. It can be unnerving to watch other boats in the fleet sail in gusts that haven't yet reached you, but it shouldn't be; remember that the new wind will reach you in advance of the boats it is favoring. You must utilize the time spent waiting to position yourself to use the coming wind to its best advantage.

The best defense downwind isn't applicable until we get fairly close to the down-wind mark. Our concern is to protect our position coming into the two-boatlength circle so that we can execute an advantageous rounding. Let's say we are over-

If we've jibed too early, boats coming in from the outside will just go around us; we are too slow to defend ourselves.

lapped by another boat which is, at the present moment, between us and the mark. We have to break this overlap. If we are on port tack with another jibe left to the mark, we can jibe over to starboard. Assuming we have enough room to complete the jibe without fouling the boat on the inside, he will be forced to respond by either taking our transom or jibing himself. If he jibes with us, we can hold him out until we are ready to jibe to enter the circle. This works very much like taking a boat beyond the layline to an upwind mark. After we jibe back, the other boat has to make a tight turn to get to the mark and will have lost the overlap. Other boats entering the circle at the same time can complicate this maneuver. In that case, we are more likely to be able to round cleanly if we are on starboard tack coming back into the mark.

If instead of maintaining his overlap our opponent has elected to take our transom and split tacks with us, we need to work low to try and enter the two-boatlength circle on starboard before we have to jibe over to port to round the mark.

The worst situation we can be in is having jibed too early for the mark. We will be ambling into the mark rather slowly. Any boat coming from the outside and reaching will be able to round in front of us; we will not have enough boatspeed to enforce our rights as inside boat. Other boats will be able to round us as well as the mark and continue on their way as we try to accelerate.

At the Downwind Mark

This last mark rounding can be confusing. There are boats coming into the mark from all angles and at widely varying speeds. Some have been tacking downwind and are approaching on a reach, and some have jibed early and are diving straight downwind.

If we back ourselves into a position where we must defend ourselves with the rules, we have done something wrong. Only in light air, when everyone is drifting around the mark en masse, should the infighting come to this; in any kind of wind, boats will be in and out too fast.

As discussed in the previous section, I favor approaching the mark on starboard tack. I want to enter the circle on starboard, establish my rights to be there, then jibe to port to round. If you jibe to port too early, you may slow through the maneuver and lose the overlap at the critical juncture. Then you are on the wrong tack, on the inside, with no rights and nowhere to go.

If you do end up inside other boats after the jibe, you face the risk of having to sail too far straight downwind to get to the mark. As mentioned above, the boats on the outside may sail around you even though you have rights—you simply are moving too slowly to stop them.

If you are ten lengths or more from the mark, you may want to take a few transoms before you jibe onto port. The stronger the wind, the more I prefer to jibe to weather; the lighter the wind, the more inclined I am to take transoms and ensure that I come into the mark sailing higher with good speed.

Exiting the mark involves the same considerations that applied at the end of the reaching legs: getting clear air and being on the favored tack. Remember the tack on which you were knocked going downwind: you will want to go in the same direction on the opposite tack when you turn back upwind. The tactician or skipper has got to determine which direction that is, while also threading the boat through the mark rounding, so don't let him or her get caught up in what the crew has to do to lower the chute.

Questions

Q How do I pick the correct side of the course on the downwind leg?

A The favored downwind side might be the same as the favored upwind side. The reason is that when you are sailing downwind, you look for headers rather than lifts. Since sailing downwind puts you on the opposite tack, where the wind lifted you sailing upwind, it will now knock you sailing downwind.

So the correct side of the course is the side that is headed relative to the median wind. If the wind oscillates, you want to sail down the headed side until the wind starts to swing behind you. This is a lift, indicating that it is

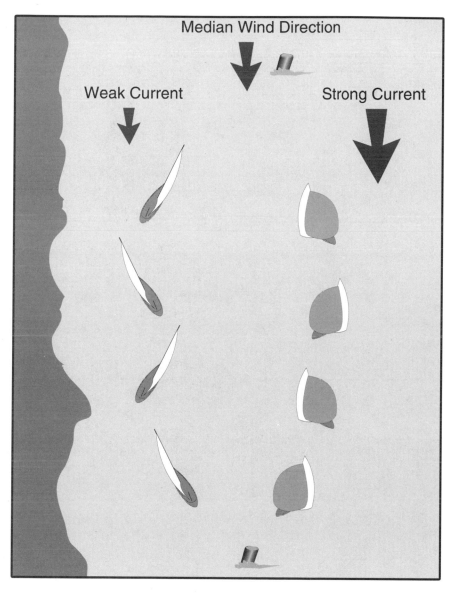

Median Wind Direction

Weak Current

Strong Current

Sail upwind against the weak current, then move into tho strongor curront to get downwind.

time to jibe over to the other tack so that the shift will be a knock. The farther forward the wind is blowing relative to the course to the mark, the better. The strength and direction of the puffs inside that shift will determine how far you should work to that side.

On the other hand, if you were sailing upwind in one area to stay out of an adverse current, when you turn and sail downwind you want to be in the stronger part of that current. In this case the favored side downwind is decidedly not the same as the favored side upwind.

Q How do I know where the crew weight should be?

A Here the answer really depends on the type of boat you are sailing. The important thing to remember is that the drag of the stern creates more problems than pushing the bow down. Some boats need weight aft to promote planing and surfing in heavy-air conditions, but in light and medium air, moving weight forward is generally better. The noise created by the water bubbling off the transom is a good indicator: the quieter the wake, the faster the boat.

The boat should be level from side to side if there is a spinnaker to balance the helm. If there is not, a heel to weather will pull the main over the boat. This brings the center of effort closer in line with the center of resistance and reduces the amount of helm input required to keep the boat moving forward. A word of warning here: the hull shape of the boat will want to push the nose down. If a sudden gust enters the sail, the top may accelerate to windward, the extra heel may start the boat turning, and a sudden jibe and swim may be the result. Overtrimming the main will alleviate this tendency.

The last consideration is wetted surface. In extremely light air some heel to leeward is best. The heel will reduce the wetted surface and thus the resistance of the boat. The forces on the rig and foils aren't strong enough to create any induced drag or steering problems. The heel also keeps the sails out there when there isn't enough wind to support them. At some point it will be necessary to make the transition from leeward heel to level or windward heel. The feel of the helm will provide the cue: when you have to exert a great deal of effort just to keep the boat going in a straight line, it's time to adjust the balance through the boat's heel.

Q How can I stop the oscillations that start in heavy air?

A This is only a problem in keelboats. Boats with centerboards would have them pulled up and can be accelerated out of the oscillations simply by heading up. A keelboat won't generate enough apparent wind through acceleration to stop the cycle.

To break an oscillation, you must understand its origin. As the puff hits to start the oscillation, it comes from farther aft; remember that the puff increases the aft component of the apparent wind. This breeze hits the chute and moves it to weather. It also flows through the top of the main and adds a sideways force at the top of the mast. The boat heels to windward, and the righting moment takes over just as the apparent wind starts to catch up with the chute. The chute then swings over to leeward and adds to the righting moment, and the boat heels over to leeward in turn; as it rights itself again, the chute once more swings over to the windward side and tries to take the rig with it. In the meantime, the keel swinging back and forth through the water is creating a lot of drag, and once the center of effort gets too far off, either to windward or to leeward, control is lost and the boat yaws around the keel.

The easiest way to dampen the oscillations is to let the pole move forward a couple of inches or feet, depending on the size of the boat. This will put the spinnaker farther out in front and will reduce its projected area. It will also reduce the flow of air across the chute, flow that can pull the masthead to windward. Choking the chute down with twings also helps discourage the oscillations. The cycle of oscillation must be broken quickly, so the crew must be ready to react when the puff hits.

Q When is it faster to head straight downwind, and when is it better to reach?

A Any boat that is fast enough to generate its own apparent wind—planing monohulls, catamarans, sailboards, and so on—should reach to build that apparent wind, and then take it downwind. As they slow, or feel the pressure dropping, they should swing back up to rebuild it. Keelboats have the same characteristics, but there are limits to how much their boatspeed can actually contribute to the apparent wind. Anytime they reach a certain speed—the "cliff" in the performance plot we mentioned—they will be better off heading straight, or nearly straight, downwind to the mark; beyond that boatspeed, the optimum angle for the true wind quickly approaches 180 degrees.

Chapter 13

The Final Leg

Having turned the last mark, our goal is in sight. We have only this last leg upwind to go, then the race will be over. There is not a lot about strategy left to discuss; the conditions we are sailing in are well known by now. This last leg is a matter of either protecting the place we have earned or making a last effort to better ourselves.

But even though the last leg of the race may be lacking in strategic complexity, there are still a great number of tactical variables to consider. We have to balance the chances of picking off boats ahead against our position relative to the boats behind us. Fatigue comes into play, both in ourselves and in the other boats. Are we still sharp enough to see the opportunities before us, or will we simply sail toward the line, hoping to hang on to our current place?

It hardly requires mention that the same factors controlling the previous legs are at work in this one as well. We need to select the correct side of the course, and we need to develop a lane of clear air. One factor is preeminent, however, to a degree it wasn't until now; that factor is simply the competition.

In our last trip upwind, we once again have to pass boats or prevent them from passing us, and this will more than ever require crisp tactical execution. We have to cover the boats behind us, or break the cover of the boats ahead of us—usually both.

In the last MC Nationals I sailed, at Lake Geneva, Wisconsin, I had been leading all around the course in one race. Then, on the downwind leg, two boats came out of the pack to close on me. One was not very close to me in the standings, but the other was a boat I had to beat every chance I could. As we rounded the mark, the two of them split. The closer one, the boat not in contention, took the side of the course I knew to be advantaged; I had used that side to gain the lead on the first leg upwind. The second went the other way, and I had no choice but to follow him. I could not afford to let a boat that was clearly a threat to me get away while I sat on someone who was having the race of his life.

Although the boat on the correct side did pass me and win the race, I succeeded in preventing the other boat from getting by me. I accomplished my overall goal (although the boat I did cover subsequently beat me in the series), and the sting of not winning the race was endurable. The point is that the competition rises above all other concerns in making decisions on the last leg.

In general, these decisions are somewhat tougher than on earlier legs, because there is no room to make up for mistakes. I've often heard people complain that they were coming on but ran out of race just before they could make their big move. That can easily happen: dropping or gaining several boats right at the end of the race is a common occurrence. Big gains sometimes become possible by chance, but they are more often the result of planning. Conversely, boats may be lost because of a lack of planning or simply because the tactician lost sight of the big picture in the final push to the line.

Strategy for the Last Leg

Somewhere during the race, the contest has changed from a fleet race to a battle with those three or four nearby boats. The fleet has stretched out, and our maneuvers or tactics are focused on passing the boat just ahead or keeping the boat just behind from passing us. We may want to get farther out to one side, where the next shift could put us over a group of boats. Even in these smaller groups, the action can get quite frantic.

If we are ahead, we want to control the boats closest to us—or those that present the greatest threat—and let the boats back in the pack go where they may. If we are behind but in the first rank, we need to maneuver ourselves into a position where any advantage on the course will favor us more than the boats ahead and the boats behind. If we are mid-fleet, we may have to concede the race to the leaders and just work on the boats in our area. Any boat we pass will improve our standing and place us in a better position for the next race. If some disaster has put us far back, we may need to gamble on a flyer to one side of the course, hoping for a favorable shift.

Generalizing about the circumstances that should lead to the selection of a particular course of action is difficult. Spontaneous opportunities will cause you to reevaluate your moves. For instance, it's not unknown for a large shift that has held off all day to come across the course during the last leg and completely scramble the picture. Or, a group of boats ahead may be so preoccupied with each other that they slow down tremendously and let you in. It's best to keep your options open and your head up.

In the race I mentioned above, I chose to control the boat that presented the greatest threat to my overall standing in the series, at the cost of winning that particular race. Had there been other boats closer to the three of us, and had they chosen to follow the fellow I let go, I would have had to take another look at the situation.

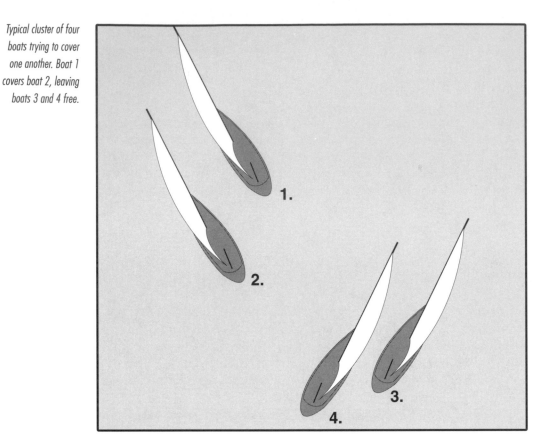

Beating one boat would not have been reason enough to go from first to fifth or sixth.

I think that in any circumstances, aspiring to lead the group of boats you are in is a fair goal. By definition these boats are close; they are not likely to scatter but rather will start to work on each other. Typically, the leader of the group—if it is not you—will cover the second-place boat, and the third-place boat will split from the first two. The fourth-place boat is left alone. The dynamics of this interaction should govern your tactics.

The situation can become very fluid. The leader may reconsider which of the boats in the group he really needs to cover. The fourth-place boat may realize that the other boats are heading toward the favored side of the course and stick with them, opting to remain in the ballgame until a better opportunity to pass comes along, or he may decide that his only chance lies in taking a different course altogether. Of course, he might also see something the other boats don't, because they are too distracted by each other to look up the course.

As mentioned, the race you are immediately concerned with is probably part of a series, and that complicates matters. We've discussed the role the competition plays

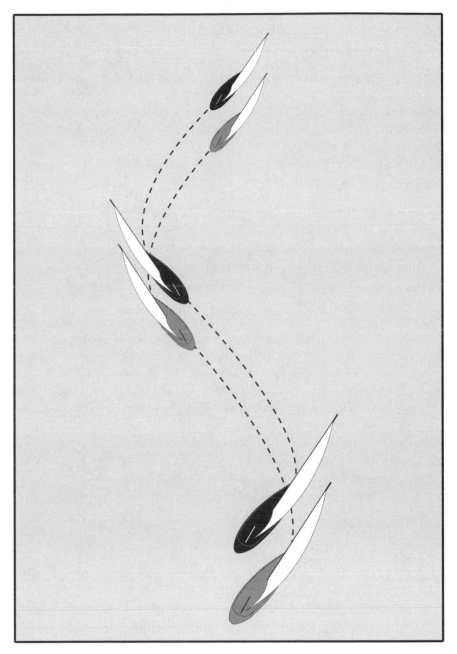

Covering means trying to prevent another boat from passing you by keeping better speed or benefiting from a favorable shift.

in the prerace formulation of strategy; in this leg our planning comes to fruition. If our rivals are safely tucked away, we can be relatively satisfied with the status quo. If they are immediately behind or in front, our decisions on this leg will be dictated by the need to pass or stay ahead of them. In the extreme case, we may have to try to drive a rival back into the fleet to force him to use a throw-out race.

The goal is simple, but the time to accomplish it is short. You have to start executing your decisions immediately upon rounding the mark. This is not the time to get the chute down, sheet in, settle down, and then look around. If you are going to be covering boats behind you, you can use the rounding to place yourself in position for this purpose. If you are behind, you need to start breaking whatever cover may be placed on you.

Covering is simply the act of preventing another boat from passing you by sailing faster or reaping greater benefit from a shift. It is done by staying between the boat you are covering and the finish line, close to the other boat and on the same side of the course. If the other boat is sailing faster than you or is very close, place yourself in a position to interfere with the wind going through his sails. The disturbed air will slow him down and increase your lead.

Conversely, in order to break a cover if you are behind, you need clear air to pass, or you need to derive more benefit from a windshift. There are a number of options, which we will discuss in detail later.

Despite the supreme importance of dealing with the competition, you cannot forget the big picture. As always, you need to stay in touch with the shifting wind. In Gold Cup courses where the last leg is a short one, the race may be over before an oscillating wind swings back. In this case, the shift you start the leg with resembles a permanent change in wind direction and should be sailed accordingly—get to the inside by sailing initially against the shift, then head for the line. Late afternoon winds often end up shifting into one direction and staying there. In Florida, the sea breeze comes in and oscillates east to east-southeast, then slowly works its way to the southeast. When it gets there, it maintains its direction but starts to blow harder. This frequently shifts the advantage to the right side of the course for the last leg.

Loose Cover

A loose cover is designed to do two things: it will prevent another boat from getting a shift that will immediately move him past you, and it will encourage him to move in the direction you want him to go.

A loose cover is called for when you have a significant lead over the boats immediately behind you and want to guard this lead without provoking a tacking duel. The cover places you on the inside of the course relative to the other boats, and that gives you greater flexibility to respond to changes in the conditions. Since the boats you're covering have clear air, they have no reason to tack and may follow docilely behind you. If they do, they are unlikely to get a private puff that hasn't come to you first. As we've discussed, the fleet tends to round in bunches; placing a loose cover on the first few boats that come out of the mark after you will allow them

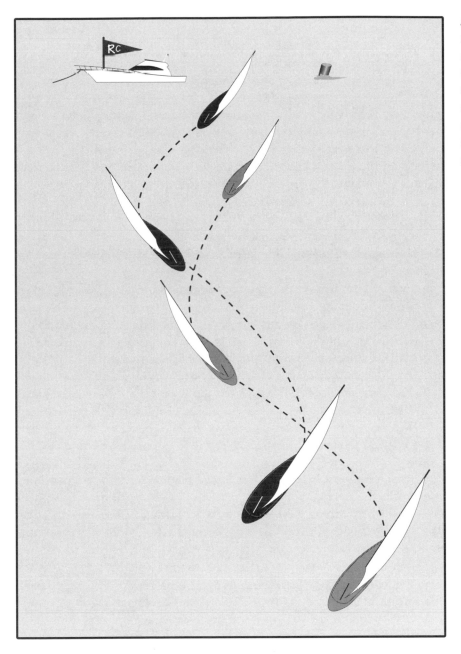

A loose cover does not interfere with the other boat's wind. The covering boat merely seeks to stay between his opponent and the finish and to ensure that both boats benefit equally from any windshifts.

to continue, then tack to place their own cover on the boats that finally split tacks. You can then tack with the entire group and keep them all under control.

A good loose cover is prepared before the next boat rounds the mark. Your crew has to get things squared away and the boat properly set up for the leg. The best cover won't protect a boat that is tangled up with itself or not set up for speed upwind. The concept of loose cover presupposes that you've gotten where you are by adequate speed, and that you will be able to maintain that speed.

The classic way to initiate a cover after rounding the mark is to sail on port tack half the distance between you and your competitor, then tack to starboard. You should be directly upwind and on the rhumb line when the other boat gets to the mark. You want to tack again here to parallel his course, assuming he will continue on port at least long enough to clear the boats approaching the mark on the downwind leg. Even if he tacks to starboard when you tack to port, you can sail on a bit, then tack with him. You are still safely on the inside of the course and should still be a bit ahead of him (see illustration on page 154).

Don't wait too long to tack with your opponent. If there is a starboard tack knock, his position on the outside will be in his favor. Indeed, it is his only defense. Any slowing of your boat from the two quick tacks should be viewed as a wise way of spending your lead.

Spending your lead is an important concept here. A loose cover may find you directly ahead of a boat sailing on the lifted tack. If the lift persists, this boat will start to lift out of your wake and onto your hip, and eventually work past you. When you foresee this you should tack, take the header, and get to the inside of your competition. The distance between you will shrink, but you will solidify your defensive position. This move is similar to the consolidation tack we discussed on the first leg.

There is a temptation to slam right on the air of the miscreant who had the guts to challenge you once you get above him. Resist it: if you lodge yourself on his air, he will tack away, and the whole process will have to be repeated. Before you know it, you will be in a tacking duel—the very thing you are trying to avoid by covering loosely.

It is important that you spend your lead playing the shifts rather than the other boats. When covering, you need to maintain your position as the inside boat, if necessary by extending your tack somewhat farther into the shift than you might like. This kind of balancing act may give you a bit of a stomach problem, but if the lead disappears before the end of the race, you'll easily be able to shift into a more aggressive covering mode for the last push to the finish.

In a handicap race, where your position in the fleet will be determined after the application of a correction factor, you may not be able to determine exactly where your closest competitor is. Even if you can locate him, you may not be able to influence him. Loosely covering the fleet is the only reasonable course of action in that situation; engaging anyone in a tacking duel would only allow other boats to gain.

As you approach the end of the leg, the considerations change slightly. You acquire an ally in your effort to control the other boats; that ally is the layline. You can use the layline as an outer boundary, holding your competitors against it so they cannot turn away from you. Let's see how this is done in practice.

As you work out to one side of the course, you face a dilemma: you are approach-

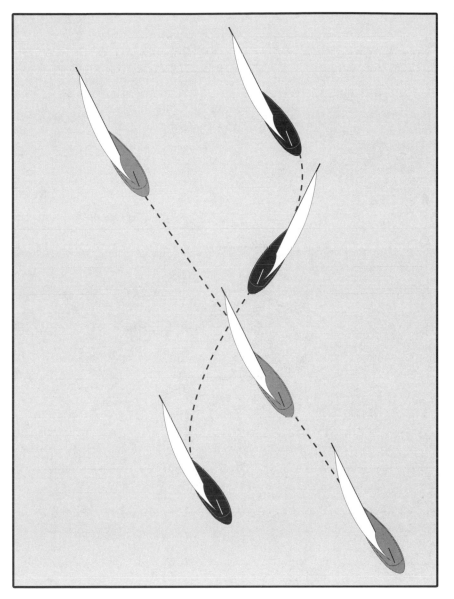

If a boat is on your hip and starting to gain, cross him so that you get on the inside of the shift, rather than tacking on his air.

ing the layline and would like to tack short, but you do not want to let the boat you are covering get to the outside of you, where a shift might place him ahead. You should sail out to the layline, tack as you normally would, then wait for the other boat to go beyond your track and the layline and tack. When he does, take one final tack over to the side of the course, then tack again for the finish. You now have the other boat pinned on the layline; he cannot tack away because he is already

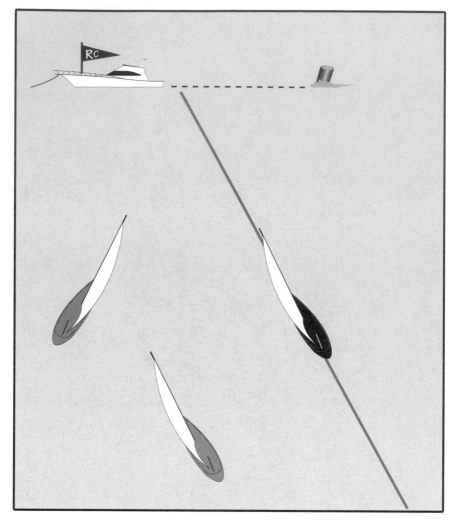

making the finish line. Since he is in your backwind, he should lose ground to you all the way into the line. His only salvation would be a massive header, which would push you both off the layline and open up room for another tack of his to the outside of the course. However, being ahead in this instance, you could tack over as well, with the advantage of being on the inside of the shift. Your competitor would simply be pushed farther back by the exchange.

The danger of a loose cover is that an attempt to stay in touch with too many boats spread over too wide an area confines the covering boat to the middle of the course, robbing him of the benefits of a clear shift to one side or the other. In fact, as you shall see later, one of the suggestions for breaking a cover and passing a boat is to keep that boat in the middle of the course. Not only does this completely deprive him of the use of leverage in a shift, it also deprives him of the use of the layline at the end of the race. Since you are concerned with covering, rather than being covered, at this point, I can only recommend that you try to keep the group of boats behind lined up and headed in the same direction. Ideally, the boats that successfully split from the group, if any, will be those that have farthest to go to reach you.

Hard Cover

If you round the leeward mark with the second-place boat right on your heels, and with a comfortable distance to the third-place boat, you are about to start one of the most exciting sequences in the sport. The entire discipline of match racing focuses on just this aspect of sailing—preventing that closest contender from passing you.

This situation, which may actually occur at any point in the last leg, calls for a hard cover. By definition a hard, or tight, cover is the tactic of staying between your opponent and the next mark, close enough to him so you are feeding him bad air and slowing him at every opportunity. A successful hard cover not only maintains your

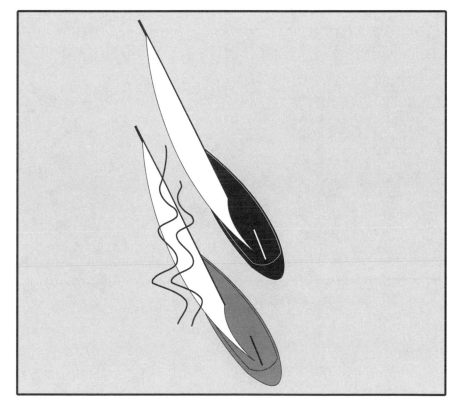

The object of a hard cover is to slow the other boat by interfering with his air.

lead, but increases it. Because of the offensive nature of the tactic, your opponent will do all he can to get away from you.

Covering in this fashion is most successful when you are faster in and out of tacks than the boat behind and can shift gears to fine-tune your rig relative to his. You need to place yourself in a position where these strengths will pay off. Late in the leg, your technical advantage will allow you to shift from a loose cover to a tighter one at your discretion. By contrast, initiating a hard cover right at the leeward mark can be difficult.

Your primary concern at the mark is to come out of the rounding as high as or higher than the boat behind you. If you can get his bow below you at the beginning of the leg, you will start feeding him bad air right away, and when he tacks away, you will be in position to give bad air to him on the other tack as well.

You need to round the mark wide and leave it tight. If your opponent slips onto your inside, you have to use speed to dig to windward in order to prevent him from accelerating into clear air. If you can slow him, he will fall into your wake as you continue on port tack. If he establishes himself above you with clear air, however,

Leaving the leeward mark, we need to prevent the boat behind from getting his bow up to windward of us.

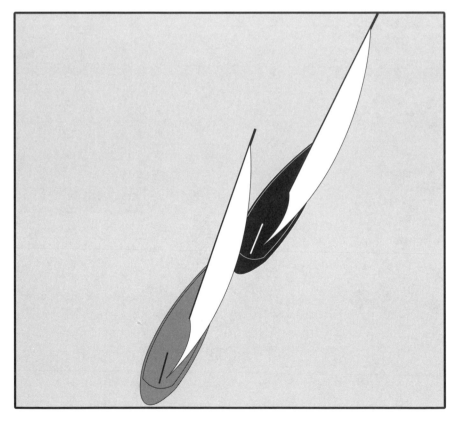

you should tack to starboard and force him to tack as well. In doing so, try to carry as much speed as possible over him; this will place him securely in your blanket when he accelerates. If you don't have room to tack, your opponent is probably being affected by your backwind, and you just have to wait a little longer. You can use the scalloping technique discussed in Chapter 11 to draw him to you.

If you must tack to challenge, be careful not to initiate a series of tacks that has the other boat continually moving to the favored side, leaving you headed the wrong way. To avoid this, you must either cross him and proceed to a position not directly on his air, or try to have him tack with you.

If the favored side is clearly evident and you succeed in getting across the other boat to a position on the inside of the shift, you can blend the techniques of loose cover and tight cover to maintain your lead. Apply a loose cover when your opponent is headed in the direction you want to go and you are in a position to benefit from the geometry of the shift. Apply a hard cover when your position isn't so favorable relative to the wind and you want him to head in the opposite direction.

If you need your opponent to finish farther down in the fleet, you might encourage him to go in the wrong direction in the hope that another boat in the fleet will pass him. Alternatively, if the wind is steady, you may want to initiate a tacking duel to slow you both down.

If the leg is long, the other boat will probably want to sail the fastest course for the early part of it. Since he is as sensitive to the other boats as you are, he will realize that inviting a hard cover early may slow both of you. So after that initial jockeying at the mark, things may quiet down for a while. This is fine as far as you are concerned unless you need other boats between the two of you; if you do, the sooner you can accomplish that goal, the better.

Sometime up the leg, you may lose control over the boat you are attempting to cover. He may have worked out from underneath you through superior boatspeed, or he might have gotten inside on a momentary shift. If that happens, you must not hesitate to take advantage of any opportunity to reestablish control. Don't go off the deep end in panic or rush things: just grab that quick knock, tack, and either force him over or tack right in front of him. (The latter is called a "slam dunk" both by those who love it and those who hate it.)

If your competitor gets clear from underneath you, you have to shift gears and try to stay high. You cannot let him build distance in front of you. If you fall into his bad air and start to slow, you must tack first before you can work on breaking his cover.

One of the hazards of covering another boat tightly is that you can get locked into a completely reactive style of sailing and forget the world around you. In fleet racing, there is rarely a situation when you can safely ignore all other boats on your way up the last leg; the boat you are covering probably doesn't want to ignore the boats immediately behind him either. If you have the luxury of a fairly substantial lead over him, you can provide him with incentive to remain in contact with the fleet. To do this, you simply camp on his air when he moves away from the rest of the boats.

When he tacks back toward the fleet, delay your tack on him until you have good
reason to tack anyway and until he has gained clear air. If he then tacks back upon
rejoining the fleet, continue to give him room to breathe. This will keep the overall
situation comfortably under control until the final stages of the race.

The main feature distinguishing a hard cover from a loose one is the ability to
affect the covered boat's wind. Even with a hard cover, though, it may not be necessary or advisable to be on his air at every moment. In general, the hard cover only

works when there is just one boat to defend against, because a third boat will almost always split from the first two. If you do want to try defending against two boats, you need to be more in the middle of the course. Only your experience on prior legs can tell you whether that tactic will be viable. Since one side is usually favored, or one boat matters to you more than the other, you usually have to make a choice. In the example cited early in this chapter, I made the right choice, but it took me to the wrong side and cost me the victory in the race.

Breaking a Cover

To look at things the other way now, nothing is more frustrating on the last leg than seeing your opponent right there whenever you look to windward, seemingly tied to you with a string. You've got to cut that string to get around him.

Breaking a cover requires patience. If the other boat is fairly far ahead, he has to be reeled in before you can even consider making an attempt. You have to be alert to the geometry of the weather leg, which gives you as the trailing boat some advantage. Remember, you control the time and place of your tack.

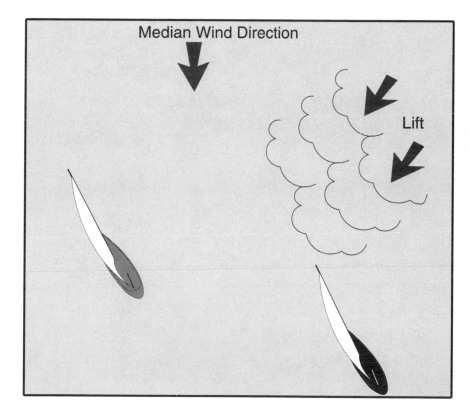

Beating the other boat to the shift will close the distance between you. He will give you an accurate gauge of the strength, duration, and magnitude of the shift, so you should be able to jump on it sooner.

Our discussion of leverage in Chapter 6 applies here as well. In the absence of a clearly favored side, you want to continue toward the side that will be favored by the next shift. If there is a favored side, though, you need to be the boat farthest out in that direction.

When you are on the outside, you can make leverage work for you. You can tack on a shift and sail on the lift toward your opponent, who must either spend some of his lead to cross you before tacking, or tack as he enters the shift, thus leaving you on the inside of the lift.

If he crosses you before tacking, you can foot out from underneath him and repeat the maneuver later, on the other tack. Alternatively, if you need to get back to the side you're coming from, you can tack as he tacks on you and get yourself out of phase with him.

If he tacks underneath or ahead of you, you can ride the lift until he feels compelled to tack back at you or until you pass him. In an oscillating situation, he might

In puffy conditions, you can break a cover by timing your tacks to be in puffs while your opponent is sailing in light air.

use his leverage on that side to capture the next shift first and regain his lead. You need to prevent him from building distance to the outside. If necessary, you might even tack away before the next header comes across to deny him the favored side. If he tacks with you, you've been successful at that; if he continues until the shift and tacks only then, at least you've split tacks with him.

This process of using leverage and cutting corners on the shifts works with differences in wind velocity as well as differences in direction. If you tack in a nice puff and force the other boat to follow you while he is in a lull, you're rewarded with the difference in acceleration plus the higher angle you can sail in the puff. Picking your spots and cutting the corners will gradually reel in your opponent.

It all works very well until you've gotten the other boat so close that he is affecting your air. Suddenly the two of you are no longer equal in speed. You are bumping up against a wall of disturbed air, and improving your position further is difficult. Now you have two options: you can initiate a tacking duel, hoping to work by your opponent and into clear air, or you can bring another boat into the picture.

A tacking duel can be started anytime during the race, and of course anytime on the last leg. It usually isn't used as a weapon until later in the leg because the frequent tacking reduces both combatants' overall speed toward the finish. Delaying this tactic gives the thundering herd behind you little time to close on you and your opponent. Unfortunately, it also gives you little time to effect a pass.

A tacking duel is simply a series of quick tacks with the goal of forcing the boat ahead to make a mistake. A bad tack or a failure to tack on his part will allow the boat behind to close the gap or achieve clear air in a position that is essentially even with the leader. The skills needed to win a tacking duel are self-evident: you have got to enter and leave your tacks faster than the boat you are trying to pass. It goes without saying that the mechanics of your tacks must be close to perfect.

The timing of the tacks can also work in your favor if you are the boat behind. As mentioned, you get to choose when and where you are going to tack. If the leading boat is in a bad set of waves or a light spot, he will either be slower coming out of the tack or will have to wait for a better time to tack. In either case, you have been able to clear your air and get farther out to one side, where you may get a favorable shift.

If the other boat delays, then tacks, you may want to tack right back at him, forcing him into another tack before he is accelerated out of the previous one. This puts him on the wrong side of the power curve and will quickly work to close the gap between you. If you tack away again, you eliminate the risk of getting so close to the other boat that he can pin you in place.

If you get too close to the other boat, he will deny you room to tack. That may mean the end of the tacking duel if you are close to the layline. The other boat will force you out to the layline, and the game will be over.

This leads us to one of the rules for passing on the last leg. You can only pass a boat by way of a tacking duel if you have room on either side of the rhumb line, so you have to coax the leading boat into the middle of the course. Otherwise, he can

use the layline to the finish just as a cornerback uses the corner of the end zone to
help defend against a receiver.

The alternative strategy to shed a defender, besides initiating a tacking duel with
him, is to bring another boat into the picture. This, too, may involve a tacking duel,
but more as a means than an end. After a series of tacks, both the aggressor and
defender will have slowed enough to bring other boats up from the ranks. Clearly,

this strategy is not without risks: the newcomer may pass both of the leaders. It is easier to find someone to peel off the boat ahead if you are in a group to begin with.

The simplest technique is to sail over to the third boat and tack so that the boat preventing you from passing has to tack into the backwind of the third boat. That will ruin his day, and it is surprisingly easy to do. Remember that the boat covering you is focused on what you are doing. He may not realize the proximity of the third boat until after he has tacked to cover you. Once he does, he will spend some time evaluating his position and probably decide he needs to make a move out of there. Hopefully this will leave you on the advantaged side of the course; you can then cross him next time you meet.

If the third boat crosses between the two of you, that alone may be enough to pull off the boat covering you. Remember, if you need to beat this boat more than you need to finish in any particular place, any element of confusion you can add to the situation will improve your chances.

Starting a tacking duel with the boat covering you or trying to peel him off has to be done while there is still enough time to finish the job. The optimal timing varies from race to race, and it is hard to make a general statement. As mentioned, if you are one of two lead boats and you start a tacking duel too early, the rest of the fleet is going to come into the picture very rapidly. If it is early in the series, you have to balance your desire to beat the boat in front of you against the need to score as well as possible. It is also inadvisable to start tacking like crazy until the boat ahead is close enough that he will have to tack immediately with you. Concentrate on cutting corners and on tacking when you are in a puff and your opponent is in a lull. These techniques should bring him closer, so that a bad tack on his part can put you through him into clear air. If your opponent doesn't feel he has to try to feed you bad air, you are too far away for any kind of aggressive tacking duel.

If you can't break away from the boat ahead, or the last leg is heavily favored to one side, you can still practice some deception to reel him in. When the helmsman looks back at you, pinch up. Even if one of the crew is doing nothing but watching you, when the helmsman looks back and sees you pointing above him, he will pinch as well. He may try and hold this course longer, while you foot to build your speed when he looks away. As the gap narrows, this may drive him quite insane. At the very least you'll succeed in closing the gap; you can then tack and drag your opponent into the middle of the course. I guarantee he will not want to let you go off on your own after you have cut his lead dramatically.

Other Considerations

We've spent a lot of time looking at covering, both from the attack and from the defense point of view. And for good reason: no matter where you are in the fleet, at some point you and the people around you are going to accept their position in the race and to concentrate on protecting it by throwing a cover on the boats behind.

If you are mid-fleet at the last downwind mark, you can take advantage of this tendency in others and make an initial move out of phase with the clump of boats you are in, or ideally the clump just ahead of you. By taking this short clearing tack, you wind up in a position where you can utilize some leverage against them. If the wind is still oscillating fairly evenly, use your slightly out-of-phase position to work the shifts in clear air. If the wind is shifting to one side, as it may do at the end of the day, be more aggressive in positioning yourself for it. Sail a little deeper into the shift before tacking: placing yourself on the inside of a new, more permanent shift will pay big dividends. The boats clumped ahead will tack with each other, and may leave the way clear for a major pass.

Obviously, the last leg is the time to pull out the stops if you need to move up. That doesn't mean that you have to shoot for a corner, but you should commit fully to the side you believe is favored, and you should be ready to jump on any mistakes made by other boats.

One other circumstance that may arise during the last leg requires special consideration: you may need another boat to finish poorly, in a situation where it doesn't matter at all where you end up yourself. This is most likely to be the case when a series includes a throw-out. You may not have had a race to throw out yet, having sailed conservatively and finished consistently, while your rival has finished ahead of you but has one bad race which, if kept, would place you in front of him. Your object here is to make him finish lower than that place in the current race, knowing you can throw out that race yourself if accomplishing this takes you too far back.

You can harry your target throughout the race, and if he allows you a clear shot, you will probably be successful early on. Concentrate on feeding him bad air at every opportunity; you can dirty up your air even more by luffing or adding more camber to your sails. You can also try to slow the other boat by pushing him past laylines and forcing him to tack excessively.

This tactic is bound to provoke a strong reaction, so you have to be very careful not to foul your opponent. (Some races don't allow a disqualification to be thrown out.) It raises some concerns about fair sailing, but in my opinion, if you have worked yourself to the point where this strategy is necessary to win a series, you are justified in using it.

It is said that the past is prologue to the future. Well, the entire race, including the last leg, is merely a prologue to the finish, which can be the most critical part of the race and the hardest to get right. We will look at the elements of a strong finish in the next chapter.

Questions

Q How can I tell if the wind has shifted or conditions have changed for the last leg?

A There are two indications. One is that your compass headings are consistently to one side of the range established on previous legs. If all the convection-related shifts—the sea breeze for example—have had time to establish themselves, they may have rotated the median wind direction. The other is a change in the look of the course: if the water looks different, the wind must be different. It is probably steadier now than it was earlier in the day; bands of clearly defined puffs may have broken up, and the velocity of the shift may be more uniform. This knowledge will assist you if you have to go to one side to pass a group of boats, but a clearly favored side may hamper you if you try to pass a single boat by initiating a tacking duel.

Q Should I start a tacking duel with other boats close by?

A If you are trying to pass an opponent and intend to continue tacking until you either pass or finish, you should probably wait until late in the leg. However, if you merely need to clear your air or split tacks with the boat ahead, you can start a tacking duel anytime. If there are other boats in the picture, your opponent will not want to waste a lot of distance by playing your game too long. As a matter of fact, two tacks will probably be enough to convince him to lay off. And he is wise to do so: he has got to cover a number of boats, so allowing one boat clear air in order to protect against three others is a reasonable trade-off.

Always be aware that if there are other boats nearby, they will pass you if you engage in this kind of protracted struggle with someone. That is why tacking duels generally take place between boats leading the race or ones that are locked together in the overall standings for a series.

Q How aggressive should my cover be?

A The shiftier the conditions, the tighter the cover needs to be. If things are fairly steady, the speed that put you in front should keep you there. If the boat you are concerned about has come charging out of the pack, his speed may be greater than yours, so he should be covered tightly. In most cases a cover should ensure that you will receive the same wind as your competitor, thereby reducing the chances of a wild-card shift shuffling the places. If you are in a place where any shift that benefits your competitor will help you even more, you've got it knocked.

Q What if I am mid-fleet and I don't want to cover, but rather improve my position?

A In this case you need to sail the leg as best you can and try to get a firm read on the finish line as you approach it (more on this in the next chapter). Pay attention to where clumps of boats may be trying to slow each other and try to get to the advantaged side of them. Watch the boats finishing ahead to determine which end of the line is favored, and try to approach it on the lifted tack. You can gamble a little if there are other boats heading for the line at the same time and slightly ahead. Tack underneath them, or try to pick them off by coming across on starboard. In short, keep working at it until you hear the horn.

Chapter 14

The Finish

T he end is in sight. No matter where we are in the fleet, approaching the finish line generates a little anxiety. Can we hang on to win, or will we be able to work by one more boat, or at the least, can we outlast that other team that seems to be charging out of the pack?

I always seem to be judging my entire race on the progress made in the last 500 yards to the finish. If I pick off a couple of boats at the end of the race, it's been a good race; if I'm hosed at the end and lose two or three boats, the whole race has been somewhat less than wonderful. I don't recommend this attitude, but it's probably a fairly natural human response.

You can't let your tactical guard down late in the race. No matter how tired, cold, or wet you might happen to be, you have to remember that everyone out there is just as cold and wet, and that your competitors are still looking to improve themselves. I've mentioned the Blue Chip regatta, the scow race that selects the top finishers from the year's racing and pits them against each other in a small fleet. These people do not want to be in the back of the fleet—they are not used to it, they don't like it. The finish area gets savage as each of them attempts to eke out that one place higher before the race runs out. In fast-tacking boats, the battle for position across the line is carried right to the end.

Types of Finishes

There are really only two types of finishes: upwind and downwind. Upwind finishes are the norm, as they are used in Olympic and Gold Cup–type courses. The boats cross the line at acute angles, which makes it easy to call close finishes, and the legs are fairly even, not favoring either the boats ahead or those behind. The most difficult problem to overcome in an upwind finish arises if the wind shifts after the line has been set, since any advantage to one side of the course greatly restricts the ability of the boats to pass each other. A shift can turn the last leg into a parade to the line.

A downwind finish shares this problem to some degree. If the wind shifts so that the leg is no longer straight downwind, the advantage goes to the leading boat. If the leg is straight downwind, however, the downwind finish favors the boat behind—in theory, at any rate. The most publicized downwind finish was that of the 1992 America's Cup series, which was employed in a deliberate attempt to make the races more interesting. Whether or not that attempt succeeded is a matter of opinion; it did not produce many lead changes.

The boat behind has the advantage on a downwind finish due to his ability to blanket the boat in front. This advantage is offset by the ability of the leading boat to block the trailing boat from getting to the line. The transition of the trailing boat from clear astern to overlapped and the resulting shift in status with respect to the rules can make for an interesting tactical situation.

Downwind finishes may be used in conventional races if the race committee wants to start another race soon after the completion of the current one. Finishing in the area of the downwind mark places the fleet in position to start another race immediately.

The structure of the finish line makes it different from other marks. Because it is a line that must be crossed, it has a mark at each end. Ideally these two marks should lie perpendicular both to the course line and the wind direction, but this is seldom the case; almost inevitably one end of the line is favored. Identifying the favored end is the key to a good finish.

The favored end cannot always be spotted before the line is nearby. Usually one

The finish line has four laylines—two from each end. Once you've determined which end you will cross, you concern yourself with the laylines for that end.

end is a buoy and the other a boat, and their difference in size makes it difficult to tell which is closer. As you approach, you start to run into the other peculiar characteristic of the finish line: having two ends, it has four laylines. When finishing to weather, the laylines are to be avoided until you are ready to cross the line, just as the layline is to be avoided at the weather mark.

We will discuss finishing to weather first, and look at the downwind finish as a special case later in the chapter.

Windward Finishes

Determining the Favored End

The favored end of the finish line is simply the one closer to the last mark. If the starting line is being used as the finish line, it may be the end that was unfavored for the start. If the race committee has moved the mark—they may shrink the line for the finish to make it easier to call the boats across and to clear the course—checking the line as you sail by on other legs of the course will give you an indication of the favored end. Race committees are much less particular about the setting of the finish line than they are about the start line. There is no reason why they should be—they just are. If they've moved the line, they've probably significantly favored one side.

Unless the line is perfectly square, it is important to finish the race at the favored end. Sailing across the middle of a favored line is equivalent to overstanding the

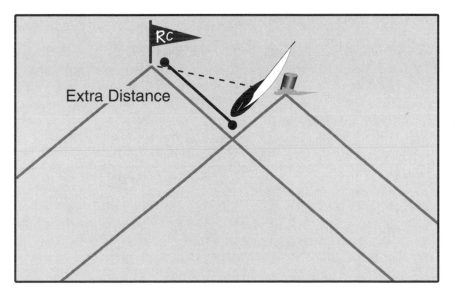

Unless the finish line is square to the wind, crossing anywhere but at the favored end means sailing farther than necessary to cross the line.

windward mark, since you have sailed extra distance to cross the line in the center. The critical point is where the two inside laylines cross. If you pass inside the inner layline to the favored end, you are sailing extra distance. By the time you reach the point where the inside laylines cross, you need to have determined which end you will cross. If you still cannot tell which end that might be, you'll need to look over the other boats and evaluate their positions and your ability to tack. If the line is so even that you can't decide upon an end, continuing on the same tack rather than tacking may be the best course. In a catamaran, or in a heavy boat in light air, you will lose as much in a tack as you might gain by crossing the line at the favored end. Ideally you will cross at the favored end without having to tack anyway. As long as you cross the line at a roughly perpendicular angle, you should be all right.

If the wind shifts during the last leg and this shift favors one side of the course substantially, you'll need to cross at the new leeward end. That will allow you to take the favored tack toward the line earlier, and you can gamble by tacking short of the leeward layline. If you find yourself lifted to the middle of the line, so be it; at least you have been moving toward the line more directly. If you are lifted all the way to the line, you can crack off a bit and pick up some speed, sailing a shorter course faster to the finish.

Failing to determine a favored end is not an excuse to cross in the middle; even the most myopic skipper needs to decide upon an end and head for it. But stay flexible if there is a massive header from the side you've chosen; the rule of sailing the lifted tack still takes precedence. I've been on boats that have suddenly found themselves paralleling the finish line because they've ignored a shift when heading for an end of the line.

The Competition and Finishing

One of the sweet agonies of sailboat racing is deciding when to end the cover on a boat and tack over to cross the line. This is a problem you face when covering on any upwind leg. When is it time to go for the layline? The solution is always the same. If you can force your opponent beyond the layline, he has nowhere to go; he can only follow you into the line and cross behind you. As a matter of fact, the closer you are to the layline, the more restricted are his options. As you approach the finish area, you will want to provide more opportunity for the boat behind to move out to the side of the course, by placing a hard cover on him as he moves into the center and a looser cover as he heads toward the outside of the course.

In a closely bunched fleet, this strategy can be costly early in the last leg, but as the leg winds down, you can afford to take one side. The time for the trailing boats to take advantage of a shift against you decreases as you approach the finish line.

If you are on the inside of the course and a tacking duel ensues, keep trying to move the other boat to one side until you are securely on one layline. He may try to

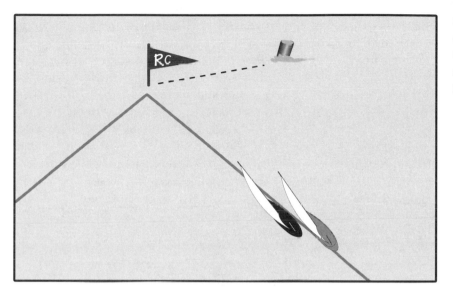

Pinning your opponent out on the layline will end his options: he has nowhere to go but to the line.

induce you to tack away once more: resist the temptation and head for the line. At this point, if you get a lift, you will finish comfortably, and if you are headed, you can tack at the line to cross on the lifted tack. If the other boat has closed in the course of the tacking duel, it doesn't make much sense to continue to play when the end is in reach. Allow him to move to the side of the course with clear air, while you tack on the layline for the finish. If the other boat continues beyond what you have deter-

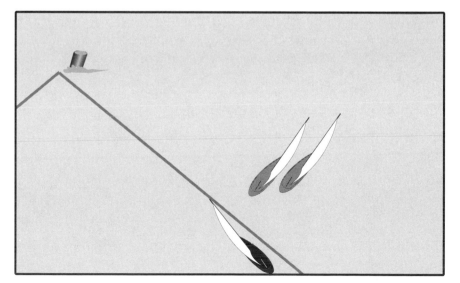

Following a boat beyond the layline is smart only if there are no other boats challenging and there is still some distance to the line. In this instance the two boats beyond the layline are about to let you sneak by.

mined to be the layline and there is still some distance to be sailed, consider one more tack to seal him out there.

This is the time to really slam your competitor. If you cross, put your backwind right into his sails. If there is a lift over there and you can't cross him, you need to tack well underneath him instead. After all, you were on the layline when you tacked away, so the lift should put you across easily. If he has overstood, he'll have to come down to you. If you have him locked outside, you can hold him out there until you get to the line. Simply stick your bow across before he can get there.

The only drawback to this scenario is that both of you have overstood the line in the process, so other boats may be crossing while you engage each other. It is this possibility that tightens everyone's stomach at the end of a race.

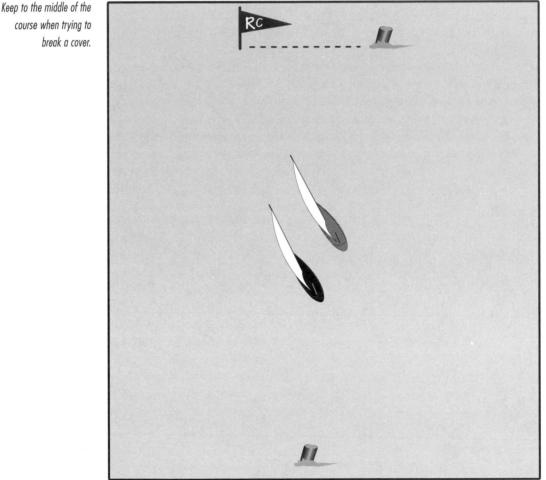

Keep to the middle of the course when trying to break a cover.

Again, it is just as interesting strategically to look at the situation from the other side. Trying to get by another boat is a matter of sailing faster while keeping him under control. I remember a race I had been leading throughout. The wind had been rising through the race, and with the end in sight, out of the pack came another boat. Try as I might, I could not hold him back, and he finally broke through my lee about 200 yards from the finish. Luck was with me, though: I tacked away back to the middle of the course, picked up a shift, and still beat him across the line. Had the other boat tacked with me, he would easily have won the race.

If you are trying to break a cover, keep to the middle of the course, where you can cut corners using windshifts and puffs. The longer you stay away from the lay-lines, the more time you have to put these shifts to work for you. When you finally do reach the layline, try to tack first; you may be able to get your bow out in front. That's all it takes.

One tactic boats ahead are using these days is to reach off so that they are right on the air of the trailing boat. If someone is doing this to you, time your tack to begin just as the other boat pulls off. If he wants to react immediately, he will have to tack through a large angle and will come out moving very slowly. A tack back

When another boat is footing dramatically to get on your wind, tack when he will have the largest turn to make to tack with you.

toward him will force him either to let you go or try another tack while moving at low speed. If he does try to come back and you are on port tack, tack over to starboard and either force him into one more tack or slam dunk him as he ducks you. This reverses the roles pretty quickly. Some people will just watch an opponent reach down and won't tack away until he is on their air. They don't realize that the covering boat has to be attacked at his weak point, which is when he is below a close-hauled course and has to tack through a wider angle; once he gets on their air, he is where he wants to be. You need three tacks to execute this pass, so you cannot be near the layline; if the first tack takes you outside the course, you are done.

Most often you are crossing in a group. You may be covering someone, but there are other boats around that you can pick off or that may get to you. In a handicap fleet, you also have to be aware of boats that may not even be in sight. You have to get across the line in the most efficient manner possible.

The simplest strategy for a good finish is to tack short of the port tack layline to the favored end. If there is a lift, you can go ahead and cross the line; if you don't make it, you can tack to starboard to cross right at the mark. If there are other boats crossing on starboard but not making the line, you can duck them smoothly, knowing that when they tack to cross the line, they will have to take your position on starboard into account.

Once you are on starboard tack, other boats will either duck you or tack underneath you. If they have room to get established on starboard tack with a safe leeward, they may be able to break the overlap and luff across the line ahead of you. They may be late in doing this, though, and you might be able to shoot across the line before them by luffing earlier. Again, timing is important, coupled with knowl-

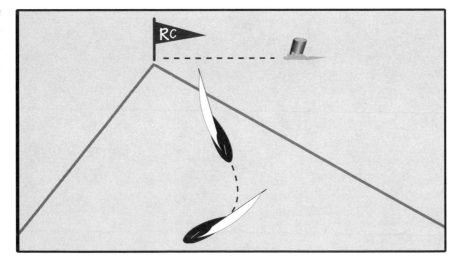

Approach a port-favored line short of the port tack layline, so you can tack onto starboard to hit the layline easily.

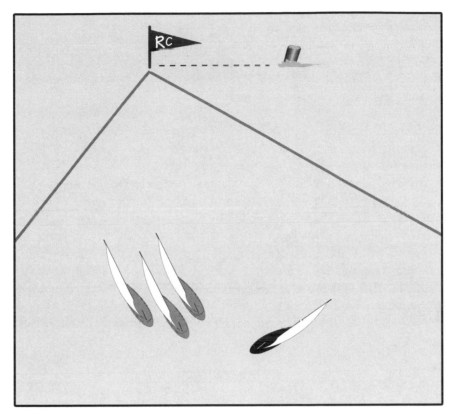

Getting out of phase with a group of boats coming into the line will give you clear air and possibly a favorable shift.

edge of the angle of the line. If you are free to roll over onto the other tack, you might take a big bite to weather and complete it as a tack.

If you are approaching the line at the end of a group of boats, get out of phase with the group; they will be tacking with each other and should ignore you. At least then, when a shift comes in, you will know that it will either lift you over a couple of boats or just leave you as you were. If you stay in phase with the other boats, no matter what happens, you will likely be left in place—at the back of the pack.

Once you are headed through the line, crossing it should be a matter of swinging up smoothly and punching the bow over. You can maximize your velocity made good (VMG) by pointing the boat straight upwind. The boat will slow rapidly, so you have to be sure you are close enough to the line to cross before your velocity bleeds away. It is important to tell your crew what you are doing: I've seen boats jam the line and roll over to windward because the crew was still valiantly hiking as the pressure left the sails. This is all right as long as some part of the boat has crossed the line, but it is embarrassing to finish by having the tip of one's mast fall across the finish line.

Downwind Finishes

Downwind finishes share all the excitement of the upwind variety. If the boats are tacking downwind, the two finish marks create the same four laylines, and any strategy must take these into account.

Finding the favored end of the line is just as important sailing downwind. Greater latitude in heading makes it easier to get to one end, and the tendency of the fleet to spread out across the course as they sail off the wind will reward the boat that finds the favored end.

Holding other boats out past the laylines is a good tactic for downwind finishes as well. As boats struggle for clear air, jibing duels develop down the leg. Holding someone out on the left side prior to jibing to port for the line will ensure that he has to stay in your wake to the finish.

On the right side of the course things get a little trickier. The boat on the outside can jibe over to starboard and force everyone above him to follow. If you are close to the finish and you know that the right end of the line is favored, you may want to use the same technique suggested above for the upwind finish. Duck behind the starboard tacker, continue for a bit, then jibe yourself. You'll be coming into the line

Determining the favored end is just as important when sailing downwind for the finish.

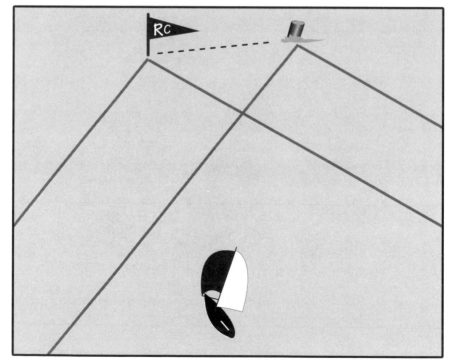

faster than the first boat, and if he has jibed early, you might squeeze in below him.

When you arrive at the line, you can maximize your VMG downwind by diving for the line just as you punch up for a windward finish. The consequences of shooting for the line early are not usually as great either. It takes longer to slow the boat down below the speed you make reaching. The downwind finishes in the 1992 America's Cup races illustrated this. During the close races, the two boats involved dove low for the line even though their best angle to sail the course was much higher. The increase in VMG was temporary but useful.

Questions

Q Why is the layline so attractive as a course to the finish, after I have been warned to stay away from it during the rest of the race?

A The answer is simply that there is a "rest of the race" to keep in mind on the earlier legs. The finish is the end: you don't have to worry about losing any places later. The fact that the fleet is compact on the first weather leg, and that an adverse shift can put one or several boats past you on the second weather leg, makes the layline less attractive on those legs. The same risks exist during the finish, but now the layline can be used to put a definite end to the chances of a boat you have taken out there, so now you have to balance a potential reward against the likelihood of another boat passing you from the inside of the course. Of course, if the boat that matters to you most is on the inside, then no, you won't be out on the layline; you will be covering him instead.

Q If I am approaching the line and get hit with a big knock, should I tack right away to cross the line, even if I am taken through the middle?

A Yes, because the knock has changed the favored end and you have already overstood. If the shift was unexpected, then you cannot do much about it except try to reduce the distance you are sailing; you still need to be aware of the favored tack, and use it to take you most directly across the line. If a shift changes which tack is favored, then you should change tacks.

Q If I am overlapped to windward with a boat approaching the line, am I entitled to room to finish?

A Yes; the finish mark is an obstruction, and the other boat has to allow you to pass on the correct side of it. Having said that, realize that he doesn't have to make it easy. He can luff prior to the circle to break the overlap, or to slow you down so that his bow will cross the line first. If you roll over him prior to the mark but don't get clear ahead, hail for room to pass the obstruction.

The worry here isn't really the boat you are overlapped with—if you are both making the mark easily, he has you anyway. He will be able to carry you above the mark, then turn and dive for it at the last moment, leaving you to watch his transom. So your real concern should be the other boats crossing the line that may sneak in if you are forced above the mark. If necessary, slow down to allow the outside boat to break the overlap so you can get across, and then protest. Seriously, if you hail for room and the overlap exists at the two-boatlength circle, you are entitled to room to finish.

Chapter 15

After the Race

Every race is an occasion for improvement. There are aspects that need to be analyzed and corrected, and aspects that deserve to be celebrated and emulated. That great spinnaker set should set the standard for all future sets. The stretch for the finish that resulted in four boats being passed should be dissected so that it can happen again. The port tack approach to the first mark that cost several boats should be relived.

Sailing is a team sport. We've emphasized this point over and over. We should take time immediately after a race to discuss our performance; that is the time when the events are fresh in everyone's mind, and we are still together as a team. On larger boats it is critical to try and get everyone, even the walk-ons, involved in the postrace discussion. The skipper has no monopoly on good ideas. If I'm steering, I may not even be aware of some of the problems that are occurring.

The Postrace Crew Meeting

The first order of business is to identify and attempt to solve the procedural problems that arose during the race. You will want to talk through the takedowns, sets, and basic boat handling problems. Most of these should have been addressed, and the relevant maneuvers practiced, long before the race; but chances are there were some new people on board, or the procedure that worked well when sailing alone broke down under the pressure of traffic. A review of the tactical considerations that led to the problem maneuver will enlighten the discussion. It gives everyone a sense of the overall priorities involved and provides the underlying guidelines for the solution.

Picture this: Approaching the windward mark, we have tacked slightly short of the layline. We need aggressive trimming on the headsail to pinch up around the mark.

Usually, the headsail trimmer will prefeed and load the guy on the approach to the mark. That isn't getting done in this case.

The foredeck crew pulls the guy out, but there is no one taking the slack behind him. He leaps up to hoist the sail, the foot droops in the water and gets pulled aft, and the chute comes up as a distinct hourglass. Oh boy!

Meanwhile, the trimmer lets go of the headsail and starts hauling aft on the guy. The genoa blows out over the guy and holds the leading edge of the spinnaker back so the sail can't fill. At about this time, the helmsman calls for a beer.

This situation is typical on new boats, boats with new crews, and boats sailing in big fleets for the first time. It is simply the result of a communication problem. When it looks as if the boat can't make the mark, genoa trim must become the overriding concern. The next person forward can take up the guy slack, without even leaving the rail, if it is explained to him beforehand what has to be done. Chances are he will get the message from his fellow crew after the chute is up, but this kind of instruction should be kept to a minimum during the race, and the problem addressed calmly afterward. Solving the problem on the spot has its advantages only if the discussion can be restricted to the two people involved, so that the other crewmembers are not distracted from preparing their next moves. Whole-boat awareness can wait until everyone is available to participate.

After the procedural glitches have been addressed, a discussion of the various tactical situations and the thinking behind them, to the extent that they haven't come up yet, is useful. Some of the reasoning may be fanciful, some may have been gone over prior to the race, but a review of the specific considerations involved, say, in deciding which side of the reaches to travel or in approaching a mark will help the crew anticipate similar situations.

This kind of discussion is an effective way to develop the crew's tactical frame of mind. They will learn to see situations arise and to anticipate them. When you tack underneath a boat, for instance, they will be ready to do what is necessary to help you climb out of there. Hiking, adjusting the sail controls, and anticipating puffs without detailed instructions should become second nature for them, so the helmsman can concentrate on steering.

Constructive postrace discussion should also result in the crew becoming of one mind. Even openly shared disgruntlement with what the nut on the tiller was doing will help get and keep the crew involved. There may be worse things, but clandestine postrace recriminations and factions are about as bad as I want to see it get. If there is disagreement, let it come out immediately. As I said, no one has a monopoly on good ideas, and a tactician or helmsman may have missed something the crew saw. If this is confirmed after the fact, at least they can be alert to similar occurrences in the future.

If the crew sees something worth noting, the afterguard has to be informed about it. Time doesn't permit long explanations in the heat of combat, but the lines of communication can easily be straightened right after the horn sounds ending the race.

"I said . . . , and that meant . . . . " Everybody has to be on the same page to communicate in the verbal shorthand that takes place on the course. I once participated in a race series in Key West that was a good case in point because it had people from all over the country on the same boat. Not until the third race did everyone understand what the others were saying. It wasn't too smart to wait that long for clarification, but usually what people were saying almost made sense, and there was that reluctance, of course, to appear dense.

Channeling the communication flow effectively is also important. For instance, why did four people yell "No!" when the hoist was called? There needs to be an acknowledged routine, and the exceptions must be explained. Let's say during the prefeed hoisting the chute, someone noticed that the guy had been hooked up under the lifelines. As he or she was straightening out the mess, people in back, who couldn't see what was happening on the foredeck, were yelling at the trimmer to prefeed. At the same time, one crewmember who could see what was going on was yelling "No, no, no!", so the poor trimmer was going crazy. If the trimmer had jerked, the guy would have reached the pole, but the chute wouldn't have been with it. After the race this kind of situation must be analyzed and the lesson applied in the future.

Another aspect of postrace discussion might be to develop some projections. Setting up a few hypothetical scenarios based on events in the race just experienced is a good way to get everyone on the boat thinking. "If *this* had happened, then we would have wanted to do *this*, so you would have had to . . . , " and so on. Such verbal rehearsals will result in a team that is more flexible and quick reacting. They also teach the new people on the boat the extent of their responsibilities and the full scope of the tasks that may need to get done in a certain situation.

Finally, the mistakes should be analyzed. The goal here is to obtain consensus on the things that went wrong and ways to avoid repetition of the errors. This discussion should include everything from the choice of starting tactics to jibing techniques. It is at this point that the communication between crewmembers can be expanded, and full explanations can be delivered. It is indeed helpful to have the entire crew in one spot for this discussion: often the person who can solve the problem may not be one of those who were directly involved. It can be as simple as having one of the people on the rail load the guy onto a winch so that the trimmer can continue to pay attention to the genoa and just turn and grab the tail, instead of having to lift it over two other people to get to the winch.

It is clearly better to address technical mistakes or awkwardness in a practice situation, but that may not always be possible. The crew you want to put together for a trip to a major regatta may differ from the one used on a weeknight beer-can race. That doesn't mean you shouldn't hold postrace discussions after a beer-can race, of course; if you can solve problems there in an orderly fashion, you'll have a larger pool of skilled people to draw upon when it is time to become serious.

The last area of discussion is probably the most important; identifying gear or systems on the boat that need work. With a new crew, after the first few races there will be some items that need to be adjusted. Every crew is different, and this will be reflected in the placement of movable parts. As the crew gels in practice or racing, the best location for these items will emerge. Boat designers often develop a standard layout that works well as a starting point; after a while, you will be able to pinpoint the shortcomings of this standard layout for your purposes.

There will probably be some ideas for long-term changes voiced in the discussion. Write them down and forget about them until after the regatta. I like to deliberate for a long time before moving hardware around or adding new complications to a system; considerations always come up later that remove some of the luster from those great ideas. Changes implemented before they have passed thorough examination away from the heat of battle can be a cause of regret. In fact, several acquaintances of mine who started out with adjustable everything have since removed most of the hardware because it rarely got used and always got tangled at the wrong moment.

If there is a major systems failure of some sort, it needs to be dealt with immediately. Someone from the crew needs to assume responsibility for handling the repair, and no one should leave the boat until it is settled who is going to perform the repair and when it will be done. If at all possible, fix the boat that same evening. Pack the sails, repair the hardware, replace the line. Do what is necessary so you can return and walk aboard a boat that is capable of winning first thing in the morning.

After the boat is ready for the next race, by all means, relax and socialize. This is one of the most pleasurable aspects of the sport and should be enjoyed. Since you know that you are prepared for the next day, there should be nothing preventing you from unwinding. This decompression is important in the process of rebuilding stamina for the next race. The postrace party is also an excellent place to gather ideas about the course and glean some go-fast techniques from the leaders. Of course, you need to be open-minded to benefit from this sharing of expertise. One scow sailor I know became so frustrated with the constantly changing theories about the best jib lead that he finally just placed a single eyebolt where the gurus of the day told him it should go. "When they say to move less than an inch in either direction, I'll put in the track. Until then, I'm willing to try most anything," was his comment.

Team Building

It is important to remember and apply some basic management skills when you assemble a crew. The most important consideration is the need to establish a common goal: if you plan to have a group of people practice with you, work on the boat with you, and invest time and money with you, you will have to have a shared interest. The goal that you plan to work toward—whether a club championship, placing above a certain point in a major regatta, or winning the world championship—should be fairly clear at the start of the season, or perhaps even at the end of the previous season. Different goals obviously require different levels of commitment, so you and your crew will be a lot happier if you all agree on the program at the outset.

As helmsman, you will be faced with some of the same questions any manager has. What kind of talent do I need to succeed here? Can I develop that talent, or do I need to go outside to get it? Once I have it, how can I make the most of it?

I like to think that once practice time is over and we are gearing up for a series, a particular regatta, or whatever, the crew is with me and all I have to do is sail. Even the best people will be watching each other the first couple of times out, but after they gel, there should be hands to help out whenever needed. That's why a good program must provide opportunity for the crew to grow together, either by racing some less important races or by practicing.

I strive for some flexibility in the people I recruit. Sometimes I'll select someone for a position he or she openly admits to feeling unqualified to fill, because anyone who places the good of the boat ahead of his or her own interests or ego has the right attitude. In my experience, attitude matters most; mechanical skills can usually be taught. Remember that it is not necessary to assemble the entire crew for a training session dedicated to one particular skill; for example, teaching a new foredeck person to handle the bow only requires as many people as it takes to handle the spinnaker.

The crew needs to be aware of the progression of events. Early races that are mere stepping stones to a major goal should be approached as opportunities to gain confidence in our own and each other's abilities. More time should be spent after these races on analyzing specific boat handling errors. After the errors have been discussed, the solutions should be practiced and then the errors forgotten. Any type of recrimination is counterproductive here: the whole point of the preliminary races is to work out the bugs for the finale, so mistakes should be welcomed as long as they point toward greater improvement.

General awareness of the season's program is also important for logistic reasons. As skipper, you've got to know when to schedule maintenance, when to buy the new sail, and when to make hotel reservations. Your crewmembers also need to make their personal arrangements; needless to say, they have responsibilities both on and off the boat, and you have to give them the chance to balance these. Besides, the longer the notice you can give for a project that will require crew assistance, the more likely you are to receive the needed help.

The Sport

Sailing is a lifetime sport. You can sail competitively at any age, even though goals may shift. At some point, world championships may no longer be your target, but the club championship may still hold an attraction. Enjoying an occasion to get family and friends together may have been your main motivation from the beginning. Whatever your situation, improving the skills necessary for successful racing will ultimately increase your enjoyment of the sport. You'll always find opportunities: as long as the wind is free and the water calls, sailors will want to test their skills against others.

We've talked in this book about offensive and defensive tactics, boat handling techniques, and overall strategic concerns. What I've tried to share here are some of the racing techniques I have used and found effective. They don't work all the time, and if the wind goes against you, they won't work at all; but in any given situation, they place the odds in your favor.

Winning sailboat races is largely a matter of avoiding fatal errors. A bad start can still result in some great sailing, because the pressure is off and the skipper and crew can relax and sail to their potential. On the other hand, a simple mistake at the end can cause the whole race to collapse like a house of cards. I like to play for the long haul and sail conservatively, trying to develop my speed to the point where I only need place myself in an advantaged position to succeed. Then I have no need to go for a home run or a miracle comeback.

Most of the top race sailors I know share this outlook. The race goes to those who make the fewest mistakes, those who take the smallest number of chances, and those who don't give up when a particular maneuver doesn't yield the hoped-for result.

As will have become apparent, it is always part of my strategy to put pressure on the boats around me. I find I can do this most effectively by always being tactically active: when an opportunity arises, I am there. I might not always be right in predicting what is most likely to happen, but I am constantly reaching for some advantage.

In short, I hope that more than teaching any particular technique, this book has managed to convey the idea that wherever we are on the racecourse, skills and alertness will gain us some advantage. There is a lot to know and apply in this sport, to be sure. We can all take some pleasure in the thought that we have plenty of room for improvement, and look forward to the process of learning. It's one of the things that keeps us coming back for more.

Index

Note: Numbers in **boldface** type refer to illustrations.

Weather mark
  approaching, 161–63
  rounding, 184
Wedge technique, 120–22
Wetted surface area, 186
Wind
  apparent, 93–98, 175,
    187
  direction, 67
  duration, 67–68
  shadow, 132, 133, 176
  shear, 172
  velocity, 36, 67
Windshifts, 35–39,
    61–63, 140, 157–59
Windward finishes,
    209–12
Windward–leeward race
    course, 26
Windward mark
  rounding, 74–88

Y
Yawing, 97, 187

Z
Zones of influence,
    100–04, 109